LOVE'S HIDDEN SYMMETRY

What Makes Love Work in Relationships

Bert Hellinger

with
Gunthard Weber
and
Hunter Beaumont

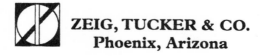

ZEIG, TUCKER & CO.
Phoenix, Arizona

Published by
ZEIG, TUCKER & CO., INC.
3614 North 24th Street
Phoenix, Arizona 85016

Library of Congress Cataloging-in-Publication Data

Hellinger, Bert
    Love's hidden symmetry: what makes love work in relationships
/ by Hert Hellinger with Gunthard Weber and Hunter Beaumont.
        p. cm.
    Translation and reworking of: Zweierlei Glück.
    ISBN 1-891944-00-2
    1. Family psychotherapy. I. Weber, Gunthard. II. Beaumont,
Hunter. III. Zweierlei Glück. IV. Title.
616.89'156--dc21   98–13152 CIP

Manufactured in the United States of America

10 9 8 7

CONTENTS

ACKNOWLEDGMENTS

Many people have contributed generously to this effort.

To John B. Cobb for teaching me to think about process—holistically and systemically.
To K. E. and H. A. for preparing the ground.
To John Hobbs for his generous gift of time and skill in correcting my grammar and style and for supporting my tenuous relationship to the common comma.
To Deb Busman for courageous and caring criticism that helped.
To Colleen, my wife, with whom I have learned most of what I know about relationships, and for the space, confrontation, love, and criticism.
To Erik and Jesse, my children, for making my life very worthwhile.
To my parents for making everything possible.
To many unnamed others—friends, relatives, students, colleagues, critics—who have contributed directly and indirectly.
To Bert Hellinger for the work, and for the abundance of support and care.

My heartfelt gratitude,
Hunter Beaumont

FOREWORD
by
GUNTHARD WEBER

In his poem, "Legends of the Origins of the Book Tao te Ching during Lao-tzu's Emigration," Bertolt Brecht describes how a customs official got Lao-tzu to declare his knowledge before he withdrew to the mountains:

> *On their fourth day among the boulders*
> *A customs man blocked their way:*
> *"Valuables to declare?"—"None."*
> *And the boy who led the oxen, spoke:*
> *"He has been teaching."*
> *And so his knowledge was declared.*
>
> *The man, in his excitement*
> *Asked: "What! Did he make a profit from it?"*
> *Said the boy: "He gained knowledge that soft water,*
> *Moving over time, defeats the mighty stone.*
> *You understand, that the hard is weak."*

I later learned that Lao-tzu's book is also important to Bert Hellinger.

For many years, I have regretted that almost nothing has been written about Bert Hellinger's work, and many others have told me that they feel the same way. Still, I can well understand his caution in committing to writing something that others might treat either as a revelation of truth or as confirmation of their prejudices. "The spirit moves like wind," he has said. What is written loses its connection to real life so easily, loses its vitality, and becomes oversimplified, uncritically generalized, and rendered into fixed patterns and empty sentences.

Bert Hellinger: "The best can't be said. The next best will be misunderstood." My doubts that writing is a suitable medium to communicate what Bert Hellinger has developed were gradually assuaged by my repeated experience of the value of his ideas—for me personally, and also for my clients in my psychotherapeutic work. His intention to retire—he became 72 in 1997—strengthened both my interest in watching him at work once more and my resolve to make his teachings available to others. I asked him in 1990 if he would permit me to be a "customs official," and he agreed.

My first plan was to videotape one of his seminars, and then to publish the transcripts. After I had taped the second seminar and he had given me copies of his lectures "The Orders of Love" and "The Limits of Conscience," as well as other material, it became clear that this plan was not adequate. The present volume is the result of an attempt to integrate his ideas about family relationships and systemic psychotherapy and to give an overall impression of his work.

In this I have attempted to allow Bert Hellinger to speak his own words, and wherever possible, I have included transcripts of his seminars. I have withheld critical commentary where my views differ from his, hoping that each reader will come to grips with the text in his or her own way.

Why did I choose to describe the systemic psychotherapy of Bert Hellinger? In my career, I have participated in many different workshops and training seminars from a great variety of psychotherapeutic schools and orientations and with a variety of teachers. The three seminars I did with Bert Hellinger in the 1970s remain indelible in my memory. In every seminar, I experienced something that continued to move me years later, to work in me, bringing me back into balance, guiding me back to myself when I became confused. I was impressed by the precision of his way of seeing—I still think of him as a "seer." I know no other therapist who is able to recognize problematic patterns so quickly, to interrupt them so effectively, and to reopen the possibility of change in areas of the soul that are seldom addressed in psychotherapy with such impeccable timing and loving humor.

As a participant, I lacked the necessary distance to discover how he does what he does; for example, how he awakens the "good that is present in the transitory moment," how his stories are constructed, how he manages to reduce and concentrate the family constellations so that they become powerful therapeutic interventions. At first, I found his ideas about the background of tragic family entanglements alien, and I felt resistance to his style of communication without understanding what he really meant.

Participants in his workshops are presented with a meeting that is clear, challenging, orienting, and encouraging, and, at the same time, free of personal investment in a particular outcome. He is separate and intimate simultaneously, thus avoiding power conflicts. With every theme that people bring, he moves the exploration inexorably toward the depth of human nature and to the existential dimension of our lives—themes such as belonging, bonding, love, the success and failure of relationships, surrendering to the unavoidable, mortality, and death. For this reason, people are deeply moved, and also because the poetry of his words allows him to address the soul directly.

Although what he says often appears to relate to the past, through his feelings and intuition he is always scanning the horizon for resolutions that set free possibilities for attaining unrealized good. The family constellations develop their deep natural force for healing because information is accessed that is nonverbal, as in a liminal state of a rite of passage. The old, which must be left behind, and the new, which is to come, meet and are one.

The content of this book is susceptible to being misunderstood and to skeptical or infuriated rejection. Those easily swayed will be tempted to interpret what they read as universal truth. He often formulates what he says as if it were an eternal or absolute truth, but careful observation of his work reveals that his therapeutic interventions are directed to a specific individual in a specific therapeutic context. If you try to make these specific statements into general truths and rules for behavior, then you keep the peel and throw away the fruit. After setting up a family constellation, he often recommends not doing anything different at all, but to let the constellation continue to work in the soul until the necessary and appropriate action has become clear.

On reading the transcripts, it will become obvious how quickly Bert Hellinger pulls back when someone tries to generalize uncritically. He also guards against his thoughts and observations being poured into specific theoretical molds. "Too much theory interferes with practice." I have followed his lead in this. He sees his work as being phenomenological. For him, what needs to be done emerges from really seeing what is happening. "I open myself to a situation in darkness, not knowing what is going on. The question is: How do I get to a truth concealed in darkness? I dive into a flowing field; I become part of it, and it reaches out beyond me. Things move in the field, some into areas of light, revealing something of whatever IS. I open myself to that and wait for something to come to me. An image for this process is: I feel my way in darkness along the walls until I find a door. When I find a place of light, I try to describe what is illuminating me with a word that is full and ripe. When the right word is found, those for whom it came grasp it at a level beyond rational thought. The right word touches and moves them, even when they don't understand how."

I will be pleased if this book is a "right word" that touches you.

INTRODUCTION

by

HUNTER BEAUMONT

The family therapist Bert Hellinger has a knack for getting your attention, rattling preconceptions, and encouraging clear thought.

"The whole purpose of being male is to serve the feminine"—to a man concerned that his wife might not have enough time for him if she were to go back to school.

"You know, most families actually function better when the woman follows the man"—to a woman concerned with the injustice of having to change jobs because her husband was transferred.

They both hit the ceiling. The man was convinced that Hellinger is a feminist and the woman that he's a chauvinist, and it took them a while to grasp what he was getting at.

Hellinger is unwavering in his calm compassion while working with families facing the most difficult problems—serious illness and death, suicide, infidelity, separation and divorce, incest, abortion—always on the lookout for solutions, for possibilities that will restore love. And it's astonishing how often he helps people to find hope and constructive action amid their suffering. Yet he can be gruff in his defense of the defenseless and the excluded. Many of his observations are startling and provocative:

"A lot of male chauvinists are dependent on some woman, and a lot of militant feminists are hung up on some man."

"Guilt and innocence aren't the same as good and evil. Religious and political atrocities, for example, are usually committed in all good conscience."

He says, "When I say what I observe without fear, even if it shocks people, then they have to wake up and think about where they stand, about how *they* see things. The authority that's good to

ix

follow is in your own soul." Waking up is the best protection against manipulation. Helping people to consult their own experience honestly is far better than getting their mindless agreement.

Listening to Hellinger on tape for the first time one evening after a psychotherapy training group I was leading, I vacillated between outrage and fascination. I thought, "How can a psychotherapist say such dogmatic and moralistic things?" But then the deeper meaning of his words caught my attention. After the initial flashes of outrage, I became fascinated and realized: "He's not moralizing, he's describing. He's describing the inside of things I've so often seen my clients doing—and have done myself. He's describing how it really is." The next day, instead of returning the borrowed cassette, I listened to it again. It was a tape of the lecture by Bert Hellinger called "The Orders of Love."

During the next two years, whenever I listened to the tape with friends and with participants in my psychotherapy training groups, many had the allergic reaction that I had had, at first believing that he was speaking with false authority: "Let me tell you what the truth is." Yet, as we listened and discussed his observations, it became clear that Hellinger has an extraordinary ability to discern and describe the hidden patterns that allow love to flow in families.

What he's really saying is, "This is what I've observed. It's helped many people to free up love. I offer my experience to you, but don't take what I say on faith. Confirm it yourselves." After a while, we didn't need to take his word for it—we could see what he describes happening in our own work—but we had to give up a lot of our preconceived beliefs.

Bert Hellinger has rediscovered something about love in intimate relationships that grasps people and changes their lives. What he's found is this: If you want love to flourish, you need to do what it demands and to refrain from doing what harms it. Love follows the hidden order of the Greater Soul. The therapeutic work documented in this book shows what happens when we injure love or ignore what it requires. It also shows the healing that happens when our intimate relationships are restored to order. It reveals how children's innocent love blindly perpetuates what's harmful, and how injuries to the Order of Love by earlier members of a family affect the lives of later members, just as the waves and ripples in a river caused by a submerged boulder upstream still twist and swell far downstream.

The systemic Orders of Love influence us as much as its environment influences a tree. If a tree is able to align itself between the force of gravity and the pull of the sun, it naturally grows vertically, with its branches equally balanced. In this form, it is most stable. If, however, the tree is unable to align itself in the usual way, perhaps because it is growing on a canyon wall, it will adapt, growing as straight as the systemic interplay of wind, soil, gravity, and sun allows. Such a tree is not less good than a more vertical tree, but it may be less stable and not as tall as its cousin in the valley. Both trees are subject to the same laws of nature, yet the dynamics of their habitats exert differing pressures on them, and each finds a systemic equilibrium in the best way it can.

Or we may compare the systemic laws of relationships to a whirlwind—we can't see it until it grasps the desert sands or fallen leaves and throws them swirling into the air. We know the whirlwind only by its effect on the visible world. The Orders of Love are dynamic, systemic forces blowing and whirling in our families and intimate relationships. We know the disorder caused by their turbulence—as leaves know the whirlwind—in our suffering and illness. Conversely, we know their harmonious flow as a sense of well-being in the world.

Not all suffering and illness are caused by disturbances in our relationships, of course, but since we often can do something about the suffering that does arise out of such systemic turbulence, it is of special concern in our work. When we understand the systemic laws that allow love to unfold, we may be able to help suffering families and individuals to find solutions and to change their psychological habitats. It's profoundly moving to observe clients approach the Orders of Love and spontaneously melt into soft and intimate love, even after a lifetime of hate and anger and abuse. Yet striving with willpower alone can't create the systemic equilibrium in a relationship that allows love to thrive. As Bert Hellinger says, "To gain insight into the Orders of Love is wisdom. To follow them with love is humility."

Because the systemic forces that constrain love in intimate relationships are invisible to the naked eye—like the beauty of Saturn's rings or the movement of a single cell—we need to amplify our powers of perception in order to study them. The instrument Bert Hellinger uses to make visible the normally hidden dynamics operating in relationship systems is the family constellation.

In setting up a family constellation, a participant chooses other group members to represent the members of his or her family and moves them in the room until their positions relative to one another "feel" like they felt in the family. The representatives become a living model of the original family relationship system. The incredible thing is that, if you set up your family authentically, the representatives begin to have feelings and thoughts very close to those the family members felt—*without prior knowledge.*

We don't know how it's possible for the representatives to feel strangers' symptoms, and Bert Hellinger refuses to speculate about it, saying, "I'm unable to explain this phenomenon, but I see that it's so, and I use it." Skeptics have a hard time believing that people representing others whom they don't know can experience in their own bodies what those persons felt, what they needed, and what will help. There are many examples of this phenomenon in the transcripts and case reports that follow, but if you are a dedicated skeptic, you won't be convinced until you have an opportunity to experience the phenomenon yourself. Still, you won't understand the material that follows unless you remain open to the possibility that hidden systemic dynamics can set representatives' feelings in motion in a family constellation as a whirlwind sets the fallen leaves in motion.

Therapists of many different schools have used family constellations for over three decades to bring the hidden dynamics operating in intimate relationship systems to light. Bert Hellinger didn't invent the method, but he did discover how it can be extended beyond making destructive dynamics visible. He found out how the same method can be used to help people identify what can be done and how to use the representatives' reactions to modify the family dynamic so that the hidden, systemic orders that love requires can be reestablished, allowing love to flow freely. Again, it's hard to believe, but sometimes the behaviors of family members who were *not even present* change for the better after a family constellation has been brought to a good resolution

Although this book is a report of empirically observed phenomena,[1] it goes beyond the customary conventions of scientific literature. The language of science demands a precision that doesn't

---

[1] Bert Hellinger, Gunthard Weber, and their associates at the Heidelberg Institute for Systemic Research are collecting a large archive of video documentation of this work, and are conducting both process and outcome research.

persuade the soul. Poetry and stories, on the other hand, filled as they are with metaphor, engage the soul in the play of exploring meaning, but are open to many different interpretations. Scientific investigation succeeds by pinning things down so that there's only one thing on which everyone can agree, but a good poem has many different meanings.

Hellinger's love of language; his interest in philosophy, stories, and poems; and his ability to cut through to the existential themes hidden in people's everyday complaints give the book a nonscientific immediacy. His language is hot; it wants to touch and move, not just to inform. In this sense, it's literature or practical philosophy, a book for everyone interested in intimate relationships.

Bert Hellinger also refuses to accept the separation of spirituality from science and literature. In contrast with the psychotherapeutic mainstream, he freely uses the words "soul" and "heart," but in a very specific way. For him, soul is embodied in experience; it's felt as real. Soul is distinct from mind and from body, yet it is at home between them. Longing and yearning, for example, are not just thoughts, but are things we feel as an ache, a wrenching, or a burning. Yet they're not identical with the body pain of a burn, a cut, or a bruise. They're something in between. Soul knows things like loneliness, hope, longing, closeness to others, and loyalty. If we listen to it carefully, it tells us what it needs and loves. The heartbeat of this work is helping people learn to distinguish what the soul loves and needs from the blind pressures of social conditioning, religious prejudice, and political ideology.

Bert Hellinger's spirituality is close to the earth, embodied, passionate, life affirming. It embraces the everyday lives of average people struggling with their suffering and with their greatness. It draws us into life rather than seeking to lift us above it. It celebrates the simple and the ordinary, speaking to everyone who is wrestling with whatever limits the soul's longing to reach its potential in the world. This book is about remembering how to listen to your soul and to the Soul of the Greater Whole.

The book began when Gunthard Weber, a prominent German psychiatrist and family systems psychotherapist, offered to record and edit some of Bert Hellinger's workshops. At that time, very little had been published on Hellinger's work. Weber's original idea was to make the material available to a small circle of professional psychotherapists. To everyone's surprise, the German edition of *Zweieerlei Gluck* [*Capricious Good Fortune*] became a best-seller and was received with national acclaim—and controversy.

Bert Hellinger and I started preparing this English version by translating Weber's German book, and then we began a three-year process of recreating it for the general reader. As a result of our dialogue, we completely rethought, rewrote, and reorganized the material. We also added new material, and expanded some points and clarified or omitted others. To remind the reader that we're describing real people living in real relationships, we added some transcripts of therapeutic work. As it now stands, it's a collaborative effort. Gunthard Weber and I have assisted in organizing, adapting, clarifying, and developing Hellinger's work in a written format, but the original integration is Hellinger's own.[2]

There are five different kinds of material in this book.

The text. The text is based primarily on Bert Hellinger's lectures. His language in these lectures is dense, poetic, hypnotic, almost prophetic—his intention being to address the soul more than the mind. Material has been omitted, but nothing has been invented. They are drawn from both Hellinger's and my psychotherapeutic practices.

The stories and poems. All of the stories and poems, unless otherwise indicated are Bert Hellinger's original work, although the reader will recognize some well-known stories, but with surprising new twists.

Questions and answers. The questions and Bert Hellinger's answers have been drawn from many sources—from questions asked in his workshops, seminars, public lectures, and interviews and from private conversations, and have been edited with an eye to the written word. In some cases, I've even asked questions that I felt needed to be answered for the sake of clarity. Although his answers are no longer exactly what he said in the workshops, they clearly

---

[2] Many different influences have been integrated into Hellinger's work during his long career, and the reader will recognize many familiar psychotherapeutic concepts and techniques, some in surprising forms. Rather than trying to note them in the text as we go along, we refer you to the Appendix for a brief history of Bert Hellinger's professional life, including the major influences on the development of his work.

reflect his style and thought. They also capture the flavor of the lively give-and-take characteristic of his seminars.

Transcripts of videotapes. These are accurate records of actual clinical work. They've been edited for clarity and extraneous material has been omitted, but as far as possible, they present "what really happened." As with any transcription, Bert Hellinger's impeccable timing and his warmth, humor, and presence could be conveyed only partially. Many people have told us that watching the videos greatly aided their understanding of the material. Some were surprised at how gentle Hellinger is.[3] We've added relevant questions and answers from other sources at the end of some transcripts, and these are clearly indicated. We've used simple diagrams to give an impression of the movement and spatial relations of the representatives during the constellations. Some of the readers have told us that they take some getting used to, but therapists find them useful in learning about the work. They're the best solution we've found. Some readers just skip them. In reading the transcripts, keep in mind that most of the participants are not professional psychotherapists, but are average people dealing with the issues that arise in their lives.

Additional considerations. Some of Hellinger's remarks have been controversial and misunderstood. I've added my own concerns at several points. Although he doesn't always share my concerns, we both hope that these additional considerations will be of use to the reader.

In reading the material, it's useful to remind yourself periodically that when Hellinger describes *Love's Hidden Symmetry*, he describes what people experience in the family constellations. He's describing what brings the profound "soul feeling" that says, "This is what's right for me!" He's not describing ethical principles that we should force ourselves to follow, nor is he addressing the superego with messages of "you must" and "you must not." His voice seeks a different organ of perception in the soul, an "ear" that listens for the resonance of the natural order of things.

Some readers who live in nontraditional relationships have wondered about the relevance of the material for them. We are family

---

[3] Video documentation in English of Bert Hellinger at work is available through Zeig, Tucker & Co., 1935 East Aurelius, Phoenix, Arizona 85020.

therapists, and our work is primarily concerned with traditional families and male–female relationships. Nevertheless, many single persons and many couples without children—both heterosexual and homosexual—have been profoundly touched by the perspective we offer. The simple fact that there are many single people and couples without children leading happy, loving, meaningful lives is proof that there are Orders of Love supporting these forms of relationship. They share many common relationship issues with those in traditional families, but they also have some different issues to resolve in order for their love to thrive. The point is not that you must have a traditional family in order to be happy, but if you want your love to flourish, you must identify the Orders of Love that constrain and support love in your particular life situation, and you must follow them with love.

Hellinger's observations have been made primarily with families socialized in European cultures. We have gathered some preliminary experience with members of Asian, Islamic, and African cultures. It seems possible that love follows the same systemic laws in these cultures as well, even when the specific roles and customs vary widely. This is an intriguing possibility that must await more careful observation for verification.

Rivers can be used as metaphors for complex systems, and in this book you'll find many rivers flowing through the stories and cases. When we sit on the bank of a river and allow its current to grasp our minds, we are reminded of a permanence in change and of the great cycle of return—clouds, rain, river, ocean, and clouds are all phases of one vast system. The following story was inspired by Bert Hellinger, and I dedicate it to him in gratitude for all that he has given. It's also an invitation to you, the reader, to dive in and swim.

The Source

A young man man sat by a river watching it ripple and whirl, feeling the current's gentle pull on his mind, and wondered, "Where does the river come from?" And he set out to find the river's source.

He followed the river until he found one branch that was longer than the rest. Before he could celebrate his discovery, it started to rain, and there were little rivers everywhere. He scurried here and there until he found the little river that was longer than the others. As he began to celebrate he saw a bird sitting in a tree, water dripping from its beak and tail. He stopped, stood back, and looked very carefully—the bird's beak was just a little higher than its tail. Then he hurried back to tell of his final discovery.

Once he was home, people asked him again and again to tell of his journey and of his discovery, and each time he told them, they were astonished and admired his achievement. In time, he became so fascinated with telling his story that he no longer went to the river.

An old man who loved him recognized the danger he was in and hurried to his aid. In a voice that was clear and gentle, he said, "I wonder where the rain comes from."

The young man despaired, "Where can I get a ladder to climb into the sky and measure so many drops of rain, and how shall I follow clouds?" He turned away, and to hide his shame, he jumped into the river and let it carry him away.

The old man thought, "That's a good answer, my son. Dive in, feel the current, let the river carry you. It's longing to go home, flowing to its source."

PART ONE

The Phenomenology of Intimate Relationship Systems

C H A P T E R   O N E

Guilt, Innocence, and the Limits of Conscience

We are led to believe a lie when we see not thro the Eye Which was Born in a Night to perish in a Night when the Soul Slept in Beams of Light.

—William Blake

If we carefully observe what people do in order to have a clear or a guilty conscience, we see that conscience is not what we are led to believe. We see that:

- A clear or a guilty conscience has little to do with good and evil; the worst atrocities and injustices are committed with a clear conscience, and we feel quite guilty doing good when it deviates from what others expect of us. We call the conscience that we feel as guilt or innocence a personal conscience.

- Our personal conscience has many different standards, one for each of our different relationships: one standard for our relationship to our father, another for that with our mother, one for the church, another for the workplace, that is, one for each group to which we belong.

- In addition to personal conscience, we are also subject to a systemic conscience. We neither feel nor hear this conscience, but we experience its effects when harm is passed from one generation to the next. This invisible systemic conscience, its dynamics and the orders of *Love's Hidden Symmetry*, is the primary subject of this book.

• Further, in addition to personal conscience, which we feel, and to systemic conscience, which works through us although we do not feel it, there is a third conscience that guides us toward the greater whole. Following this third conscience requires great effort, perhaps even a spiritual effort, because it tears us away from obedience to the dictates of our family, religion, culture, personal identity. It demands of us, if we love it, that we leave behind what we have known and follow the Conscience of the Greater Whole. This conscience is ineffable and mysterious and it does not follow the laws of personal and systemic conscience, which we know more intimately.

The Question

We know our conscience as a horse knows the riders who ride it and as a helmsman knows the stars by which he sets his course. But many riders ride the horse—and many helmsmen steer the ship, each guided by a different star. The question becomes: Who shall command the riders and which course shall the captain choose?

The Answer

A disciple asked of his teacher, "Tell me what freedom is."
"Which freedom?" asked the teacher.
"The first freedom is foolishness. That's like a horse that throws its rider with a triumphant whinny, only to feel the saddle girth pulled tighter.
"The second freedom is remorse. Remorse is like the helmsman who goes down with the ship, after he has sailed it onto a reef, rather than seek safety in the lifeboat with the others.
"The third freedom is understanding. Understanding comes, alas, only after foolishness and remorse. It's like a shaft of wheat that bends in the wind, and because it bends where it's weak, endures."
The disciple asked, "Is that all?"
The teacher said, "Many think they're seeking the truth of their own soul, but it's the Greater Soul that is thinking and seeking in them. Like nature, it allows great variety, but replaces with ease those who try to cheat. But to those who allow it to think in them, it allows, in turn, a little freedom, helping them like a river helps a swimmer

cross to the other shore if she surrenders to the current and allows herself to be swept along."

PERSONAL CONSCIENCE AND OUR FEELINGS OF GUILT AND INNOCENCE

In all our various relationships, fundamental needs interact in a complex way:

1. The need to belong, that is, for bonding.[1]

2. The need to maintain a balance of giving and taking,[2] that is, for equilibrium.

3. The need for the safety of social convention and predictability, that is, for order.

We feel these three different needs with the urgency of drives and instinctual reactions, and they subject us to forces that challenge us and demand compliance, that coerce and control us. They limit our choices and commit us, whether we like it or not, to objectives that conflict with our personal wishes and pleasures.

These needs constrain our relationships, and also make them possible, because they both reflect and enable our fundamental human need to relate intimately to others. Our relationships succeed when we are able to fill these needs and to balance them with one another, and they become dysfunctional and destructive when we can't. With every action we take that affects others, we feel guilty or innocent. Just as the eye discriminates continually between light and dark, so too an inner organ continually discriminates between what serves and what hinders our relationships.

---

[1] Konrad Lorenz described the phenomenon of imprinting among animals. John Bowlby and his students have described the bonding that occurs between a mother and her children. Bert Hellinger has recognized the importance of the bonding between sexual partners, which ties them together quite independently of the love they may feel for each other. However the bonding referred to here is primarily a social bond that ties an individual to his or her group of reference.

[2] The importance of balanced giving and taking in family dynamics, as well as the importance of the hidden bonds and loyalties operating in family systems, has been described by Ivan Boszormenyi-Nagy.

When our actions endanger or damage our relationships, we feel *guilt*, and we feel freedom from guilt, or *innocence*, when our actions serve them. We call our experience of guilt and innocence—that is, our sense of what serves or endangers our relationships—*personal conscience*. Thus, our feelings of guilt and innocence are primarily social phenomena that do not necessarily orient us toward higher moral values. On the contrary, by binding us so firmly to the groups that are necessary for our survival, *our feelings of guilt and innocence often blind us to what is good and evil.*

DIFFERENT NEEDS
REQUIRE DIFFERENT BEHAVIORS

Our needs for belonging, the equilibrium of giving and taking, and social convention work together to maintain the social groups to which we belong, but each need strives toward its own goals with its own particular feelings of guilt and innocence, and so we experience guilt and innocence differently according to the need and the goal being served.

- Guilt feels like exclusion and alienation when our belonging is endangered. When it is well served, we feel innocence as intimate inclusion and closeness.

- Guilt feels like indebtedness and obligation when our giving and taking are not balanced. When they are well served, we feel innocence as entitlement and freedom.

- Guilt feels like transgression and as fear of consequences or punishment when we deviate from a social order. We feel innocence with respect to social order as conscientiousness and loyalty.

Conscience demands in the service of one need what it forbids in the service of another, and it may allow us in the service of one what it forbids in the service of the others. For example:

Love and Order

A mother told her son to play alone for an hour because he had broken a family rule. If she had allowed him to remain in his room for the whole hour, the need for social order would have been served, but he would have felt justifiably lonely because love and belonging would have been neglected. For this reason, the mother, like many parents, released her child from a portion of the punishment. Although she neglected the full requirements of social order and was guilty in that respect, she served love with innocence.

Conscience serves all these needs even when they conflict with one another, and we experience the conflicts between them as conflicts of conscience. Whoever reaches toward innocence with respect to one need simultaneously reaches toward guilt with respect to another; whoever rents out a room in the house of innocence soon discovers that he or she has sublet to guilt as well. No matter how we struggle to follow our conscience, we always feel *both* guilt and innocence—innocence with respect to one need and guilt with respect to another. The dream of innocence without guilt is an illusion.

How Conscience Guards Bonding

Acting in the service of our need to belong, conscience bonds us to the persons and groups necessary for our survival regardless of the conditions they set for our belonging. Although an oak tree doesn't choose the ground in which it grows, its environment affects it and it develops differently in an open field, in a deep forest, in a protected valley, or high on a windy hill. In the same way, children accommodate without question to the groups into which they are born, and they bond to those groups with a tenacity reminiscent of imprinting. Young children experience their bonding to their family as love and good fortune, no matter how the family nourishes or neglects them, and they experience their family's values and habits as good, no matter what the family believes or does.

In the service of belonging, conscience reacts to everything that enhances or endangers our bonding. Our conscience is clear when we act so that our continued belonging to our group is assured, and we have a guilty conscience when we deviate from the norms of our group and must fear that our right to belong is jeopardized or damaged. Like an apple on a stick held before the pony's nose and a whip in the driver's hand, guilt and innocence have the same goal. They entice us and drive us in the same direction, jealously guarding our connection to our family and intimate community.

The conscience that guards our bonding does not stand above the false beliefs and superstitions of the groups to which we belong, guiding us to a greater truth. Instead, it serves and maintains those beliefs, making it difficult for us to see and know and remember whatever it forbids. The bonding and belonging so necessary for our survival and well-being also dictate what we may perceive, believe, and know.

Conscientiously Denying the Obvious

A doctor told a group how his sister had called one morning and asked him to visit her as she wasn't feeling well and wanted his medical opinion. He visited as she asked, and they talked for an hour without coming to any clear conclusion. He recommended that she visit a gynecologist. She did and was delivered of a healthy son that same evening.

The doctor had not perceived that his sister was pregnant, nor had she been aware of her pregnancy, although she, too, was a physician. In their family, children weren't allowed to know about pregnancy, and all their medical studies hadn't enabled either of them to remove the perceptual block.

We Have a Different Standard for Each Group

The *only* criteria followed by conscience acting in the service of bonding are the values of the group to which we belong. For this reason, persons who come from different groups have different values, and persons who belong to several groups act differently in each group. When our social context changes, conscience changes its colors like a chameleon in order to protect us in our new situation. We have one conscience with our mother and another with our father; one for the family and another for the workplace; one for church, another for an evening out. In each of these different situations, conscience strives to guard our belonging and to protect us from abandonment and loss. It holds us to our group like a sheepdog holds the sheep together in a herd, barking and nipping at our heels until we move together with the others.

But what leaves us innocent in one relationship may make us very guilty in another. In a group of thieves, members must steal, and they do so with a clear conscience. In another group, stealing is forbidden. In both cases, members experience the same sensations of guilt or innocence as the penalty for violating their group's conditions of membership.

What serves one relationship may damage another. For example, sexuality is the fulfillment of one relationship and a violation of another. But what happens when our belonging in one relationship collides with our belonging in another? When what makes us guilty in one relationship is demanded of us in the other? Then we stand before different judges for the same act, and one may find us guilty while the other may declare us innocent.

Dependency Strengthens Bonding

Conscience ties us most firmly to our group when we are most powerless and vulnerable. As we gain power in a group and independence, both bonding and conscience relax, but if we remain weak and dependent, we also remain obedient and loyal. In families, children occupy this position; in a company, the lower employees; in an army, the enlisted soldiers; in a church, the faithful congregation. For the good of the stronger in the group, they all conscientiously risk health, happiness, and life and make themselves guilty—even when their leaders, for what is called "higher purposes," unscrupulously misuse them. These are the meek who stick out their necks for the stronger, the hangmen doing others' dirty work, unsung heroes holding their positions to the last, sheep faithfully following their shepherd to the slaughter, victims paying restitution. These are the children who leap into the fray for their parents and relatives, who carry out that which they didn't plan, atone for what they didn't do, and bear burdens they didn't create.

No Room

An old man approaching the end of his life sought out a friend to help him find peace. As a young father, he had once mildly reprimanded his son and the boy had hanged himself that night. The son's reaction was out of all proportion to the father's admonishment, and the old man had never recovered from the great weight of his loss and guilt.

In talking with his friend, he suddenly remembered a conversation with his son a few days before the suicide. His wife had mentioned during dinner that she was going to have another child. The son, quite beside himself, had cried out, "Oh my God! We haven't got enough room."

As he remembered this conversation, the old man understood this tragedy in a larger context: His son had hanged himself to take on some of the burden of his parents' poverty, and to make room for another—not just as a reaction to the mild punishment. The old man, understanding that his son had loved too, found meaning. He said, "I'm at peace at last, as if I were sitting by a quiet mountain lake."

Belonging Demands the Exclusion of Those Who Are Different

Wherever conscience acting in the service of belonging binds us to one another in a group, it also drives us to exclude those who are different and to deny them the right to the membership that we claim for ourselves. Then we become frightening for them. The conscience guarding our belonging guides us to do to those who are different what we most fear as the worst consequence of guilt—we exclude them. But as we treat them badly in good conscience, so do they in turn treat us in the name of the conscience of their group. The conscience that guards belonging inhibits evil within the group, but lifts this inhibition in regard to those outside the group. We then do to others *in good conscience* what our conscience forbids us to do to members of our own group. In the context of religious, racial, and national conflicts, suspending the inhibitions that conscience imposes on evil within a group allows members of that group to commit, in good conscience, atrocities and murder against others who belong to different groups.

Thus, *guilt and innocence are not the same as good and evil.* We do destructive and evil things with a clear conscience when they serve the groups that are necessary for our survival, and we take constructive action with a guilty conscience when these acts jeopardize our membership in these same groups.

Additional Considerations

The testimony of former members of the South African secret police before the Truth and Reconciliation Commission gained international attention and it is an excellent illustration of the phenomenon we are describing here. The decision of Nelson Mandela's government to grant amnesty to members of the former secret police who were willing to testify publicly about their former activities created an atmosphere in which the effect of membership in social groups on the perception of good and evil is clear. In the context of their membe.:ship in the secret police during the apartheid government, they tortured and murdered, believing they were doing good, acting in defense of their endangered nation. Now, in a different political context, having been granted amnesty, many view their former activities differently, reporting genuine and deep remorse. [H.B.]

The Appearances of Guilt and Innocence Can Be Deceiving

Guilt and innocence often exchange their garb so that guilt appears as innocence and innocence as guilt. Appearances deceive, and it's only by the final outcome that we know the truth.

The Players

They declare themselves
Opponents.
Face to face
They play
On one common board
With many figures,
And complex rules,
Move for move,
The ancient Game of Kings.

Each sacrifices
Many pieces
In their game,
And seeks advantage
Until there are no moves to make
And then their match is done.

Then, changing sides
And colors,
They begin another round
Of that same Game of Kings.

But whoever plays enough
And often wins

And often loses
Becomes a master

—Of both sides.

Just as appearances of guilt and innocence may deceive, the conscience of the group also gradually shapes the child's experience of the world. It colors the child's perception of what *is* with the family's beliefs.

Learning to Be Good

A child goes into the yard and feels amazement at the growing things. Mother says, "Look, how beautiful." Now the child must attend to words; looking and hearing are interrupted, her direct engagement with what exists is replaced by value judgments. The child can no longer trust her own experience of being enthralled by what *is*, but must defer to an external authority, who defines what is beautiful and good.

Conscience then becomes the great pretender, setting feelings of guilt and innocence in the place of knowledge of good and evil. The good that brings reconciliation must overcome the false appearances created by virtue of our belonging to various groups. Conscience talks; the world *is*.

CONSCIENCE AND BALANCE IN GIVING AND TAKING

Our relationships—and our experiences of guilt and innocence—begin with giving and taking. We feel entitled when we give and we feel obligated when we take. The oscillation between entitlement and obligation is the second fundamental dynamic of guilt and innocence in every relationship. It serves all our relationships, since both giver and taker know peace only when both have given and taken equally.

A Gift of Love

A missionary in Africa was transferred to a new area. On the morning of his departure, he was visited by a man who had walked several hours to give him a small amount of money as a going-away gift. The value of the money was about 30 cents. It was clear to the missionary that the man was thanking him, because when the man was ill, the missionary had been concerned and had visited him several times. He understood that 30 cents was a huge sum of money for this man. He was tempted to give the money back, perhaps even to add a bit to it, but upon reflection, he accepted the money and thanked the man. Having given in love, he was obliged to take in love as well.

When we receive something from someone, we lose our innocence and our independence. When we take, we feel indebted and beholden to the giver. We feel this obligation as discomfort and pressure, and we try to overcome it by giving something back. We can't truly take anything without feeling the need to give. Taking is a form of guilt.

Innocence in the service of this exchange becomes manifest as the comfortable feeling of entitlement that comes when we take fully and when we give a little more in return than we have taken. We feel innocently carefree and lighthearted when we've taken fully and our needs have been satisfied, and when we've also given fully in return.

There are three typical patterns people adopt for achieving and maintaining innocence with respect to exchange in relationships: fasting, helping, and full exchange.

Fasting

Some people cling to the illusion of innocence by minimizing their participation in life. Rather than taking fully what they need and feeling beholden, they close themselves off and withdraw from life and need. They feel free from need and obligation, and because they don't feel need, they need not take. Although they feel beholden to no one and innocent, theirs is the innocence of the uninvolved observer. They don't get their hands dirty, so they often consider themselves to be superior or special. Nevertheless, their enjoyment of life is limited by the shallowness of their involvement, and they feel correspondingly empty and dissatisfied.

This posture can be observed in many people who struggle with depression. Their refusal to welcome what life offers develops first in the relationship with one or both of their parents, and later is carried over to other relationships and to the good things of the world.

Some people justify their refusal to take with the complaint that what they were given wasn't enough or was not the right thing. Others justify not taking by pointing to the errors and limitations of the giver, but the result is the same—they remain passive and empty. For example, people who reject or judge their parents—regardless of what their parents may have done—typically feel incomplete and lost.

We observe the opposite in people who have succeeded in taking their parents as they are, and in taking from them everything that was given. They experience this taking as a continuous flow of strength and nourishment that enables them to enter other relationships in which they, too, can take and give richly—even if their parents treated them badly.

Helping

Other people try to maintain innocence by denying their need until after they've given enough to feel entitled. Giving before taking allows a fleeting sense of entitlement that dissolves as soon as we've taken what we need. Persons who prefer to maintain their feeling of entitlement rather than to allow others to give to them freely say, in effect, "It's better for you to feel obligated to me than for me to feel obligated to you." Many idealists hold this posture, and it's widely known as the "helper syndrome."

Such self-centered striving for freedom from need is fundamentally hostile to relationships. Whoever wants only to give without taking clings to an illusion of superiority, rejects the bounty of life, and denies equality to his or her partner. Others soon want nothing from those who refuse to take, and become resentful and withdraw from them. For this reason, chronic helpers often are lonely and eventually become bitter.

Full Exchange

The third and most beautiful path to innocence in giving and taking is the contentment that follows a plentiful exchange of giving and taking, when we have both given and taken fully. This exchange is the heart of relationship: The giver takes, the taker gives. Both are giver and taker equally.

Not only is the balance of giving and taking important to this innocence, but so also is the volume. A tiny volume of giving and taking brings no profit; a high volume makes us wealthy. High-volume giving and taking bring with them a feeling of abundance and happiness.

Increasing Volume

A man loves his wife and wants to give her something. Because she loves him, she accepts his gift gratefully, and, as a result, feels a need to give. Obedient to her need, she gives to her husband in return, and just to be on the safe side, she gives a little more than she has taken. Because she has given in love, he desires to take what she offers and also reciprocates with a little more. In this way, conscience maintains a dynamic imbalance and the couple's loving relationship continues with an increasing volume of giving and taking.

Such joy doesn't just fall into our laps, but is the consequence of our willingness to increase love by needing and taking in intimate relationship. With such high-volume exchanges, we feel light and free, just and content. Of all the ways of knowing innocence in giving and taking, this is by far the most deeply satisfying.

Balancing Giving and Taking When Reciprocity Is Impossible

In some relationships, the discrepancy between giver and taker is insurmountable; for example, that between parents and children or between teachers and students. Parents and teachers are primarily givers; children and students are takers. Of course, parents take from their children and teachers from their students. However, this only reduces the discrepancy, it doesn't nullify it. In all situations in which balance cannot be attained by reciprocal giving, equilibrium and contentment must be acquired by different means.

Parents were once themselves children and teachers were students. They achieve a balance of giving and taking when they give to the next generation what they took from the earlier generation. Children and students may do the same.

Börries von Münchhausen describes this beautifully in the following poem

The Golden Ball

For the love my father gave to me
I did not give him due.
As child, I didn't know the value of the gift.
As man, became too hard, too like a man.
My son grows to manhood now, loved with passion,
as no other, present in his father's heart.
I give of that which I once took, to one from
whom it did not come, nor is it given back.

When he becomes a man, thinking as a man,
he will, as I, follow his own path.
I'll watch, with longing free from envy as
he gives on to his own son the love I gave to him.
My gaze follows the game of life
deep through the halls of time—
each smilingly throws the golden ball,
and no one throws it back
to him from whom it came.

What's appropriate between parents and children and between teachers and students can also be applied wherever an equilibrium of giving and taking cannot be achieved through giving in return and full exchange. In all such situations—for example, people without children—we still may relieve ourselves of obligation by giving to others what we have taken.

Expressing Gratitude

Expressing genuine gratitude is another way to balance giving and taking for those who must take more than they can reciprocate. We mustn't misuse the expression of gratitude to avoid giving other things when it's possible and appropriate, but sometimes it's the only adequate response; for example, for handicapped persons, for the seriously ill, for the dying, and sometimes for lovers.

In such situations, in addition to the need for equilibrium, an elementary love comes into play that attracts the members of a social system to one another and holds them together as gravity holds the planets and stars. This love accompanies giving and taking and it becomes manifest as gratitude.

Whoever feels genuine gratitude affirms, "You give without regard as to whether or not I can repay, and I take your gift with love." Whoever accepts such gratitude affirms, "Your love and recognition of my gift are more valuable to me than anything else you might give to me."

With our gratitude, we affirm not only what we give to one another, but also what we are for one another.

Gratitude Worthy of God

A man once felt he owed God a great debt because he had been saved from life-threatening danger. He asked a friend what he should do to express his gratitude in a way worthy of God. His friend told him a story:

A man loved a woman with all his heart and asked her to marry him. She told him she wouldn't marry him because she had other plans. One day, as they were crossing the street together, the woman stepped in front of a car and would have been run over if the man hadn't pulled her back. Then she turned to him and said, "Now I'll marry you!"

"How do you think that man felt?" asked the friend. The man grimaced, but didn't answer. "You see," said the friend, "perhaps God feels the same way about you."

We tend to experience unearned good fortune as threatening, something that creates anxiety, secretly believing that our happiness will arouse the envy of others or of fate. We all tend to feel that happiness breaks a taboo and makes us guilty, as if by being happy we put ourselves in danger. Genuine gratitude reduces this anxiety. Nevertheless, affirming good fortune in the face of another's misfortune requires humility as well as courage.

Home from the War

Childhood friends were sent off to war where they experienced indescribable dangers, and, although many were killed or wounded, two came home unharmed.

One of the two had become very calm and was at peace within himself. He knew he had been saved by the whim of destiny and he accepted his life as a gift, as an act of grace.

The other got into the habit of drinking with other veterans and reliving the past. He loved to brag about the dangers he had escaped and about his heroic acts. It was as if, for him, the whole experience had been in vain.

Giving and Taking Constrain and Are Constrained by Love

Giving and taking in intimate relationships are regulated by a mutual need for equilibrium, but no meaningful exchange develops between partners without the willingness of both to experience periodic imbalance. It's similar to walking—we stand still when we maintain static equilibrium, and we fall and remain lying down when we lose mobility completely. But by rhythmically losing our balance and regaining it, we move forward. As soon as equilibrium is achieved, the relationship either can be concluded or it can be renewed and continued by new giving and taking.

Partners in intimate relationships are equal—although different—in their exchange, and their love succeeds and continues when their giving and taking are balanced in the negative, as well as in the positive. Their exchange ends when they achieve a static equilibrium. When one takes without giving, the other soon loses the desire to give more. When one gives without taking, the other soon doesn't want to take any more. Partnerships also end when one gives more than the other is able or willing to reciprocate. Love limits giving according to the taker's capacity to take, just as it limits taking according to the giver's ability to give. That means that the need for a balance of giving and taking between partners simultaneously limits their love and their partnership. In that way, our need for equilibrium constrains and limits love.

But love also constrains equilibrium. When one partner does something that causes pain or injury to the other, then the injured person must return something that causes a similar pain and difficulty in order to maintain a balance of giving and taking—but in such a way that love is not destroyed. When the injured person feels too superior to stoop to the appropriate retribution love requires, then equilibrium is impossible and the relationship is endangered. For example, one of the difficult situations couples may face arises when one of them has an affair. Reconciliation is impossible after an affair if one partner stubbornly clings to innocence, polarizing guilt and innocence.

On the other hand, if the injured partner is willing to make himself or herself also guilty by returning a portion of the hurt, then it may be possible for them to resume their relationship. But if the injured person loves his or her partner and wants the partnership to continue, the hurt returned must not be exactly as much as received because then no inequity remains to tie them together. Nor may it be more, because the wrongdoer then becomes injured and feels justified in seeking retaliation, and the cycle of harm escalates. The hurt returned must be a little less than was originally given. Then both love and fairness receive their due, and the exchange can be resumed and continued. In this way, love constrains equilibrium.

Some people find it uncomfortable to realize that, in such situations, the reconciliation that allows love to flow abundantly isn't possible unless the innocent become guilty by demanding just compensation. Nevertheless, as we know the tree by its fruit, we need only to compare couples who try the one approach with those who live the other to recognize what is truly good and what is harmful for intimacy and love.

The Way Out

A man told his friend that his wife had been resentful for 20 years. He said that a few days after their marriage, his parents had asked him to go on a six-week vacation with them because they needed him to drive their new car. He had gone with them and had left her behind. All of his attempts to explain his actions and to apologize had not achieved resolution.

His friend suggested, "Tell her that she can choose something or do something for herself that costs you as much as what you did cost her."

The man beamed. He recognized the key to unlocking the solution to their problem.

It sometimes happens that both partners cause increasing hurt to each other and act as if what injures their love were good. Then their exchange in the negative increases and this exchange binds them tightly to each other in their unhappiness. They maintain a balance of giving and taking, but not in love. We can recognize the quality of a relationship by the volume of giving and taking, and by whether equilibrium is usually achieved in good or in harm. That also points to how we can restore a weakened partnership and make it satisfying; partners move from exchange in harm to exchange in good, and increase it with love.

False Helplessness

When someone is wronged, he or she suffers helplessly. The greater the helplessness of the victim, the harsher we judge the wrongdoer. But injured partners seldom remain completely helpless once the harm is past. They usually have possibilities in action, either to end their partnership if the injuries have been too great, or to demand just atonement from their partners, and by doing so, to put an end to guilt and to enable a new beginning.

When victims don't take advantage of a possibility to act, then others act for them—with the difference that the damage and injustice done by those acting on their behalf are often much worse than if the victims had acted themselves. In human relationship systems, repressed resentments emerge later in those who are least able to defend themselves; most often, it's the children and grandchildren who experience an earlier anger as if it were their own.

False Martyr

A mature married couple attended a seminar together, and on the first evening, the woman took their car and left, reappearing again the next day just in time for the workshop. She placed herself squarely in front of her husband and announced in front of the whole group in a very provocative way that she had just come from her lover.

When this woman was with others in the group, she was as nice as her husband was: attentive, empathic, sensitive. But when she was with him, she was as mean to him as she was kind to the others. The others couldn't understand what could possibly be going on, especially inasmuch as her husband didn't defend himself.

It turned out that as a child this woman, with her mother and her siblings, was sent to the country during the summer while her father stayed in the city with his mistress. He and his mistress would visit from time to time, and his wife was always friendly and waited on them both as if nothing were wrong. But inwardly, she was furious. She repressed her anger and her pain, but the children noticed it anyway.

We might be tempted to call the mother's behavior commendable, but it was false innocence and its effect was destructive. The daughter avenged the injustice done to her mother by punishing her husband for her father's deed, but she also demonstrated her love for her father by acting exactly as he had acted—she treated her husband as her father had treated her mother. The better resolution would have been for the mother of this woman to have confronted her husband with her anger. Then he would have had to make a decision, and they could have either come to a mutual agreement or made a clean separation.

Whenever the innocent continue suffering although appropriate action is possible, more innocent victims and guilty victimizers soon follow. It's an illusion to believe that we avoid participating in evil by clinging to innocence instead of doing what we can to confront wrongdoing—even when we ourselves then do wrong as well. If one partner insists on a monopoly on innocence, there's no end to the other's guilt, and their love withers. Not only do those who ignore or passively submit to evil fail to preserve innocence, but they sow injustice. Love requires the courage to become guilty appropriately.

Premature Forgiveness

Similarly, premature forgiveness prohibits constructive dialog when it covers up or postpones a conflict and leaves the consequences to be dealt with by others in the family. This is especially destructive when the one who was wronged tries to release the wrongdoer from his or her guilt, as if victims had that authority. If reconciliation is desired, then the one wronged not only has the right to demand restitution and atonement, but also the obligation to do so. And the wrongdoer not only has the obligation to carry the consequences of his or her actions, but also the right to do so.

The Second Time Around

A man and a woman who were married to other partners fell in love. When the woman became pregnant, they divorced their respective partners and married. The woman had previously been childless. The man had a daughter from his first marriage, whom he left with her mother. The man and his new wife both felt guilty about the man's first wife and their dream was that she would forgive them. In fact, she was very resentful of them, because she and her daughter were paying the price for the couple's happiness.

When they spoke to a friend about their wish to be forgiven, he asked them to imagine what would happen if their wish were fulfilled and the ex-wife really forgave them. When they did so, they both realized that they had avoided feeling the full weight of their guilt and that their wish for forgiveness didn't do justice to the dignity and needs of the man's first wife. They decided to admit to his first wife and to his child that they had demanded a great sacrifice for their own happiness, and that they would meet all just demands from the two who had been injured. They then stood by their decision.

Love is well served when the victim's demands for compensation remain appropriate.

Forgiveness and Reconciliation

Forgiveness that is truly healing preserves the dignity of the guilty person as well as that of the victim. This forgiveness requires that victims not go to extremes in what they demand, and that they accept the appropriate compensation and atonement offered by the perpetrator. Without the forgiveness that acknowledges genuine remorse and accepts appropriate atonement, there's no reconciliation.

An "Aha" Experience

A woman divorced her husband in order to be with her lover. After many years, the woman began to regret her decision. She discovered that she still loved her ex-husband and wanted to be married to him again, especially as he had remained single. When she spoke to him about her feelings, he avoided answering, either positively or negatively, but agreed to talk the matter over with a counselor. The counselor asked the man what he hoped to get from the meeting. He laughed halfheartedly and said, "An aha! experience!"

The counselor asked the woman what she had to offer that would make her former husband interested in living with her again. She said that she hadn't really thought about what she had to offer, and was unable to answer convincingly. Not surprisingly, the man remained cautious and uncommitted.

The counselor suggested that she must, first of all, recognize that she had caused her ex-husband pain, and then give him cause to believe that she was prepared to make reparations. The woman thought it over for a while, and then looked directly at her former husband, and said convincingly, "I'm truly sorry for what I did to you. I want to be your wife again, and I will love you and care for you so that you will be happy and so that you can trust me."

The man remained noncommittal. The counselor said to him, "It must have hurt you a lot and you don't want to risk a repeat." The man had tears in his eyes and the counselor continued, "A person like you, to whom something painful was done, often feels morally superior and assumes the right to reject the other." He added, "Against such innocence, a guilty person has no chance." The man smiled and turned to his former wife.

"That was your "aha" experience. Pay me my fee," said the counselor, "and what you make out of your "aha" is up to you. I don't even want to know."

When We Must Cause Pain

When one partner's action in an intimate relationship results in separation, we tend to believe that he or she made a free and independent choice. But it's often the case that, had that partner not acted, he or she would have suffered some injury. Then the roles would have been reversed, the guilt and consequences exchanged. Perhaps the separation was necessary because the soul required more space to grow, and the one who left was already suffering. In such situations, suffering is unavoidable. Our choices are limited to acting so that something constructive emerges out of the unavoidable pain we must cause or suffer. Often partners stay in a painful situation until they have suffered enough to compensate for the pain their leaving will cause the other.

When partners separate, it isn't only the one who goes who has a new chance. The one who is left often also has a chance to make a new beginning. But when one partner stays stuck in pain and rejects the constructive possibilities presented by the separation, he or she makes it difficult for the partner who left to start a new life. Then they remain tightly tied to each other in spite of their separation.

On the other hand, when the one who was left manages to accept the opportunity for something better, then he or she also grants the former partner freedom and relief. Making something truly good out of misfortune is probably the most constructive form of forgiveness in such situations because it reconciles even when the separation remains.

Submitting to Fate

People sometimes feel guilty when they gain some advantage at another's expense—even when they can do nothing to stop it or change it. Here are two examples.

My Advantage at Your Expense

A boy was born, but his mother died. No one thought of holding the boy responsible for his mother's death, but his knowledge of his innocence didn't assuage his feeling of guilt. Because fate had tied his birth to his mother's death, the pressure of guilt remained inexorable, and he unconsciously created failure in his life in a vain attempt to atone for something he hadn't done.

Blowout

A man's car had a blowout, went into a skid, and crashed into another car. The driver of the second car was killed, but the first man lived. Although he had been driving safely, his life remained tied to the death of the other man and he couldn't escape his feelings of guilt. He was unable to enjoy his success until he came to see that the deceased man was demeaned by his misery, not honored.

We're helpless against such guilt and innocence at the hands of chance and happenstance. If we were guilty or we deserved a reward because of our freely chosen actions, we would retain power and influence. But in these situations, we recognize that we're subject to forces we can't control, forces that decide whether we live or die, are saved or perish, thrive or decline—independently of our actions for good or evil.

Such vulnerability to happenstance is so frightening to many people that they prefer to spoil their unearned good fortune and to repudiate the bounty of life rather than to accept it gracefully. They often attempt to create personal guilt or to accumulate good deeds after the fact in order to escape the vulnerability to unearned rescue or undeserved suffering.

It's common for persons who have an advantage at the cost of another to try to limit their advantage by committing suicide, becoming ill, or by doing something to make themselves truly guilty, and then suffering the consequences. All such solutions are connected to magical thinking and they are a childlike form of dealing with unearned good fortune. They actually increase guilt rather than diminish it. For example, when a child—as in the example above—whose mother died at the child's birth later limits his or her happiness or commits suicide, then the mother's sacrifice was for nothing, and she's implicitly made responsible for the death of her child as well.

If the child could have said, "Mother, your death shall not have been in vain. I will make something out of my life in memory of you, because I know its value," then the pressure of guilt at the hand of fate could have become a force for good, allowing the child to reach goals impossible for others. Then the mother's death would have had a good effect and could have brought the child peace for a long time.

Here, too, everyone involved is subject to a pressure toward equilibrium—whoever has received something from fate wants to give back in kind, or when that's not possible, then at least to compensate with failure. But these remain vain attempts, as destiny is utterly indifferent to our demands and attempts at compensations and restitution.

Humility in the Face of Fate

It is our innocence that makes our suffering at the hands of happenstance so difficult to bear. If we were guilty because of our own actions and were punished, or if we were innocent of wrongdoing and were spared as a result, we could assume that the condition of circumstance follows a moral order and the rules of justice and fair play. We could believe that we control guilt and innocence with our good behavior. But when we're spared regardless of our personal guilt or innocence while others perish without regard for their worthiness or unworthiness, then we know that we're completely vulnerable to the forces of chance and we're unavoidably confronted with the capriciousness of guilt and innocence. When guilt and damage reach tragic dimensions and become our fate, reconciliation is only possible if we relinquish compensation completely.

The only possibility then open to us is submission, to choose to surrender to the inexorable force of destiny, to either our advantage or our disadvantage. We may call the inner attitude that makes it possible to surrender in this way *humility*; that is, a humble forgiveness and submission to true helplessness. In such situations, when both the wrongdoer and the one wronged submit to their inevitable fate with humility, they put an end to guilt and compensation. It allows them to enjoy life and happiness—as long as they last—independently of the price others have paid. It allows them to consent to their own deaths and to the difficulties life presents regardless of personal guilt and innocence.

Where's My Grandson?

A young man who had just learned to drive had an accident. His grandmother, who was a passenger, was fatally injured. As she came to consciousness in the hospital just before she died, she asked, "Where's my grandson?" As he was brought to her, she said, "Don't blame yourself. It's my time to die."

Unbidden, the thought welled up in him with the tears, "I submit to carrying the weight of being the instrument of your passing. When the time comes, I will do something good in your memory." And one day he did.

This humility lends us seriousness and weight. When we feel true humility, we realize that it isn't just we who determine our fate, but also that it is our fate that determines us. Happenstance acts to our benefit or harm according to laws whose secrets we cannot—and must not—fathom. Humility is the appropriate answer to guilt and good fortune at the hands of fate. It puts us on a level with the less fortunate, enabling us to honor them—not by diminishing or disregarding the advantage we have at their expense, but by gratefully taking it in spite of the high price they paid, and by seeing to it that others profit from it as well.

CONSCIENCE IN THE
SERVICE OF SOCIAL ORDER

The third necessity for the success of love in intimate relationships is order. "Order" refers, first of all, to the rules and social conventions that constrain the communal life of a social group. All enduring relationships develop norms, rules, beliefs, and taboos that are binding on their members. In this way, relationships become relationship systems with order and structure. These social conventions constitute the surface convention to which all group members consent, but which vary widely from group to group. Such orders set the boundaries of membership: Those who conform belong and those who don't follow the conventions of the group soon leave. We can see this systemic dynamic clearly when watching a flock of birds in flight. Within the flock, every bird flies its individual path, but when it deviates too widely from the flight of the others, we see it leave the flock. Social orders constrain our behavior within our group and give form to our roles and functions, but we don't feel such deep guilt at violating them as when we injure bonding or the balance of giving and taking.

Additional Considerations

In earlier times, the consequences of being excluded from one's group or family must have been much more serious than today (although such exclusion still carries profound consequences in some rural areas). We live in a time of rapidly changing social orders, and while this social evolution increases flexibility, mobility, and personal freedom of choice, it also simultaneously increases alienation, disorientation, the loss of roots, and may limit the sense of well-being that naturally comes with clear belonging. Many of the individual and family problems that people bring to therapy are the result of the breakdown of old social and family orders and the difficulty of developing new orders that both stand the test of time and serve love. For example, the traditional orders that defined the roles and division of labor between men and women are changing so rapidly that many couples must expend enormous effort to develop new ones appropriate to their situations. We frequently observe how unpredictable the long-term effects of these new orders are on their children and on their love, and that their efforts are not always rewarded with success. They work very hard to achieve an order in their togetherness that once was freely given by the norms of their community. Many have been pleased to discover that they can maintain bonding and balance of giving and taking within their family even when they deviate from the traditional social orders of their group or community. [H.B.]

THE SYSTEMIC CONSCIENCE
OF THE GREATER WHOLE

In addition to the feelings of guilt and innocence that we consciously feel in the service of bonding, the balance of giving and taking, and social convention, there's also a hidden conscience operating in our relationships that we do not feel. It's a systemic conscience that has priority over our personal feelings of guilt and innocence and which serves other orders. These orders are the hidden natural laws that shape and constrain the behavior of human relationship systems. They are, in part, the natural forces of biology and evolution; in part, the general dynamics of complex systems becoming manifest in our intimacy; and in part, the forces of Love's Hidden Symmetry operating within the soul.

Although we are not directly aware of it, we can recognize the orders of this hidden conscience by their effect, by the suffering that results from their being violated, and by the rich and stable love they support. We often violate the Orders of Love when we follow our personal conscience. Tragedies in families and in intimate relationships—as we will see in the following chapters—are often associated with conflicts between the conscience guarding bonding, giving and taking, and social convention and the hidden conscience guarding the family system. But love flourishes when personal conscience and social convention submit to the orders and hidden symmetry of love.

Breaking the Magic Spell

Whoever desires to solve the mystery of Love's Hidden Symmetry enters a complex labyrinth and must carry many balls of twine to distinguish the paths that lead to daylight from those that lead deeper into the abyss. We are forced to feel our way in darkness, confronting the deceptions and illusions that weave themselves around us, dulling our senses and paralyzing our understanding as we try to unravel the secrets of the good beyond guilt and innocence. Children are led into this surreality when they're told that babies are brought by storks, and weary prisoners must have felt it as well when they read the sign above the gate of the death camp, "Work will make you free."

Nevertheless, many have had the courage to enter the labyrinth, to peer into the darkness, and to break the spell of false belief. Then they are like the minstrel waiting quietly on the corner to play a countermelody to waken the spellbound children as the Pied Piper marches past. Or like the boy, upon watching a crowd cheering a demented dictator, exclaimed what others knew but were afraid to admit, "He's naked!"

The Emperor's New Clothes

At an academic symposium, a well-known professor of philosophy was much applauded when he eloquently defended the idea that the greatest personal freedom is achieved when an individual is no longer dependent on anyone else.

As the thunder of applause died down, one of the participants stood and said, in a loud voice with childlike simplicity, "That's not right!" A wave of shock and indignation swept through the room.

After the audience had calmed, the man added, "Everyone can see that at any moment we are dependent on many things—on the air we breathe, on the farmer who grows our food, on our friends and family. We are all parts of a greater whole, and we depend on it as it depends on us. What freedom is that when we refuse to see what *is* and are condemned to live in the illusion that things are different than they are? The freedom that I love comes when I acknowledge reality as it is and consent to it. Then I can pay in full measure what I owe and I am free from debt, and I can take in full measure what is given to me and I am free to need."

The intelligence of the systemic symmetry of love operating unseen in our relationships watches over love. It is easier to follow than to understand. We recognize it, if it is important to us, in the subtle movements of our inwardness and in the careful observation of our relationships. We recognize its laws only when we see the consequences of what we have done for ourselves and others—whether love increases or it is diminished.

How we recognize the limits of personal conscience, where they help us as well as where we must overcome them, and how we may know the intelligence of the Greater Soul that supports love are described in the following chapters.

It is the path of the knowledge of good and evil beyond feelings of guilt and innocence, and it serves love.

Helping Revelations

A young man seeking further knowledge sets out on his bicycle into the countryside. He is driven by the joy of exploration and his enthusiasm knows no bounds. Far beyond his usual territory, he finds a new path. Here there are no more signs to guide him, and he must rely on what his eye can see and what his pedaling legs can measure. Now what was only an intuition becomes experience.

His path ends at a wide river and he gets off his bicycle. He sees that going on requires leaving everything he has on the riverbank, leaving the safety of solid ground, putting himself in the hands of a force that is stronger than he is, and allowing himself to be overpowered and swept along. He hesitates, and then retreats.

This is his first revelation.

Riding home, he admits to himself that he understands very little that could be helpful to others, and even that little which he knows, he could scarcely communicate. He imagines himself to be following another bicycle rider whose fender is rattling. He imagines calling out, "Hey, your fender's rattling!" The other answers, "What?" He imagines yelling louder, "Your fender's rattling!"

The other answers, "I can't hear you. My fender's rattling."

He realizes, "He didn't need my help at all!"

This is his second revelation.

A short time later, he asks an old teacher, "How do you manage to help other people? Many people come to you asking for advice, and they leave feeling better even though you know little of their affairs."

The teacher answers, "When someone loses courage and doesn't want to go on, the problem is seldom lack of knowledge, but rather wanting safety when courage is called for, and seeking freedom where necessity leaves no choice. And so he goes in circles. A teacher resists appearance and illusion. He finds his center and waits for a helpful word, as a ship with sails raised waits to catch the wind. When someone comes seeking help, the teacher is waiting where the visitor himself must go, and if an answer comes, it comes for both of them, for both are listeners."

And then the teacher adds, "Waiting at the center is effortless."

CHAPTER TWO

Man and Woman: The Foundation of Family

The foundation of family is the sexual attraction between a man and a woman. When a man desires a woman, he desires what he, as man, needs and does not have. When a woman desires a man, she, too, desires what she, as woman, is missing. Male and female form a complementary pair of partners who mutually define and complete one another. Each is what the other needs, and each needs what the other is. If love is to succeed, we must give what we are and take from our partner what we need. Giving ourselves, taking and having our partner, we become man or woman, and with him or her, we become a couple.

The expression of love in sexual intimacy, and sometimes the act of sexual intercourse alone, often bonds partners to each other whether they want it or not. It isn't intention or choice that establishes the bond, but the physical act itself. This dynamic can be observed in the sense of protectiveness that some rape and incest victims feel toward the perpetrators, and in those casual sexual encounters that leave lifelong traces.

Our shyness in naming and affirming this most intimate aspect of a couple's relationship is related to the fact that sexual passion is still regarded in some circles as being demeaning and undignified. Nevertheless, sexual consummation is the greatest possible human act. No other human action is more in harmony with the order and the richness of life, expresses more fully our participation in the wholeness of the world, or brings with it such profound pleasure and, in its consequences, such loving suffering. No other act brings such rewards or entails greater risks, demands more from us, and makes us so wise, knowing, and human as when we take each other, know each other, and belong to each other in love. In comparison, all other human actions seem merely a prelude, an encore, a solace, or a consequence—an impoverished imitation.

The sexual expression of love is also our most humble action. Nowhere else do we expose ourselves so completely, uncovering our deepest vulnerability. We don't guard anything else with such deep shame as this inner place where partners show each other their most intimate selves and give those selves into each other's keeping. Through the sexual expression of love, both men and women leave their mothers and fathers and "cleave" to one another—as the Bible describes it—and they become one flesh.

Whether we like it or not, the special and, in a very deep sense, indissoluble bond between partners arises out of, and is the result of, their sexual union. Only this act makes them a couple, and only this act can make them parents. For this reason, if their sexuality is limited in some way—for example, by inhibitions or by one partner's having been sterilized—the bond doesn't form completely, even if the couple desires it. This is also true of platonic partnerships in which partners avoid the risks of sexuality and confront less guilt and responsibility if they separate. Once partners have established a bond by sharing sexual intimacy, separation without hurt and guilt is no longer possible. They no longer can walk away as if their togetherness didn't exist. Although this bonding causes hardship for parents who separate, it also protects their children from capricious or self-centered separations.

The crucial role that sexuality plays in a couple's bonding makes apparent the supremacy of the flesh over the spirit, as well as the wisdom of the flesh. We may be tempted to devalue the flesh in comparison with the spirit, as if that which is done out of physical need, desire, longing, and sexual love has less value than what we gain through reason and moral will. Physical desire neverthe-less demonstrates its power, and sometimes its wisdom, at the point at which reason and morality reach their limits and recoil. Desire still rises to serve after reason's cold constraints have wea-ried or grown callous. The higher reason and the deeper meaning that arise out of our instinctual physical urges overpower and con-trol rationality and will. They are closer to the heart of life and are more enduring.

The Spirit Is Willing, the Flesh Is Wise

Some say that body
in comparison to Spirit
—is less.
As if that done in longing
and sexual desire
—were less
than that chosen out of
Reason and by Moral Will.

But desire displays
courage and wisdom
when Will and Reason
cower and shrink and
dare not to serve Life.

In the Desire of the Flesh
hides a higher reason
and burns a deeper meaning
outshining rationality and
overpowering the will.
Desire is closer to the Heart of life,
more obedient,
and more enduring.

It is the flesh that rules the will.
I say,
The Spirit is willing, but
The Flesh is Wise.

Additional Considerations

Hellinger's insistence on the creative and life-affirming nature of sexual desire contrasts sharply with the views of those who consider "desires of the flesh" to be a nuisance or even sinful, and also with the views of those who see sexuality merely as a pleasure unconnected to parenthood.

"Male" and "female" denote—among other things—the physiological specialization necessary for procreation. In this sense, male and female need one another, complement and complete one another, but it would be a grave error to reduce maleness and femaless to this biological dimension alone. Nevertheless, our psychotherapeutic work shows that people who downplay or ignore its importance regularly encounter difficulty in their intimate relationships. When Hellinger speaks of the sexual expression of love between a man and a woman, he isn't excluding or discounting other forms of loving, sexual relationships, but he is insisting on honoring this inescapable aspect of parenthood.

Increasing numbers of men and women are living in nontraditional families. There are singles and couples who neither have nor desire children, just as there are men who desire men and women who desire women. Faced with a population explosion, nature increasingly demands and supports couples foregoing parenthood, providing them with alternative expressions of humanness and love. Still, many people with whom we have worked feel a painful loss at foregoing parenthood and work hard to accept their loss without minimizing it, to find lifestyles that bring meaning and the deep satisfaction of soul that come automatically to parents in a healthy family. When they succeed, they know that they serve and are supported by life in what they do, and participate fully in its bounty and mystery. Still, many continue to look wistfully at families with children and do wonder what it would have been like to have been parents. This is especially true as they grow older and approach death. Their loss—no matter how appropriate—is a heavy burden and deserves full acknowledgment and appreciation. [H.B.]

CARING FOR DESIRE

If the sexual desires of one of the partners aren't reciprocated, he or she is in a weak position because the other has the power to reject. Although the one who meets a desire needn't take any risks, he or she appears to be stronger. The one who desires appears to be needy and taking rather than generous and giving, and the one who meets the desire although he or she may be loving, appears to give and to help without taking. In this dynamic, the one who desires must feel grateful, as though he or she had taken without having given, and the one who withholds need and meets desire feels free, and perhaps even superior, as though his or her giving involved no taking.

Some partners hold on to the power and superiority of being the giver, but they damage their togetherness. For a relationship to succeed over time, the risk of rejection, as well as the joys and pleasures of giving, must be shared. Desiring is still difficult for many women because they must break strong cultural taboos, and they still may be rejected or feared at first when they expose their desire. Nevertheless, in therapy, something interesting often happens when a woman tells her mother, "Sometimes I can hardly wait to make love with my husband"—even if she says it only in her imagination.

Partners who care for desire can agree that when the most intimate self of one is open and vulnerable—as it is when desire is exposed—then the other must respect the desire, even if he or she doesn't fulfill it. We are especially vulnerable when we desire, so a partner shouldn't have to risk a humiliating rejection when he or she feels and expresses desire. If couples honor this, they can risk desiring again, and their relationship can achieve depth and intimacy. Both must desire, and each must treat the other's desires with respect and love. When sexuality serves the relationship as well as being its goal, both the sexuality and the loving partnership are deeper, freer, and more authentic.

Because both men and women fear such profound need with the naked dependency it implies and the danger of devastating rejection, many people seek to develop the opposite gender within themselves. Men seek to become like women, as if they could be women, and women seek to become like men, as if they could be men. If they succeed in this, they no longer need a partner, and their relationship becomes essentially a matter of convenience.

In order for a partnership between a man and a woman to fulfill its promise, the man must be a man and the woman must be a woman. In partnerships between a man and a woman, she remains interested in him only when he is a man and remains one, and the reverse is true for him. This means that a man who desires to love a woman as his equal partner must preserve his need for her by preserving his incompleteness. Instead of developing the feminine in himself, he must allow his partner to offer it to him as a gift, and he must take from her the feminine she offers. A woman who desires to love a man must also accept the masculine from her partner. When a man and a woman both want and need what the other has, and have what the other needs and wants, then they are equal in their incompleteness—and in their ability to give. When both respect their limitations and preserve their need, their mutual needs complement and complete one another, and their giving and taking strengthen their bond.

This systemic view is exactly the opposite of the popular idea that men should develop the feminine in themselves and that women should develop their masculine potential. Persons who do so don't need a partner to give them what they're missing, and they often prefer to live alone.

The Basso Continuo

A couple's relationship is conducted like a baroque concert: a variety of the most beautiful melodies rings in the upper register, and below, a basso continuo supports and leads the melodies and gives them weight and depth. In a couple's relationship, the basso continuo is: "I take you, I take you, I take you, I take you to be my wife, I take you to be my husband. I take you to myself and give myself to you with love."

LOVE BETWEEN PARTNERS

Love between partners requires the renunciation of our first and most intimate love, our love as a child for our parents. Only when a boy's attachment—either loving or resentful—to his mother is resolved can he give himself fully to his partner and enter manhood. A girl's attachment to her father must also be resolved before she can give herself to her partner and be a woman. Successful togetherness demands the sacrifice and transformation of our earlier child bond to our parents—the boy to his mother and the girl to her father.

A boy lives his prenatal and early childhood years primarily within his mother's sphere of influence. If he remains there, her influence floods his psyche, and he experiences the feminine as all important and all powerful. Under his mother's dominance, he may well become a skillful seducer and lover, but he does not develop into a man who appreciates women and who can maintain a long-term loving relationship. Nor does he become a strong and dedicated father to his own children. To become a man capable of joining fully in a partnership of equals, he must give up the first and most intimate love of his life—his mother—and move into his father's sphere of influence.

In earlier times, the process through which a boy left his mother was socially structured and supported by rites of initiation and passage. Having passed through these rituals, a boy had a firm place in his father's world and couldn't return to live in his mother's house as a child. In our culture, the formal rituals that once supported this process have disappeared and the process of moving out of the mother's sphere is often painfully difficult. Even the military service that once served to help boys leave their mother's sphere and enter their father's has lost its viability for many young men.

A girl also enters life within her mother's sphere of influence, but she experiences the feminine and attraction to the masculine differently from her brother. Her father holds a fascination for her, and if all goes well, she can practice the art of attracting men in the steady safety of his love. If however, she stays in her father's sphere of influence, she becomes a "daddy's girl." She may become someone's lover, but she doesn't mature fully into her womanhood; she has difficulty relating as an equal partner and becoming a generous, giving mother to her children. To become a woman, it's necessary for a girl to leave the first man in her life—her father—and to return to stand by her mother.

Questions and Answers

Question: Can't a child have an equally balanced relationship with both the father and the mother?

Hellinger: Of course. This happens when boys move into their father's sphere of influence and girls return to their mother's. If you look at real people, you see that a son who is connected to his father has more respect and appreciation for his mother than does a son who remains tied to her—and the mother doesn't lose anything. Likewise, a daughter who has moved from her father's sphere of influence back to her mother's doesn't lose her father, nor does he lose her. Quite the contrary, she develops more respect and appreciation for him. Even more important, the parents' relationship is stronger when the sons are near their father and the daughters are near their mother. Then there's no confusion in the family.

Question: Have I understood you correctly that when I affirm my mother's right to womanhood, I've taken my proper place next to her?

Hellinger: No. Any daughter who assumes she has the authority to affirm or deny her mother's right to womanhood has set herself above her mother.

Question: And if I simply accept her?

Hellinger: Accepting her implies a superior generosity on your part. Accepting and affirming your womanhood as a gift from her is humble.

Rainer *(group participant)*:   It's strange that so much has been written about the mother–child relationship and so little about the father–child relationship.

Hellinger: Do you have a daughter or a son?

Rainer: I have an eight-year-old daughter.

Hellinger: Then it's about time that you let her go back to her mother's sphere of influence.

Rainer: Yes, I've thought a lot about the process of letting go of my daughter, but at the same time, I know that there's nothing I can do to make it happen.

Hellinger: Of course there is.

Rainer: I mean that I can't force it. I can't make it happen.

Hellinger: Certainly you can!

Rainer: But that's not what I want.

Hellinger: Well, at least that's a clear message. What I've been saying does have definite implications for action—otherwise I'd save my breath.

Rainer: So what could I do?

Hellinger: Well, for one thing, when you look at her, you could admire your wife in her.

Rainer: That's a great idea. I like it *(laughing)*.

Hellinger: Or you might tell your daughter that she's almost as wonderful as her mother.

Rainer: Another thing that's bothering me is . . . .

Hellinger: *(Interrupting him and speaking to the group)* He's changing the subject, but that's okay. He's noticed that things are getting serious. He's starting to realize what he has to deal with. Sometimes, when a father holds on to his daughter, it's hard for her to return to her mother's sphere of influence. She feels important, believing that she could fill his need, but that job's too big for a child. Compared with a wife, a daughter is a consolation prize.

Question: Last night, after I went to bed, I kept thinking about the "spheres of influence" of the mother and father. You said that a macho man is one who has remained bound to his mother for too long. What about an effeminate man? Would you say that this tendency is a result of staying too long in the father's sphere of influence?

Hellinger: No. In this respect, a macho man and an effeminate man are the same—they've both remained in the mother's sphere of influence. A Don Juan is also a mother's son who hasn't made it to manhood. He's hoping that by having many women he can continue to participate in womanhood forever. Needing to have a lot of partners is a quality of being stuck in mother's sphere. A man who's moved out of his mother's sphere can take what he needs from a partner, and he can give himself and become a partner. Bragging, strutting, macho types are mothers' darlings.

Question: Would you elaborate on your concept of sphere of influence?

Hellinger: I'm trying to avoid defining concepts. What we're discussing aren't concepts that are true or false. I'm trying to describe difficult experiences in a way that enables us to deal with them better and will be more helpful to people in need. There's nothing more to it than that. As soon as we claim that our descriptions are the "Truth," then they're a false theory and will immediately be discredited. What I'm describing isn't absolutely "true." It's a phenomenological description of certain dynamics I've observed in my work with couples and families over the years. I want to leave it at that. Please don't make more out of what I say than I intend.

So being in someone's sphere of influence simply describes being under the person's influence. For example, when it's especially important for a girl to please her father, then she's in his sphere of influence. Or, in some families, the mother and son collude to scorn and be condescending to the father. That's basically all I mean.

Question: A daughter also experiences her first relationship with her mother. If she has to return to her mother's sphere of influence, that means that she must have already moved away from her mother to her father, and then can go back again.

Hellinger: Exactly! *(Laughing)* That's the reason it's so easy for women—they can go back. A son experiences the feminine as so all-powerful, attractive, and pervasively important that he feels too weak to give it up. He can't quite leave under his own power. If he's to give up being a boy and become a man, he has to connect to his father and grandfather, and to the world of men. That's where he finds the strength he needs to move out of his mother's sphere.

Question: Doesn't a girl miss something if she just stays in her mother's sphere of influence? Isn't it important for her to leave and then return?

Hellinger: That's right. First, she has to move to her father, and then back to her mother. If she knows only her mother's influence, she doesn't experience the attraction of the masculine with her father.

Question: You said that a woman has a difficult time fully accepting a man if she hasn't relinquished her father. I keep thinking about that.

Hellinger: When a woman is still tied to her father, she often secretly believes that she would be a better partner for him than her mother is. That's a child's belief. If she looks honestly at the real consequences for her of being his partner, she puts that child belief in an adult context. There's a sentence that can help her give up the unhealthy tie to her father. She can tell him, "Mother's a little better for you than I am."

Question: What's the masculine in a woman and the feminine in a man? What are masculine and feminine at all? At least, what's your opinion?

Hellinger: That's something I haven't been able to figure out yet *(laughing)*. For a man, there's always something hidden about women, and the other way around. I don't even completely understand the masculine yet. But what we're talking about doesn't have to do with conceptual understanding. I'm not proposing a theory of masculinity and femininity. I'm trying to describe what people experience in the family constellations and in their relationships, and also to open up a space for you to come into contact with certain things that can be known only by experiencing them. Trying intellectually to understand an experience is like trying to hold a fire. If you try to grasp such things intellectually, then from the fire you've only got the ashes.

Question: It seems to me that what you're describing is just the old Oedipus stuff in a different language. I can't see the difference between what you're describing and the psychoanalytic Oedipus complex.

Hellinger: There's a basic misunderstanding of phenomenology implied in your question. When you immediately place your experience here in the context of something you already know, you can't observe anything new.

Of course, psychoanalysis has a deep understanding of what happens in parent–child relationships, but what I'm describing isn't the same as the Oedipus complex. Psychoanalytic thinking is different from systemic thinking. As soon as you say "Oedipus complex," the phenomenology of the system dynamic disappears and you're left with the psychodynamic construct you already know. You're moving in a different thought world. I'm not talking about how one thing causes another, nor am I trying to describe unconscious processes. I'm describing what I've actually seen people do. I'm describing their actual feelings and behaviors and looking at how they are systemically associated with one another. No causality is implied, just systemic association. That's a different level of abstraction than psychoanalytic theory.

If you're interested in observing the system dynamics of human relationships, you need to focus your attention on what people actually do. That's the phenomenological method. Otherwise, all you have are the words and concepts dissociated from experience. That's not enough to be of real help to anyone.

RENEWING MALENESS AND FEMALENESS

When partners enter a relationship, each brings his or her individuality to their togetherness, and in their togetherness, they lose it. A woman confirms her husband as man, but she challenges his maleness and takes it from him, and his maleness decreases in the course of their partnership. Likewise, a man confirms his wife's womanhood, but he also challenges her femaleness and takes it from her, and she becomes less of a woman. If the partnership is to remain exciting for both, they must constantly renew their maleness and femaleness.

A man renews his maleness in the company of men and a woman her femaleness in the company of women, so they must leave their relationship from time to time in order to refresh their maleness and femaleness. The actual content of the exchanges among the men or the women is unimportant. It might be at a coffee klatch, the corner bar, a club, a consciousness-raising group, or on a sports team. What matters is being together with other men or with other women and doing things men and women do when they gather among themselves. If a couple does this, the relationship retains its creative tension, and can continue to develop and deepen. This element of relationship is overlooked in the romantic ideal of love, which envisions a loving couple giving each other everything each needs.

THE BOND BETWEEN PARTNERS

The bond between a man and a woman requires that the man want the woman as *woman* and that the woman want the man as *man*. Their bond doesn't develop fully if they want each other for other reasons: for example, for recreation or adornment, or as a provider; or because one of them is rich or poor, Catholic or Protestant, Jew or Muslim, Hindu or Buddhist; or because one wants to conquer or protect or improve or save the other; or because one wants the other primarily to be the father or mother of his or her children. Partners who come together for such reasons don't develop the strength of togetherness that enables them to weather serious crises.

If a man remains a son looking for a mother, or if a woman remains a daughter looking for a father, their relationships, although they may be intense and loving, aren't relationships of adult women and men. People entering into relationships with the hope—acknowledged or not—that they'll get something they didn't get in their relationships with their mothers or fathers, are looking for parents. The belonging that then develops is that of child and parent. It sometimes happens that a man looking for a mother finds someone looking for a son, or that a woman seeking a father finds someone hoping for a daughter. Such couples may be very happy for a while, but should they have children, they and their children will experience difficulties as they adjust their partnership.

Love is limited in exactly the same way when one partner acts toward the other with the authority of a parent, and attempts to teach, improve, or help the other. Every adult has already been brought up and taught how to behave, and all attempts to do that again are certain to damage love. It's no wonder that the partner who's being treated like a child reacts by pulling out of the relationship—the way a child pulls away from the family—and seeks relief outside the relationship. Most power conflicts in intimate partnerships occur when one partner tries to treat the other as a child, mother, or father.

Bonding in Second Relationships

A second loving partnership is different from the first because second partners sense their partners' former bonds. We see this in the caution with which we approach new partners, and also in our slowness to give ourselves and to take and have our new partners as freely as our earlier ones. Both partners experience their second partnership in the shadow of the first, even when the first partner is deceased. For this reason, a second love succeeds only when the bond to the first is acknowledged and honored, when the new partners know that they follow the first and are indebted to them.

Our second togetherness doesn't have the same strength or quality as the first, and it isn't necessary. This doesn't mean that a second relationship is any less happy or loving. In fact, a second partnership is often happier than the first, and a second love much more satisfying. Still, the density of the bond generally decreases with each successive relationship. That's the reason why the guilt and sense of responsibility resulting from a second divorce are generally less than from a first, and why a second divorce is usually easier and less painful than a first. We can gauge the strength of the bond by the amount of guilt, pain, and loss that accompanies a separation.

My Second Wife

A man objected to the observation that bonding decreases with each relationship. He maintained that his bonding to his second wife was much stronger than his bonding to his first wife had been.

Everyone could see that this man and his second wife were very happy together and that their love was true and deep. He told how painful and damaging his first marriage had been, and it became clear that he never again wanted to be so vulnerable as he had been then. He had stayed in his first marriage, in part, to be near his son. He and his second wife had no children.

When asked what would happen if his second marriage were to sour and become as his first had been, he responded that, although he couldn't imagine that happening, he would leave before he would repeat what he had experienced before. Then he understood that, although he loved his second wife more, he was bound to her less tightly than he was to his first wife.

Sweethearts

A woman from a small town married her first sweetheart shortly after graduation from high school. They had four children and a normal life together. Her husband died in his late 50s, but she lived 25 more years. She never looked at another man, and never considered a second partnership. She said, "I can't imagine being with another man. We had always been together."

An 84-year-old woman told how she had survived three husbands. She had lost her first two husbands in two different wars and the third to old age. She said, "The third was the nicest and I had him the longest, but I miss the first the most. We were so young then, and so in love."

Examples from Seminars

Question: I asked my husband about his first wife. It hurt to hear him talk about her, but it was also good for me.

Hellinger: Not long ago, a man came to a session with his girl-friend. They had decided to get married. He'd been married before and had a son from that marriage. We set up the constellation, of his present family, which included his first wife, his son, and his present girlfriend. When I asked him who was missing, he said, "Oh yes, I was married once prior to my last marriage, but it was only a stu-dent love, and it wasn't really important." We brought his first wife into the constellation, and it was immediately clear that she was the decisive person. She hadn't been acknowledged or honored. As the constellation developed, it became very clear to the woman repre-senting his second wife that she had left him out of unconscious solidarity with his first wife. When we put the girlfriend and her husband-to-be into the constellation, she felt uncomfortable stand-ing close to him, and better when she moved away a bit. That's a typical position for a second or third wife.

A second wife doesn't completely trust herself to take her hus-band in the same way as a first wife does. She has him, but the first wife and the previous children have given him up. Her feeling of guilt is the price she pays. Standing apart from him, she could see that she was his third wife and that she followed the other two. From that position, it was easier for her to honor their roles in the man's life.

At our next session, the girlfriend said she was feeling really down. She said when she thought about the other wives, she felt that she really had no chance herself. I said to her, "There are three women who must be fully honored, the first, the second, *and* the third."

Question: Does that still apply if a couple meets after they have already divorced their first partners?

Hellinger: It has to do with the discrepancy of gain and loss for everyone, and it's independent of motivations, morals, or personal histories. The first partners have lost their mates, and the second partners have gained them. If there are children who have lost a parent, that carries even more weight. New partners take the place of the earlier partners, but their systemic obligation to the earlier partners and their feelings of guilt prevent them from taking their new partners as completely as they took their earlier partners.

The situation improves if they admit to themselves that their gain is the first partner's loss, and that they couldn't have their new partners unless the earlier partners had given them up. Honoring all the others in the system is crucial to achieving systemic balance. A man and his second wife can then move closer together, but they still have an obligation to the first wife, and their relationship will never be the same as a first relationship. The same is naturally true for a woman who's gained her husband at another woman's expense. A new relationship has a better chance for success if the partners recognize their indebtedness to the earlier partners, allow themselves to become aware of their feelings of guilt, and acknowledge the guilt and indebtedness that come with their relationship. Their relationship then deepens, and they have fewer illusions.

BALANCING GIVING AND TAKING

Love flourishes between partners when they are well matched, balancing each other like hanging scales when both dishes are alternately filled with different things of equal weight. Like the scales, their relationship system tilts from side to side as the needs or contributions of the one or the other temporarily become more important. If one is especially strong at one time, love requires the other to be equally strong at another time; if one has special potentials or liabilities, then the other must offer an equivalent. When they're well matched, their love may develop in a partnership of equals.

Being well matched means that partners give themselves to each other equally and take one another equally; that they need and satisfy one another equally; and that each acknowledges and respects equally the functions and values of the other. Although they are equal, they are also different. Only then can their relationship be a partnership of equals.

Being well matched allows partners to maintain a balance of giving and taking in which each gives to the other what he or she has to offer and takes fully from the other what is needed. The fundamental balance of giving and taking that love requires is threatened when one partner habitually gives or takes more, or when what is given in love is not taken in love.

Overcoming Limiting Roles and Norms

Because the roles and functions of men and women depend, to a large extent, on the norms of culture, class, and social group, they vary widely from group to group and from culture to culture. But love follows natural laws that are more fundamental than the habits and customs of culture, and it sometimes demands of us what our family and our culture forbid.

Perhaps an image will help in your understanding the difference between cultural habit and what love requires. In every country, people cook their food according to their particular recipes, with certain herbs and spices. Children raised in that country then develop a taste for those foods. It may happen that someone who was raised on mild food cannot eat food prepared with the fiery spices of another land. The grubs or oily fish prized by some may be disgusting to others. What recipes one follows and what foods one likes are largely learned choices. The intelligence of nature, on the other hand, dictates that we must eat to live, and must not eat what is poison. What and how we eat are largely matters of convention and the availability of food, and may be modified as opportunity and need allow. Malnutrition, whether caused by famine or by over-eating, results in illness, and eventually death. This is a natural law that is unchangeable. The social customs that guide the roles and functions of men and women vary greatly from group to group, like recipes and spices. But across all cultures, there are some things that nourish love and other things that damage it.

When two people join in a partnership, each brings a model for partnership and for the roles and functions of men and women based on the values of his or her family of origin, and they both follow these rules, patterns, and norms out of habit. They feel good when they follow these old patterns even if the patterns are destructive, and they feel guilty if they abandon them for new ones, even if the new ones are better. For love to succeed, it is often necessary for partners to rise above the dictates of the conscience binding them to their reference groups. Thus, the price of love is often guilt.

Consenting to Guilt: 1

A young couple, very much in love, decided that they wanted their partnership to be based on equality. Rather than carefully attending to their sense of systemic balance, they followed a rigid concept of balance and scrupulously divided all of their tasks 50/50 between them. This arrangement functioned without serious problems until they decided to have children. They eventually sought counseling in a state of utter exhaustion and frustration, on the verge of separation. They gradually came to understand that the only measure of equality in a partnership is the mutual feeling of balance and satisfaction. Upon dividing their tasks and responsibilities according to their inner sense of balance rather than their concept of fairness, they soon recovered their health, and love began to flow between them once again.

Consenting to Guilt: 2

Another young couple, also very much in love, decided that they wanted to live their partnership according to the principles of their fundamentalist religion. They divided the roles and functions of man and woman according to the dictates of their faith. The woman stayed at home and did the things women in that religion do, while the man worked and did the things proper for a man in that system. Unlike many other couples in that religion to whom this style of relationship brought joy and the flowering of love, this young couple became unhappy. The wife, who had a professional education, discovered that she missed her work and the company of other professionals, while the man, who was affectionate and playful, missed having more time for his children. They sought the help of a friend and were able, in a long and painful process, to rise above their original concept of balance, to learn to attend to the inner flow of their togetherness and, thus, to find a larger balance that did support their love.

Both couples faced the same systemic problem and solved it by consenting to guilt. Although the specific requirements of their consciences differed, each had to rise above the social beliefs they had brought to their relationship and learn to feel the presence or absence of a true systemic balance.

Two Styles of Love

A South American woman married a Northern European man. She longed for the stability his European reserve promised, and he for the emotional warmth and liveliness that burned in her. Nevertheless, they began to have difficulties shortly after their first child was born. The man was used to keeping his distance and to respecting a woman's personal space. He feared excessive closeness. She felt his distance not as respect, but as abandonment, and reacted with panic and resentment. He was frightened by her "irrational heat" and withdrew even more, resenting her demands and control. Both hoped that the other would adopt a different way of doing things. Their differences soon escalated until they were no longer able to talk to each other.

The love they felt for each other and for their child was barely adequate to contain the pain of their differences. They found a solution only when both were willing to surrender parts of their identities—their cultural and family habits and styles of communication—and could agree on a third way of being together.

The systemic conscience that guards equality in partnerships isn't swayed by good intentions or wishful thinking. Whether or not the roles and functions of partners in a relationship are in balance can be seen only in the degree of their love and satisfaction and not in what the partners may claim or believe. Sometimes unbalance becomes clear only in the course of time.

For a partnership to succeed, the partners need to carefully reevaluate the values and the patterns that they've inherited from their families and exchange some of them for ones that are better for the partnership. While doing this, both families must be respected even when they don't meet the other's standards. For example, if they do not belong to the same religion, it's much easier today than formerly for them to respect both families and to combine their confessions on a new level, perhaps by joining a different faith or by becoming active in a social service.

An image portrays this process: Two people are standing on opposite banks of a river. If they simply call out to one another, "This is my position," nothing changes, and the river continues to flow by, indifferent to their shouts. If they want to know the love that's possible to equal partners, they both have to get into the river and allow themselves to be carried by the current. Only then can they come together, feel the river's force, and know what life offers and demands.

When people have been hurt or damaged in their relationship with their original family, they carry that hurt and suspicion into the new partnership. They can't avoid bringing their old system into the new one. In fact, unresolved attachments to the family of origin are a major cause of difficulty in relationships.

My Husband, My Grandmother

A man and a women felt deeply connected to each other, yet they frequently had severe conflicts that they couldn't understand.

Although they had three children, they separated for six months. One day, as they met with a therapist, he noticed the woman's expression changing, until she looked like an old woman unreasonably berating her husband. The therapist asked, "Who is this old woman?" The woman thought a while and then suddenly remembered how her grandfather, who owned a bar, often pulled her grandmother around by the hair, humiliating her in front of the patrons.

As she remembered this, she recognized a similarity between the anger she often felt against her husband and her grandmother's toward her grandfather. When she became angry at her husband, she saw him as her grandmother had seen her grandfather, and now she could see her husband as he really was.

Sometimes people treat their partnership in the same way that they treat membership in a voluntarily chosen group. Instead of closely attending to what their sense of belonging requires, they act as if they could arbitrarily set the goals, duration, and structures of their relationship, and change them as they wish. They may recognize too late that a loving partnership only flourishes when the partners respect their bond and the constraints it imposes on them. The interdependence of love and systemic order is inescapable.

Saint Augustine's suggestion, "First love, and then do as you will," is doomed to fail. Many mistakenly believe that love alone is enough, or that love can make up for whatever else is missing from a relationship. The illusion that love alone can be enough prevents us from perceiving the limits of what we can and cannot do.

My Love Will Change Him

A young woman, against her parents' wishes, married a man who was fond of drink, gambling, and women. After many miserable years together, he died, leaving her destitute with four children, three of whom still needed her care. In talking with a friend, she realized that, as a young woman, she had believed that if she loved her husband enough, her love would change him. Rather than admit to herself the error of her belief, she stayed with him, giving him more and more, and paid heavily for her hubris with suffering. She also came to realize that her mother had hoped to improve her father, who, like her husband, had successfully resisted all efforts to be improved.

Because it's an emergent quality of systemic order, love develops, flows, and blossoms only in an environment of systemic balance. Attempts to compensate a systemic imbalance by increasing love

are bound to fail. Like a seed in fertile ground, love doesn't try to
change the soil. Love develops between humans and is essential to
us, but it can't influence the larger system that gave it birth—and
our love for one another plays only a minor role in the larger universe of galaxies and stars.

Hierarchy Between Parents

Certain dances, like the waltz and tango, are most beautiful when
partners are well matched in skill and style, and when one leads and
the other follows. Skillful dancers usually agree that they feel best
when their respective skills make it natural for the man to lead and
the woman to follow.

Time, weight, and function interact to determine who leads and
who follows in intimate relationships. Since partners enter a relationship simultaneously, the time factor is neutralized, but among
siblings, the elder siblings take precedence over the younger ones.

In spite of outward appearances, in relationships between parents, the woman almost always has greater weight. Perhaps because
of the immediacy of her body's involvement in pregnancy, birth,
and nursing her children, her bond to them is naturally intimate
and powerful. Through them, she also is bound to life and feels an
importance her husband must work hard to achieve. Such a woman
is the center around which her family is organized, and although
she may be more restricted than her husband, she exudes a secure
contentment and confident freedom that, paradoxically, are granted
by her greater weight.

But children who remain centered around their mother too long
find it difficult to achieve autonomy, and the mature, personal love
of well-matched partners does not develop when one or the other
dominates. Correspondingly, we observe repeatedly in constellations that all members of a family immediately feel better when the
family's center of gravity can appropriately be shifted to the man's
sphere—children feel the exuberant security necessary to explore
the world, and the couple's love rekindles and comes to life.

Love is usually well served when a woman follows her husband
into his language, his family, and his culture, and when she agrees
that their children will follow him as well. Such following feels natural and good to women when their husbands lead with heartfelt

concern for the family's well-being, and when they understand the mysterious systemic law that the masculine serves the feminine. Men and their families suffer grave consequences when this service is avoided, is distorted, or remains unfulfilled.

In addition to the hierarchy established by time and weight, the division of function also plays a role in determining which partner leads. Although this is changing in many countries, the families with which we work still generally function better when the woman carries the primary responsibility for the family's internal well-being, and the man is responsible for the family's security in the world and is followed where he leads.

Obviously, this traditional division of functions cannot, and must not, be maintained in some families. Sometimes men can't protect their families because of circumstances of war or loss of income, or because they fall ill or become disabled. Some men lack the strength to lead in a healthy way because they have not completed the movement of leaving their mothers' spheres of influence and connecting to their fathers, their grandfathers, and the healthy world of men. Some women refuse to follow because they remain bound in their fathers' spheres of influence and have been unable to connect to their mothers, their grandmothers, and the primal force of womanhood. Others cannot follow because they continue to have an important function in their family of origin, perhaps because of exceptionally difficult or tragic happenstance. Then the woman must not follow her husband, but she still must agree that their children follow him as he guides them to the greater safety of his family's sphere of influence. At times the damage in the man's family is so great that the family can only find peace and good order when he and the children move into the woman's sphere, and he must follow her there. Such couples must then take extra care to ensure that their giving and taking remain balanced, and that the woman doesn't become a substitute for her husband's mother or father.

Example

A participant in a workshop reacted with outrage to the idea that love flows most easily when men lead and women follow. She told with dignity how her first husband had become violent to her, how her second husband had begun to molest her daughter sexually, and how her third husband, although a good and loving man, had no ambition and was content with his modest earnings and simple life. She said,

"Are you telling me I should follow these men?" The group leader paused, and answered, "Obviously love would not have been served had you followed. But imagine for a moment that your present partner were to change as you desire and assume full responsibility for you and your family. How would you feel?" The woman immediately beamed, "Then I could relax at last."

Many women are surprised to discover the profound relief, the deep contentment, and the ease they spontaneously feel when a family system is brought into symmetry, and they find themselves naturally following a man who leads in the true service of his family. And men often experience a strange transformation when their service is acknowledged and appropriately valued.

Additional Considerations

This observation by Hellinger has caused considerable controversy, and some people have wrongly understood him to be advocating that women return to traditional roles and functions. Certainly these observations at first appear to challenge much of the good that the woman's movement has gained. About two-thirds of the families with which we work are happier and function better if they can find the hidden symmetry that allows the man to lead well and the woman appropriately to follow. Far from being a moral position, this describes a spontaneously felt body reaction that is clear to see in all family members if such a symmetry is found, especially the children. As representatives in a constellation many women have been surprised (and sometimes a little embarrassed) to feel the sense of "rightness" this hidden systemic symmetry gives them, and to see how it frees their children. The need to protect their family's well-being is one of the deepest feelings men normally have, and failure in this leaves deep wounds. Many men have been surprised (and also a little embarrassed) at the welling-up of dignity and emotion when their efforts are "good-enough," and their service is recognized and valued.

It's not clear whether this is a matter of socialization alone, or if evolutionary factors are involved. We may speculate that, from the point of view of evolution, once fertilization has taken place, the father is more expendable than the mother and child, and that he continues to have a life-serving function when he contributes to their survival and well-being. Bert Hellinger does not explain this phenomenon, saying, "I do not know why this is so, but I see that it is a deep movement within the soul that has a powerful effect for good, especially on the children in a family, and I respect it."

Some people confuse the term "follow" with being subservient or inferior, while others confuse domination and belligerence with "leading." Love, in contrast to evolution, requires both partners to be equally present and equally important throughout their partnership. Love requires the symmetry of their togetherness to be authentic and it isn't deceived by false assertions or good intentions.

Each situation is unique, and the constellations are one means to determine who appropriately leads or follows in a specific family. [H.B.]

GROWING TOWARD DEATH

The deeper a relationship develops and the longer it endures, the more death enters and becomes a part of it. We may enter a partnership with an expectation that it will fulfill us and end our need or loneliness. The reality is that it ultimately leads to death. Even when love thrives in a partnership, an incompleteness of the soul remains for each partner that the partnership cannot fill. Dealing with this profound and most human incompleteness leads us to the greater mysteries of life, to the spiritual and religious dimension. As illusions fade and die, couples whose love remains vital into old age confront both the limits of partnership and these greater mysteries. Sacrificing the hope that their partners will satisfy what no partner can, they begin to look more lovingly at each other, releasing each other from their earlier expectations and surrendering to a process whose outcome remains unseen.

Every intimate relationship is carried by the flow of time, moving toward its own end and making room for what comes next. For example, parents lose freedom when a child is born, but the joy of having a child and the sense of fulfillment in being parents replace what they surrender. The peak intensity in a relationship between a man and a woman usually occurs with the birth of their first child. After that, the relationship changes orientation, turning outward; other factors increasingly play a role; and gradually the intensity of the original togetherness decreases. These sacrifices of intimacy are appropriate. They bring us back to earth, freed from naive expectations of what a relationship could be.

Every crisis enables a couple to practice dying. It requires partners to give up something they have cherished, but their love continues on a deeper, more enduring level. As the coverings of unrealistic hope are peeled away, partners are increasingly exposed and can be seen and loved as they are—and see and love their partners. Such a love is beyond illusion and abides in what is.

With each surrender and loss, the new that enters the relationship is more modest and more relaxed. At the same time, their love becomes more nourishing for the soul than the love of newlyweds. As the couple's relationship moves back down to earth and becomes more modest, they grow close to death and must befriend it. Thus, one can often see expressions of profound serenity on the faces of happily married older people because they no longer fear loss and death.

Fullness

A youth asked an old man:
"What is the difference between you,
who are now almost part of what has been,
and me, who is still becoming?"'

The old man replied:
"I have been more.

"The dawning day seems greater
than the one before because
the day at dusk is mostly past.
But the new day, although it's yet to come,
can only be what it already is,
and so, it too grows more by fading.

"It climbs like yesterday
steeply toward the noon,
reaching zenith just before the greatest heat;
rests a while on high, or so it seems,
until, as if drawn by its own increasing weight,
which grows with the advancing hour,
it bows deeply to the night.

And like the day that went before,
it reaches its completion when it, too, is fully past.

"But nothing that has been can ever really disappear.
It remains because it has existed.
Although it now is past, its effect continues
and becomes still more through the new that follows.
Like a round drop of rain falling from a passing cloud
dissolves in an ocean, which remains.

"Only what never could come into being
because we dreamed of it but did not act,
thought of it but failed to implement the thought—
all that remains unknown to our experience,
all that for which we feared to pay the price—
all that is lost.
"Experience unlived is lost forever.

"Thus, the god of the right and fitting moment
appears to us like a youth
with a lock of hair in front and a bald patch behind.
We grasp him by his curls in front
and from behind we clutch at emptiness."

The youth then asked: "What must I do
to become what you have been?"

The old man answered: "Be!"

QUESTIONS AND ANSWERS REGARDING SPECIAL ISSUES

Abortion and Its Effect on Partnership

Question: How does an abortion or miscarriage affect the family system?

Hellinger: Miscarriages don't usually affect the system at all, as long as the mother's health hasn't been jeopardized. My observation has been that an abortion doesn't usually affect the other children in the family, but it does affect the parents' relationship. It may be different in other cultures, but in our culture, abortion has an effect deep in the soul that's quite independent of whatever the parents may consciously believe about abortion—although this varies somewhat from family to family.

The main problem with abortion occurs when people approach it as though it could undo something that has already happened. In fact, partners often find the burden of guilt and the consequences of an abortion worse than the burden of having the child.

In some situations, abortion may be the least destructive of the available alternatives, but it's an option that carries a heavy price. I've worked with couples whose decision to abort I honor and respect— they made the decision consciously and they accepted the consequences of their choice with a sense of reverence for the child. The unborn child appeared before them as a person who needed and deserved to be seen. If the decision to abort can be made in the presence of the unborn child, with all of the pain and guilt that entails, and with a full awareness of what's being asked of this child, then the decision brings deep suffering. That kind of abortion has a very different quality than an abortion done to avoid the consequences of our own choices. It affects the partners for a long time, but it also has the potential to draw them closer together and to deepen their love.

One frequent consequence of an abortion is that the partnership is over, and the parents have to start again if they want to stay together. If the partners aren't married, they often drift apart. When an abortion occurs in a marriage, then the sexual relationship often becomes difficult, or stops altogether. It isn't necessary that this be so, and there are solutions, but if the partners try to avoid the consequences of their actions and their feelings of guilt—perhaps by minimizing the gravity of what they've done, or by avoiding confronting their unborn child as a person—they pay the price for their neglect somewhere else.

Both parents have equal responsibility for an abortion, just as they have equal responsibility for the pregnancy, and one partner can't push it off onto the other without damaging their relationship or themselves.

Question: I've been thinking about the importance of family members who have been excluded. I'm wondering if it isn't important for siblings to know that there's been an abortion.

Hellinger: It's none of their business. This is something private between the parents, and it should remain there. I've rarely seen a case where it made difficulties for the other children.

Question: You said that relationships are disrupted after an abortion. Is that true even if the abortion is a fourth or fifth child?

Hellinger: That's been my observation, yes.

Question: And if the child was that of another man or another woman?

Hellinger: In that case, the marriage as it was is over. Even when partners stay together after the abortion, their relationship is certain to be different from what it was before. If the child was conceived with another person during the marriage, that's the start of a new system, and the old partnership is over anyway. Some people tend to treat abortion as if it were harmless, but if you work with men and women who have gone through it, you see that it often has consequences much more serious than they expected.

Question: What if the father doesn't know about it?

Hellinger: If the mother doesn't tell him, their relationship is already over. If he were to know, he'd have to take a position. An abortion is an extreme case of giving and taking because the child gives all and the parents take all. Fathers who know nothing about an abortion still gain an advantage from the child's death, and their actions still have consequences. They have the right to know and should be told.

Some people condemn themselves to death following an abortion. They actually contract a serious illness or commit suicide. Such decisions aren't made merely out of depression or superficial feelings of guilt, and they deserve to be understood in their depth and profundity. If an unborn child is asked to give up life, the parents have an obligation to see to it that it wasn't in vain. Rather than dying, they honor the child better by living fully.

When an aborted child is set up in a family constellation, that has an exceptional effect on the representatives of the parents and the child. How was that for you, Claude? *(Claude had represented an aborted child in a constellation earlier in the workshop.)*

Claude: I felt completely alone. I had no sense of life.

Hellinger: That's a typical reaction. The child feels alone, rejected, abandoned, unseen, and unacknowledged. The solution is for one or both of the parents in the constellation to make a connection with the child (it happens symbolically through touch), and to take the child into their hearts. Then the child can accept his or her fate. Such a solution is only possible if the parents feel genuine grief and accept their pain. Their willingness to endure their grief and pain honors their child and reconnects them with the child.

Young children have a basic willingness to die for their parents. They instinctively understand that death and life go together and can't be separated, so they don't feel the need to hold on to life at any price. When parents are able to recognize an aborted child as a person and to acknowledge that this child has sacrificed life for them, there's peace in the system. This peace comes only after the child has been acknowledged as a real "other" and has been taken into the parents' hearts.

In a constellation, a healing ritual can be performed by having the child's representative sit in front of the parents and lean against them. The parents can then lay their hands on the child's head, and feel the connection with love and grief. That often has a good effect on the whole constellation, and there's a profound change in the parents if they succeed in allowing the child to become a real person to them. When both parents allow themselves to feel the pain of their loss and of what they have asked from their child, there can be a deep atonement and reconciliation. Their pain honors their child so that the child feels included, finds his or her place, and is at peace. By accepting their pain and guilt, the parents become whole, and their wholeness gives them strength. Their partnership can grow again, but it will be on a new level. If only one of the partners experiences the pain, the partnership is broken, and they usually separate.

Another healing exercise after an abortion is for the parents to imagine themselves taking the child by the hand and showing him or her good things of the world. Perhaps for a year or two, the parents imagine showing the child the things they do and the places they visit, just as they would show a living child. After that, the child can really be dead and find peace.

This is an exercise that must be carried out with great caution and with utmost respect. Through suffering with full awareness and consent, a fullness is gained that's often not possible when people hide behind a façade of joy and cheerfulness. That fullness is the parents' reward for consenting to the fullness of their guilt and their loss. Something good or special can also be done in remembrance of the child. It doesn't have to be anything big, but it should be something that wouldn't otherwise have been done.

When the subject of abortion comes up in seminars, I do my best to avoid it. It's practically impossible to know what the ultimate gains and losses are in such situations, and so it's very difficult to know what the best solution is—or the least destructive. What I've offered are a few generalizations, but each situation is different, and therapists need to look very carefully at the individual persons in actual situations.

I've only been reporting what I've seen in my work with families, and I don't want to say anything more about it. It's a very difficult subject. *(Long silence)* I'll tell you a meditative story.

The Guest

Where the Wild West once was, a man with a backpack was wandering through the lonely land. He had walked for hours, the sun was high in the sky, and his thirst was growing. He saw a farmhouse on the horizon and thought, "Thank God, at last another human being in all this loneliness. I'll stop there and ask for a drink, and perhaps we'll sit on the porch and talk a while before I set off again." And he imagined how nice it would be.

But as he drew near to the house, he saw the farmer working in the garden, and he began to have second thoughts. "He's probably very busy and doesn't have time, and if I bother him, he'll feel annoyed. He may think I'm rude." When at last he reached the garden gate, he waved to the farmer and walked on.

The farmer had seen him in the distance and felt pleased. "Thank God," he had thought, "at last another human being in all this loneliness. I hope he comes here. We could drink something together, and perhaps sit on the porch and talk a while before he goes on his way." The farmer went into the house and prepared something cool to drink.

But as the walker came closer, the farmer began to think. "He's most certainly in a hurry. If I speak to him, I'll put him in an awkward situation. He may feel that I'm pushing myself on him. But perhaps he's thirsty and will come over on his own. The best thing would be for me to go into the garden and act busy. Surely he'll see me, and if he wants anything, he'll ask me." When the walker only waved in passing, the farmer thought, "Too bad!'

The walker walked on and on. The sun was hot and his thirst was growing. It was hours before he saw another house on the horizon. He thought to himself, "This time I will approach the farmer, even if I'm a nuisance to him. I am so thirsty that I simply must have something to drink."

As the farmer saw the walker in the distance, he thought to himself, "Oh God! Just what I don't need when I have so much to do. I can't take care of anyone else right now." He continued his work without looking up.

The walker watched him go out into the field and followed him and said, "I am very thirsty. Could you please give me something to drink?" The farmer thought, "I can't send him away, it wouldn't be right." So he took the stranger into the house and gave him something to drink.

The stranger said, "I saw your garden. It's clear that someone has worked here who understands gardening and loves plants." The farmer said, "So you like gardening?" Then they sat down on the porch and talked for a long time. Finally, the stranger said, "I must be on my way now." The farmer answered, "But the sun is getting low. Stay the night with me. We'll breakfast early in the morning and you can be off then." The stranger agreed.

As evening came, they sat on the porch and watched the vastness of the western sky transfigured in the evening light. In the darkness, the stranger talked about how his world had changed when he had begun to feel that someone was accompanying him step by step. At first, he said, he had refused to believe that another was always there, and that when he stopped, the other stopped, and when he went on, the other went on as well. And it had taken a while before he had understood who his companion was. "My constant companion is my death," he said. "I have grown so accustomed to his presence that I would miss him now if he weren't there. He is my truest and best friend. When I don't know what's right or what to do, I stop a while and wait for his answer. I have abandoned myself to him, and I know he's there and I am here. Without hanging on to my own desires, I wait for his message to come to me. When I am centered and have courage, a word comes from him to me, and, like a lightning flash, illuminates the dark and I become clear.'

The farmer found this talk strange, and gazed silently into the night. After a long time, he saw his own death as his companion. And he bowed his head to him. And as he paid his respects to his own death, it was as if the rest of his life were changed. It became precious as the love that anticipates a parting, and like such love, filled to overflowing.

In the morning, they broke their fast together, and the farmer said, "Even though you are leaving, my friend remains." They went outside, shook hands, and said goodbye. The stranger went on his way and the farmer returned to his field.

Examples from Seminars

Adrian: *(Adrian had left his wife and children to live with Jennifer, who then became pregnant.)* I just wanted to say that Jennifer, my partner, is probably having an abortion today, and I can't do anything about it. *(His voice drops.)* I feel so confused and helpless. I wish there were something I could do, but here I sit, 300 miles away. I just have to accept it.

Hellinger: Adrian, if she goes through with it against your wishes, you'll be touched by death. A part of you will die too *(pause)*. That will mean that your partnership with Jennifer is probably over. It's likely that you'll lose Jennifer, but you'll lose your first family for sure. You're free to consent to that, or not. If you consent to this dying, a new strength may develop in you. It comes from the guilt that you share, from the unborn child's sacrifice, and from your loss of your family. If you can consent to all of that, a load will fall from your shoulders, but if you try to find the easy way out, you'll have a heavy burden to carry. *(Adrian breathes deeply, and withdraws in a mood of self-pity.)*

Hellinger *(to the group):* What he's doing now is self-damaging. It has a quality of heaviness and self-centeredness that's inappropriate; his loss is certainly less than the child's.

Adrian *(very softly):* You're asking quite a lot.

Hellinger: The healing option isn't always the easiest. *(Pause)* There's a dramatic quality to your reaction that's inappropriate. It's channeling your energy into self-pity and away from effective action. There's no advantage in that. So we'll let you chew on it for a while.

June: I was deeply touched by what you said about abortion. I feel a lot of pain about my abortion *(begins to cry)* and a lot of anger.

Hellinger: *(After a long pause)* That kind of anger is a distraction. It's an indication of trying to push responsibility onto someone else. You have to accept your share of the responsibility, because, with an abortion, your share of the responsibility can't be pushed off onto your partner—or anyone else.

June: I've been thinking about it, trying to remember when my husband and I started talking about separating. It's been exactly a year and a half—shortly after the abortion. That would have been our third child.

Hellinger: *(With reference to June's family constellation, in which she looked in a different direction, away from her husband)* You were looking at that child, June. *(June starts to cry again, this time more sincerely)* Let the pain have all the room in you that it deserves. That's a healing pain that honors the child. The pain will help you see what to do, so that your unborn child's sacrifice won't have been in vain. *(Pause)* Are there any other questions about this?

Louis: Could you say more about the role of miscarriage in the family system?

Hellinger: As I said before, miscarriages generally don't affect the family system, and seldom affect the relationship between a man and a woman. They should be treated as things that just happen and not attached to any personal guilt. For example, a mother who has miscarried may feel guilty and ask, "What have I done to cause this to happen?" That's an inappropriate question. It's presumptuous to ask such a thing, and only creates craziness. If a therapist says, "You've had five miscarriages, so you must be responsible in some way," I'd consider that a destructive intervention.

Louis: I was asking because of a client of mine. One of his dreams made me suspect that there had been miscarriages in his family, which he then confirmed. That's why I was wondering if that could be important.

Hellinger: Were they his siblings?

Louis: Yes.

Hellinger: It sounds as if he could be an exception to what I just said. It could be that they have importance for him. If so, the solution would be for him to honor their fate and say to them, "You didn't come into the world. I did come into the world. You're dead, I'm alive." Then he'll have to deal with the guilt of being the survivor, of being alive when the others have died, even though he could do nothing about it. You already know the magic formula: "You're dead. I will live a little while longer, and then I, too, will die." This formula reconnects the living and the dead, and the living no longer need to feel that they're somehow taking advantage of the dead.

This example of yours shows how dangerous it is to try to make a comprehensive general theory from a limited observation. I'm giving you my general orientations, but don't let them get in the way of your seeing what's actually the case with the people with whom you work.

Artificial Insemination

Question: What about artificial insemination? I'm working with a couple who can't have children, and they're going to great lengths to make artificial insemination possible. What are the consequences for them?

Hellinger: There shouldn't be any problem if the semen is from the man.

Question: No, they want to use semen from a semen bank.

Hellinger: Why on earth would they do that? If they use semen from another man, they go outside the boundaries of their partnership, and they'll be in danger of splitting up. Their partnership might already be in jeopardy anyway. I know that many people believe that it doesn't matter, but my observations have been different. When partners are faced with a particularly difficult fate, such as not being able to have the children they want to have, they need to be extremely careful about what they do to try to change that fate. It isn't as easy to change fate with technological interventions as many people like to think, and the consequences for the system are unexpected, and usually greater than they like to admit. For example, if a husband can't have children and his wife sleeps with another man or is artificially inseminated in order to become pregnant, she's not accepting her husband as he is, and that bodes ill for their partnership. If she desires to be in partnership with him, then she would be well advised to accept him as he is, including his limitations. Otherwise, she should separate from him, with all of the consequences that carries.

I'm Going to Marry Him

A man who couldn't conceive children because of an illness he had had told his wife that she should find a man who was willing to inpregnate her and they would raise the child together as their own. She found a well-known actor who was willing, and she became pregnant and delivered a healthy baby girl. Shortly thereafter, the marriage collapsed. She met another man, became pregnant again, and married him. The first daughter thought that the mother's first husband was her father. But the strange thing is that whenever she saw the actor on television, the daughter would say, "I'm going to marry him." The woman eventually told the child the truth.

The Couple Comes Before the Children

Question: I work with a lot of families in which the partners put the children's needs above everything else. I've the impression that the children don't feel safe when they have too much freedom or too much attention. Could you say something about the relationship between parents and children as you see it?

Hellinger: The fundamental relationship in a family is the relationship between the father and the mother. It's the foundation of parenthood. The strength necessary for good parenting flows out of the couple's relationship. As long as that relationship is good and is the foundation of the family, the children feel secure.

Children feel best when their father honors and respects himself and his wife in them, and when their mother also honors and respects herself and her husband in them. Then the parents' relationship with their children is a continuation and a fulfillment of their relationship with one another; the children are the crowning and the completion of their love for each other. Children feel free when their parents love one another.

Crucial here are the direction and the quality of the love. When a father's love for his daughter has a good effect, it flows to her through his wife; it takes a detour through her. The same is true of a mother's love for her sons, which flows to them via her husband. When parents love their children in that way, their love for the children brings them closer together, and the children feel free and secure.

When a man and a woman join together, they are a couple first, and only later do they become parents. The partner relationship comes before the parent relationship and takes precedence. Their togetherness becomes manifest in their children, and their children are an expression of their maleness and femaleness. A man and a woman are physically and visibly united in their children.

Although the continuation of life and of the species is the biological function of their coupling, the couple's relationship maintains systemic precedence over the relationship with their children. The parents' love for their child should be the continuation and the crowning of their love for each other as a couple. This is so because their love as a couple came first, and as the roots of a tree support and nourish its branches, that love supports and nourishes the children.

When parents in a family allow their love for their children to become more important than their love for each other as a couple, then the order of love is disturbed and the family is in danger of becoming dysfunctional. The solution is for the couple's relationship to be given priority over their relationship with their children. When this happens in a constellation, you can see it immediately. The children experience their parents as a couple, they relax, and everyone feels better.

When Father Acts Like a Man

A man and a woman married because he hoped to have needs met that remained unfulfilled from his childhood, and she wanted to love him as a mother loves a child. They were quite content until they had a child. Then the woman's love appropriately began to flow to her biological son. Her husband began to feel neglected and jealous, and to compete with his son for his wife's attention. The woman felt abandoned by her husband and felt a great longing for a partner who was her equal.

The son was caught between his parents, was unable to relate appropriately to either, and fell into a deep depression.

He was freed from his depression when his father assumed his appropriate place beside his wife as a man in a partnership with a woman, and as a father in relation to his son. Then the boy felt peace and could be a child at last.

Singles and Couples Without Children

Question: I'm single and I'm now too old to bear a child. I feel excluded and devalued by what you're saying. Is there no place for people like me in the symmetry you describe?

Hellinger: Single men and women and couples without children obviously are not excluded from finding love and meaning in their lives, but they have some special issues to face and resolve. As you must already know from your own experience, facing loneliness and finding meaning in life can be especially painful for a single person who has no children. That can be a very difficult situation. My interest is in understanding what people in such circumstances can do to ensure that their potential for love and meaning comes to fruition.

In the constellations we've done, you've seen that we all share in our family's fate and guilt. That means that we share in suffering the consequences of what others in our system do, just as what we do affects them. People who freely choose to be single also freely accept the consequences of their choice, and they don't usually seek therapy. However, many people aren't single because they want to be, but because they're caught in a systemic entanglement, or are paying a debt they didn't incur. For example, a father abused his wife, and because she felt dependent on him, she endured the abuse without leaving. Their daughter developed a lifelong distrust of men and of intimacy and remained single. Being single, in order to be happy, she must organize her life very differently than she would if she were married. In many ways, she has more freedom than her married friends have, but she also pays a heavy price. She can't know the freedom that paradoxically comes from being bonded to a partner and from having to meet the demands placed on a mother.

I know it's not in vogue to say it, but there are still families in which a woman finds fulfillment and achieves her greatest psychological weight and dignity by having many children and a large, loving family. You can still see such women in the rural villages of some countries. There's a look of profound serenity on their faces, and they radiate a quality of being at peace and grounded in life. Theirs is a simple and completely natural greatness. This also applies to their husbands, although to a lesser degree. The demands on such parents are enormous; they have had to learn to let go, and to be patient and take what life gives them.

The path to finding fulfillment by having a large family has been blocked in our culture for both women and men, but that doesn't mean that we're free to demean it. Because this profound and natural human fulfillment is no longer possible, women must seek other forms of fulfillment, primarily in a career. There's a culturally evolved illusion that helps them in this—that a career is more fulfilling for a woman than is being trapped at home with children. I can't imagine that sitting in an office, staring at a computer all day, is intrinsically more fulfilling than being at home with children. However, I do believe that the illusion is necessary so that women can do what's demanded of them by the evolution of culture and still experience satisfaction in their lives.

Women often don't even notice this loss of possibility, or they deny that it's a loss and discount it, as if it were unimportant. When they do that, they devalue what once was the greatest fulfillment of womanhood, and scorn what's no longer possible. Having children is devalued, homemaking is devalued, and men are devalued. This makes it possible for women to commit themselves to a career, but the price is that they lose the connection to and respect for an important aspect of being a woman.

That's the way it is with everything—doing one thing means not doing something else. Everything we do is surrounded by the things we decide against, the not-chosen potentials that remain unrealized. If what isn't chosen is scorned or demeaned, then whatever has been chosen loses value and importance. On the other hand, if we honor and value all of the not-chosen and unrealized possibilities, what has been chosen is enriched.

There are situations in which it's neither possible nor desirable for people to have children or to live in a partnership. Women who are fully aware of the value of what they've given up and who make their choices consciously can rescue the feminine from this implicit devaluation and carry its fullness into their new lifestyle. And men can rescue the masculine in a similar way. Honoring what wasn't chosen brings a different quality into their lives. Something else is won with a conscious relinquishment of lost possibilities.

If such a loss is acknowledged and a conscious decision is made to forego family or partnership without *devaluing them*, then what isn't chosen adds something to what has been chosen. The process of acknowledging loss works in the soul and can bring something positive on a completely different level. Even though it remains unrealized, what's not chosen goes on working when it's honored and valued.

Getting Needs Met Isn't Enough for Love

Question: I've really become aware of my need for tenderness and for being held. I fall in love and have the feeling for a while that I've found the right partner and that all my needs will be met. Then something changes, and either he leaves me or I lose interest in him.

Hellinger: Most partnerships actually start out that way, with someone looking for a partner to fulfill his or her needs and long-ings. The problem is that the other person is usually looking for the same thing. I suspect that falling in love reactivates the needs of our inner child, and the partner tends to get put in the position of a mother. When men and women are on the lookout for someone to fill their needs, at the deepest level, they're all looking for a mother, and that necessarily leads to disappointment.

A partnership is a difficult undertaking, and it's very different from an affair, even an extended one. A partnership, at least what I mean by a partnership, has a completely different depth. As you said, you may find a man for a few months, but he doesn't take you seriously, in the sense of wanting to make his life with you. Because you see him as an opportunity to get what you want, he'll see the relationship as a temporary opportunity to get you to meet his needs as well.

That vision is large enough for a love affair, but too small for an enduring partnership. But if, in your heart, you allow a vision to grow that's worthy of your full dignity and the full power and depth of your womanhood—a vision worthy of your full human poten-tial—then a man may come along who can offer you a worthy response. If love develops—and perhaps even being in love a little too—that's fine. Falling in love is blind, but love is alert. Love truly accepts and wants the other just as he or she is. That touches some-thing very deep and allows love to develop.

That's some advice from an old man to a young woman.

Bruno: While we're on the subject of feelings, I've got a feeling I'm trying to understand and would like to talk about it. I can't remember that I've ever had this feeling before and I don't know exactly how to deal with it. The feeling is that I've found the right woman for me. Just that. She's the right one. There's no passion or desire, but only the feeling that she's the right person for me.

Hellinger: I'd be suspicious of that sentence. If the sentence were "She's wonderful," it would be different, but when you say "She's right," without passion or desire, it sounds as if you mean that she's the person with whom you'll have to change the least.

Bruno: Caught! *(Laughter in the group)* On the other hand, that's very nice, because I can be the way I am.

Hellinger: No, it's not good, and it'll very quickly become a burden. The feeling that change isn't necessary limits your partnership in a way that isn't healthy. It's better if she is simply "good," and you are too.

Homosexual Couples

Question: I'm gay, and there doesn't seem to be any place for homosexuals in your approach. What can it mean for me when you say that a man "becomes a man" in a relationship with a woman or that a woman becomes a woman in a relationship with a man? That makes heterosexuality the only way of being human.

Hellinger: First, I want to say a couple of general things about the systemic view. Everyone is an integral part of the relationship systems in which he or she lives, and everyone has an equal value in the functioning of those systems—*everyone* in the family system is essential to the system.

Differences in a social system add to its durability and stability. The conscience that seeks to exclude individuals from the group because they are different operates on a different level than does the systemic conscience that seeks to balance the system as a whole by guarding the right of every member to belong to the system. It has very serious consequences for the younger members of a family system when someone is excluded from the system because he or she is different. I've seen many cases in which younger persons suffered terribly because they had to identify with an older relative who was excluded from the family because of his being homosexual. This fundamental commitment to the intrinsic dignity and value of all persons makes it possible to view differences openly.

Having said that, there's an inescapable fact that homosexual couples face: Their love can't lead to their having children together. Procreation's insistence on heterosexuality has consequences that can't be ignored as if they didn't exist. In any partnership without children, the partners can separate with less guilt—they only hurt one another. But when parents separate, that has enormous consequences for their children, and they must be very careful or their children will be harmed by what they do. This added guilt makes it more difficult for parents to separate, but, paradoxically, it also supports their partnership. Couples without children—including homosexual couples—don't have the support of these consequences to hold them together during crises.

Homosexual couples, like other childless couples interested in long-term, loving partnerships, especially need to make clear and conscious decisions about the purpose and goals of their partnership. Some goals are more conducive to long-term stability in relationships than are others. Wanting to avoid loneliness or the feeling of emptiness, for example, isn't a goal that supports a long-term partnership of equals.

Everyone has his or her own path in life—part of it we choose, but part of it just comes with life and isn't really chosen. That's the part that's hard to deal with. The homosexuals with whom I've worked—even those who maintain that they chose their sexual orientation freely—have been caught in systemic dynamics, experiencing in their lives the consequences of what others in their system did or suffered. They've been inducted into the service of the system, and as children, they couldn't defend themselves from the systemic pressures to which they were subjected. So that's the second thing they have to deal with, that they're carrying something for the family.

I've rarely worked with someone who wanted to "get over" being homosexual. When I work with homosexual persons, homosexuality isn't the primary issue. I merely try to bring to light any entanglements that might be limiting the fullness of life, but I have no intention of trying to change someone's sexual orientation.

I've observed three patterns of systemic entanglements in conjunction with homosexuality, but I don't know whether they're actually its cause:

- A child was pressured to represent a person of the opposite sex in the system, because a child of the same gender wasn't available. For example, a boy had to represent one of his deceased older sisters, because none of the other surviving children was female. Or another boy had to represent his father's first fiancée, who had been treated unjustly. This is the most painful and difficult of the three patterns I've seen.

- A child was pressured to represent someone who had been excluded from the family system—or who had been vilified by the system—even though that person was of the same gender. Homosexuals living in this pattern have the position of being "outsiders." For example, a boy was systemically identified with his mother's first fiancé, who contracted syphilis and withdrew from the engagement. Although the fiancé had acted honorably, he was scorned and despised by the boy's mother. The boy's feelings of being scorned were very similar to what the man must have felt—as if they were his own feelings.

- A child remained caught in the sphere of influence of the gender-opposite parent, and was not able to complete the psychological movement of taking the same-gender parent.

If It Would Have Helped, I Could Have Borne My Pain

In a training group for therapists, a woman stood in a constellation of her family of origin and was visually confronted for the first time with what she had known but had not acknowledged—the extent of the loss, need, and damage in her family system. Nowhere in three generations was an intact relationship to be seen. Her parents' relationship was one of hate and disdain, and she was chosen to fill her father's emotional and sexual needs from the time she was eight years old until she was able to leave home at the age of 18. The sexual acts were brutal and painful, and had occurred with her mother's knowledge and implicit consent.

In her previous therapy, she had explored her rage, pain, and sense of betrayal, and had found relief, but no lasting resolution. As she stood before the representative of her father, the therapist suggested, "Tell him: 'It hurt!'" As she did so, the deepest sobbing welled up and burst forth, and she spontaneously added, "And it didn't help. I couldn't take away your loneliness. I could have stood my pain, if only it had helped your terrible loneliness." She put her arms around the man representing her father, who also was weeping openly, and they held each other tenderly for a long time. She consciously felt for the first time as an adult her child's love for her father and her secret willingness to sacrifice herself for the good of her parents.

After a while, she told him, "I promise you that no more children will be hurt as I was. I'll pay the price. It will stop with me." When she then turned to the group and said, "I'm a lesbian," she did so with enormous simplicity and with the full human dignity commensurate to her situation.

A year later, she still felt the freeing effects of her accepting the role that fate had given her, accepting as a conscious choice what she had previously unconsciously carried and could not change.

Viewed in this way, homosexuality demands a heavy price. Those who manage to affirm their sexual orientation and construct a happy, loving, meaningful life have a very different inner support than do those who fight against their destiny or demean their loss—whether or not they consciously chose it, or would want to change it if they could.

Infidelity and Three-Way Relationships

Question: My husband has been having an affair with another woman for many years. At first, I had difficulty accepting it, but over the years, I've given up trying to change him. Would you say something about infidelity and extramarital relationships?

Hellinger: When a woman treats her husband like a child, trying to improve his behavior and acting as if she knows what's best for him, he often takes a lover. His lover is then his true partner. If he has a good relationship with his wife but still has a lover, then the lover most likely represents his mother. The same is probably true for a woman who takes a lover—either she's being treated by her husband as if she were a child, or she's seeking in her lover someone to represent her father or mother.

As a rule, a woman who is content to live in a three-way relationship is her father's daughter. If she were looking for a solution, she'd need to leave her father's sphere of influence and return to her mother's. A man who lives in a three-way relationship often is a mother's son, and the solution is for him to move into his father's sphere.

A relationship outside of a marriage is often viewed as morally unacceptable. In such a situation, the so-called innocent partner sometimes behaves as if his or her claim on the other partner were exclusive and permanent. That's presumptuous. The conscience that watches over relationships isn't impressed by such claims. It respects only the real quality of bonding and the ecology of give and take. Instead of winning the partner back with love, the injured partner often torments the other, as if such demands for exclusivity, without regard for the fulfillment of need and desire, would make him or her want to return.

I argue for something more realistic. I have a deep respect for fidelity, but not the kind of fidelity that demands, "I'm the only person who's allowed to be meaningful for you and from whom you're allowed to take what you need." It often happens that you meet someone who becomes important to you, and that fact must be respected, just as the feelings of hurt and loss that arise must be respected. Such a meeting can have a very positive effect on a partnership. No matter how it turns out, a truly satisfactory resolution is only possible with love.

Jealousy

Question: Would you say something about jealousy? I have attacks of jealousy and imagine my partner's doing all kinds of things.

Hellinger: The systemic nature of jealousy can be seen when we look carefully at what it actually accomplishes. Occasionally, jealousy brings a couple closer together. This happens, for example, when a woman's jealousy protects her children and her husband from a capricious affair, or from another woman's interference in her family. But usually jealousy accomplishes the opposite of what it purports to desire, driving the partners farther apart. If you have attacks of jealousy, look at the situation honestly and you will probably discover a secret systemic pressure pushing you away from your partner—the jealous person unconsciously wants the partner to leave.

There are many unconscious systemic dynamics that make us push our partners to go:

- To confirm an earlier belief that we're not worthy of love, for example, or that we'll cause unhappiness. Some people fear they'll be abandoned and unconsciously push their partners out. They create what they fear, as if being abandoned were preferable to a chosen separation.

- To be loyal to the beliefs and examples of your family. For example, to do as your parents did when they didn't fully take one another, when they separated, or when one of them died early in their relationship;

- To fulfill an unconscious identification with another person who's owed something by the system. For example, a woman didn't marry because she was taking care of her elderly parents. Her younger niece unconsciously identified with her and she also didn't marry;

- To compensate for some personal obligation. For example, a man abandoned an earlier family in order to enter the present partnership. His second wife became very jealous of him and wanted to leave him. In the family constellation, it became clear to her that she felt a solidarity with and an obligation to his first family.

Often when one partner is jealous, the partnership is already over, but the participants haven't yet admitted it, or they don't want to see it. If both partners are willing, it's sometimes possible to bring a partnership back into order after jealousy has broken out, but this requires them to confront the systemic pressures that are pushing them apart. They usually have to face some painful experience, perhaps guilt, loneliness, or a fear of loss or inadequacy. Partners can say to each other, "Sooner or later, I will lose you." That's a very painful sentence to say authentically, but it can restore order to the partnership.

It's often not possible for partners to bring a relationship back into order after jealousy has surfaced. Then they must choose between two kinds of pain: the pain of separation and the pain of staying in an unsatisfying relationship. If they choose to stay, it's better for them to consent to continuing their relationship the way it is and to give up their hopes and expectations that it will change. The worst choice they can make is to stay in an unsatisfying relationship and keep on hoping that things will be different. However, that's the choice most couples prefer.

Enjoy Him While You've Got Him

A woman told a therapy group how she tormented her husband with jealousy and, although she saw her behavior as irrational, she could not stop. As she spoke about her jealousy, its systemic function became clear to the group leader and he showed her a solution. He said, "You will lose your husband sooner or later. Enjoy him while you've still got him." A few days later, the husband called the leader and said, "Thank you. I have a wife again."

Her husband had participated in a workshop led by the same group leader many years earlier with a woman with whom he had lived for seven years. During the group, he had told the woman he was with that he had a younger girlfriend, and was planning to marry her. He attended a second workshop with his new partner, whom he had married shortly after she became pregnant. Outwardly, his new wife acted as if her husband had no bond to his earlier partner, and she sustained her claim on him through jealousy and public pressure. Secretly, she felt a bond between her husband and his ex-wife and her own guilt for her part in their separation. Her jealousy was, therefore not the consequence of her husband's actions, but rather her secret acknowledgment of her own indebtedness to his former partner. Her jealousy resulted in an inner separation from her husband and thus reflected his still-existing bond with his first partner and expressed solidarity with her.

In spite of this insight, she and the man separated several years later.

Love Sets Limits on Freedom

Question: From what you're been saying about systemic entanglements, it begins to sound as if everything were predetermined. Do partners who want to live what you call "a partnership of equals" have any personal freedom, or is everything set by the systemic constraints?

Hellinger: In every relationship, the boundaries are set differently; some are broader and more permissive and others are more restrictive. Guilt begins as soon as you cross the boundary of your relationship system. You feel free and innocent within the boundaries, and there's no freedom or innocence without clear boundaries. This process is clear in schoolchildren, for example, who often become distraught if their teacher hasn't set clear limits. When the boundaries have been tested and are clearly defined, the area of freedom is also clearly recognizable.

Fulfillment and satisfaction are found within the boundaries of a partnership. When we go beyond the boundaries, we damage the relationship, sometimes so much that we no longer can return to it. For example, it sometimes happens in a couple's relationship that the limits are too narrow, and one partner or the other (or both) takes a lover to stretch the boundaries and create new free space. If the boundaries become too loose and what the partners hold in common too unclear, the relationship is threatened. Then they must turn back and redefine their limits, or separate.

Their belonging to one another sets limits on their freedom, and such limits are an integral aspect of every relationship system. There's a point at which our freedom of choice is limited by the consequences that our choices have for our sense of belonging. We may choose to go beyond the set boundaries of a relationship, but not without paying a price of guilt, not without consequences for our own and our partner's happiness, and not without endangering our relationship. This reflects a natural law of systems—that there's a limit beyond which a system cannot change without evolving into a different system.

Separation

Question: I work a lot with couples in the process of separating. Sometimes it goes pretty well, and sometimes there are horrible problems. Are there any systemic dynamics that influence that?

Hellinger: People often allow themselves to suffer a long time before they feel free to leave a bad situation because they don't want to hurt their partner, or because they're afraid of what others might think or say. Usually one person wants a new and bigger space, and doesn't feel justified in taking steps to get it, because it will hurt someone. The person acts as if his or her own suffering could neutralize the partner's pain or justify the person's action in the eyes of others. That's one reason that divorce proceedings take so long.

When a separation is finally accomplished, both parties have the opportunities for and the risks of a new beginning. If one partner rejects the opportunity to make a new beginning and ignores the chance to create something good, and instead clings tightly to his or her pain, then it's difficult for the other partner to be free. On the other hand, if both accept the possibilities presented and make something out of them, then both partners are free and unburdened. Of all of the possibilities for forgiveness in situations of divorce and separation, this is the best because it brings harmony even when separation occurs.

When a separation doesn't go well, there's often a tendency to look for someone to blame. Those involved try to get out from under the weight of their fate by blaming someone else. As a rule, a marriage doesn't end because one partner is at fault and the other is blameless, but because one or the other is entangled in the unresolved issues of his or her family of origin, or because they are being led in different directions. By blaming one partner, an illusion is created that something different could have been done, or that some new behavior could rescue the marriage. Then the gravity and the depth of the situation are ignored, and the partners begin blaming and accusing each other. The solution to overcoming this illusion and the destructive blaming is for both to surrender to the deep grief they experience because their partnership has come to an end. This grief doesn't last long, but it goes very deep, and it's extremely painful. Once they've allowed themselves to go through their grieving, they can talk about what needs to be talked about and arrange the things that need to be arranged with clarity, reason, and mutual respect. In a separation, anger and blame are usually substitutes for the pain of grieving.

When two people can't manage to separate cleanly, it's often because they haven't fully taken from one another whatever has been given. Then one must say to the other, "I take the good you've given me. It's a great deal and I treasure it. All that I've given to you, I have given gladly, and it's yours to keep. I take responsibility for my part in what's gone wrong between us, and I leave your part with you. I leave you now in peace." If they manage to say this to each other authentically, they can separate in peace.

In such situations, sometimes telling a simple story is helpful.

The End

Two people, backpacks fully packed, set out together. Their path leads through blooming gardens and meadows, and they're very happy. Then the path gets steep. Eventually, one of them runs out of provisions, and sits down. The other continues a little further and a little higher. The path gets rocky and more difficult, and eventually the second also eats the last of the food and sits down. Looking back at the glorious colors of the meadows below, the person begins to weep.

Partners often behave as if their participation in the relationship were like a club membership that has been freely chosen and can be freely terminated. But the unconscious and relentless conscience guarding love teaches otherwise. If we were free to terminate our partnerships, separation would be less agonizing. Frederich Hölderlin describes this in a poem.

The Lovers

Separate! It seemed so smart and good.
Why are we so shocked now, as if we'd murdered love?
Ah! We know so little of ourselves!
There's a hidden god in us who rules.

In a serious partnership of equals, we are bound to our partners and can't separate without pain and guilt. The consequences are invariably destructive when partners separate irresponsibly. For example, if one partner says, "I'm going to do something for myself and my development, and whatever happens to you is your problem," it's not infrequent that a child will die or commit suicide following the separation. Such a separation is experienced by the child as a crime that requires atonement. Bonding is both the reward and the price of love.

Mother, I Leave the Consequences of Your Going with You

A woman had frivolously separated from her husband, and her daughter became seriously ill shortly after the separation. In the family constellation, the representative of the mother felt best when she was placed outside the circle and the children were placed near their father. When her daughter said to her, "Mother, I leave the consequences of your going with you," she felt free, and everyone in the constellation felt a sense of harmony.

Question: Who decides whether a separation is irresponsible?

Hellinger: No one decides; it's just felt. When a separation occurs, everyone knows immediately whether it was irresponsible.

Transcript

ERNEST, AND A CHILD'S SUICIDE

Following a family constellation, Ernest reacts to the suggestion that a picture of a deceased child be put up in the home.

Ernest: If I were to put up a picture of my son [who committed suicide], the other children would get very upset. They don't want to have anything to do with their deceased brother, and they don't want to be reminded of his suicide.

Hellinger: If that's the way they feel, then they're in danger of becoming suicidal, too. We could set up a constellation of your family, and see what's going on. Would you like to do that?

Ernest: Yes.

Hellinger: Okay. We'll set up your current family. How many children do you have?

Ernest: There are two more.

Hellinger: And the boy who killed himself, which position in the family did he have?

Ernest: The youngest.

Hellinger: Have either you or your wife ever been in a previous relationship?

Ernest: No.

Hellinger: Then we need you, your wife, and the three children. Go ahead and set it up. You've seen how it's done. Start with your representative and lead him to his place. Stay centered in yourself. Whatever comes from your head won't help us. Feel your way into the situation and put everyone where it feels right. *(Ernest places representatives with the exception of a representative for his wife.)* And your wife?

Ernest: I can't put her in.

Hellinger: What does that mean?

Ernest: She doesn't want to see it.

Hellinger: Then move her to the place where someone who doesn't want to see must stand.

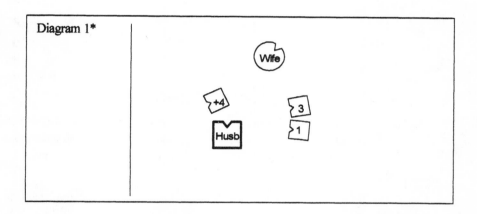

Diagram 1*

Hellinger: What's happening for the father?

Ernest's Representative: I feel very tense in this confrontation, and I can't tell what else is going on.

Hellinger: What's happening for the wife?

Wife: My throat feels like it's being choked, and my arms are paralyzed.

Hellinger: What's happening with the eldest?

First Child: I feel a great weight, and my heart is pounding.

Third Child: I'm afraid of my youngest brother. It makes me unhappy that there're all looking somewhere, but no one looks anyone else in the eye.

---

*Legend: Husb—Ernest's representative; Wife—Ernest's wife's representative; 1—first child, a son; 3—third child, a son; +4—fourth child, a son, died in infancy.

Hellinger: How's the youngest feeling?

Deceased Child: I've got a pounding heart and I'm shaking. No air.

Hellinger *(to deceased child):* Go out, and close the door after you.

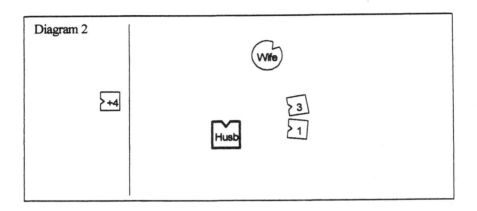

Diagram 2

Hellinger: What does that change for the father?

Ernest's Representative: That's a relief.

Hellinger: For the mother?

Wife: Better *(surprised)*.

Hellinger *(to first child):* And for you?

First Child: Worse.

Third Child: That's much better. I can breathe much more easily.

Hellinger *(to group):* Why does a child commit suicide? Out of love. The representatives' reactions of relief show that this family needed someone to disappear. The question is: Who really needed to go?
(To Ernest): So, who really was under pressure to go?

Ernest: There were so many. Even in my grandparents' generation.

Hellinger: So who all died?

Ernest: An uncle and my grandmother, also by suicide.

Hellinger: Whose brother was the uncle?

Ernest: He was my mother's brother. The grandmother was my father's mother.

Hellinger: And they both committed suicide?

Ernest: Yes. And then two of my brothers died when they were young, and a little daughter.

Hellinger: Your daughter?

Ernest: My daughter, very young *(murmur of surprise in the group)*.

Hellinger *(to group)*:   Do you notice how forgotten persons are still present, even when they're deceased? *(Brings representative of youngest son back into constellation.)*
(To representative of youngest son):   How did you feel out there?

Deceased Child: Better.

Hellinger: Come back in and take the exact place you had before you went out. Did you hear that you have a younger sister?

Deceased Child: Yes.

Hellinger *(to Ernest):*   Was the daughter who died the eldest?

Ernest: She was the second.

Hellinger: Put her in the constellation. *(Ernest places her next to her deceased brother.)*
(To Ernest)   Get centered. Where must she go, exactly? Look at the whole constellation and feel where her place is.

Ernest: Here *(next to her brother)*, she's together with the dead. Over there *(by the other brothers)*, she's with the living.

Hellinger: That's a thought. That's not a feeling.
(To group:)   When people set up a constellation according to a concept, it doesn't work.

Ernest: Here, she's with the dead.

Hellinger: That's only a theory you're stuck on.
(To Ernest's representative): Where does she belong?

Ernest's Representative: By her mother.

Hellinger: Where?

Ernest's Representative: To her left. *(Representative moves to indicated position.)*

Hellinger *(to wife's representative)*:   Exactly where does she need to be for you?

Wife: I'm suddenly icy cold. I can't see her.

Hellinger: Where does she need to be for you?

Wife: In front of me.

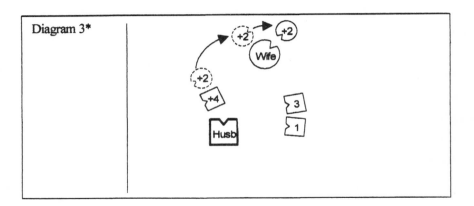

Diagram 3*

Hellinger *(to wife)*:   Take her in your arms. Breathe. *(Mother and daughter hold each other tenderly.)*
(To Ernest):   Of what did she die?

Ernest: She couldn't breathe. Her lungs were undeveloped. She could only breathe for two days.

Hellinger *(to Ernest's representative)*:   How are you doing now?

Ernest's Representative: My heart's very warm.

Hellinger *(to youngest son)*:   How are you doing?

---

*Legend addition: +2—second child, a daughter, who died in infancy

Deceased Child: I'm much better now.

Hellinger *(to group):*   When she's there, he can stay.
(To eldest son):   And you?

First Child: I'm relieved.

Third Child: Me too, but I'd like it better if she'd come over here to us.

Hellinger: We'll do that later.
(To deceased daughter):   How are you doing?

Deceased Daughter: I'm remembering that when I was a little baby, I almost died. I couldn't breathe and I was very often in a sanitarium with asthma and bronchitis.

Hellinger: That's your personal memory. For now, just stay in the role. Obviously, Ernest didn't choose you by chance alone. But how is it for you to be by your mother?

Deceased Daughter: Good.

Hellinger: And how's the mother doing?

Wife: I feel calmer. It's also become very warm in here.

Hellinger *(to group):*   Now we can try to find an order for the family, that is, we'll look for what could be a good order for them.

(Hellinger moves the parents next to each other with the deceased daughter sitting on the floor in front of them, her back leaning against them. The other children are across from them.)

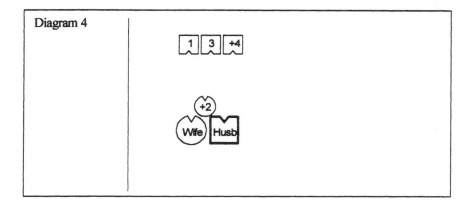

Diagram 4

Hellinger *(to parents):* Lay your hands gently on the dead girl's head or shoulder so that she's really together with you. Look at each other while you feel the presence of your child.
(To deceased daughter): How do you feel there?

Deceased Daughter: I feel threatened.

Hellinger: Threatened? Then go over to your brothers . . . close to them . . . really in between them, in your place.

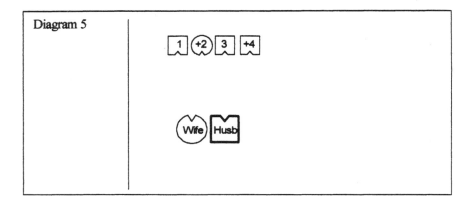

Diagram 5

Hellinger: How's that for you?

Deceased Daughter: Very protected.

First Child: Good!

Third Child: Also good.

Deceased Child: Not so good.

Hellinger *(to Ernest's representative):* How are you doing?

Ernest's Representative: Good.

Wife: I feel slightly cramped on my right side.

Hellinger *(to parents):* Switch sides. Is that better or worse?

Wife: Better.

Ernest's Representative: Better.

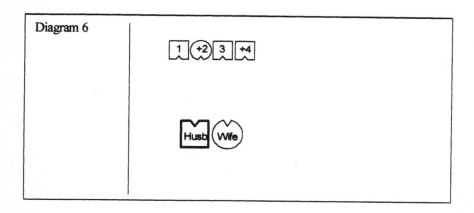

Diagram 6

Hellinger *(to youngest son):*   How are you doing now?

Deceased Child: My heart's pounding and I'm shaking like I was at the start.

Hellinger *(to Ernest):*   Once more, what happened in your family?

Ernest: Earlier?

Hellinger: Who died?

Ernest: My father's mother; then my mother's brother, two very young brothers of mine, and my father.

Hellinger: So, we've still got a whole gallery of dead people. How old was your father when he died?

Ernest: Fifty-five.

Hellinger: How did your grandmother die?

Ernest: She committed suicide.

Hellinger: How old was she?

Ernest: Thirty-four.
(Hellinger asks the parents to switch places once again. Then representatives are added for Ernest's father, his younger brothers, and his paternal

grandmother. Several configurations are tried, with the representatives'
help, until correct positions are found.)

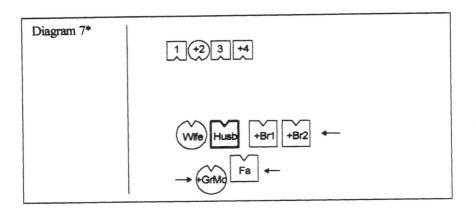

Hellinger *(to Ernest's representative):*   How do you feel when you
see them all?

Ernest's Representative: I feel good. My father gives me
strength.

Hellinger *(to youngest son):*   How do you feel now?

Deceased Child: Much better. But I need to be able to see my
grandfather clearly.

Hellinger: Okay, we'll slide them over a bit. He's the most important for you.

Deceased Child: As the grandfather came in, I immediately felt
better.

Hellinger *(to group):*   My hunch is that with so many deaths and
suicides in this family, Ernest unconsciously wanted to commit sui-

---

*Legend: +Br1—Ernest's brother, died young; +Br2—Ernest's brother, died
young; Fa—Ernest's father, died at age of 55; +GrMo—Ernest's paternal grandmother, committed suicide at age of 34.

cide, or had the feeling that he needed to die young in order to follow all of those who had gone before. His youngest son did it in his
place.

That's a dynamic we often see in families that have experienced
serious illness, frequent accidents, or suicide. It's called, "Better I go
than you, dear Father, or dear Mother." That's the case here. The
first constellation Ernest set up showed that very clearly—the
youngest son was standing in front of his father to keep him from
leaving.

(To Ernest):   What shall we do with you? Put yourself in your place
in the constellation so that you can feel how it is to be there.

Ernest: I have another intuition.

Hellinger: Put yourself into the constellation first. *(Ernest takes
his place in the constellation. Hellinger watches his reaction.)*

(To group):   I don't think he'll be able to set that right. He's too old
to be able to really resolve that dynamic. We need to respect that.
There are limits to what we can do that are set by our age. In principle, the worst has already happened. His youngest son has already
committed suicide, and it's too late to save him.

The question is whether or not we can do anything for the other
sons. He could save them if he would give his deceased son a place
in his heart and say to him, "I know that you did it for me, and I
carry you in my heart so that you live on in me. I'll do something
good in memory of you"—whatever that might mean to him. And
he can say to his other sons, "He has a place in my heart, and I'm
asking you to give him a place in your hearts too. Also, look at your
sister who is standing between you and who belongs to us."

That would be an Order of Love, and a resolution through love.
(To Ernest):   Is that clear enough for you? *(Ernest nods, pause, repre-
sentatives sit down.)*
(To group):   Are there any questions?

Participant: My son constantly puts his life in danger. Must I
wait until it has happened?

Hellinger *(looks at her for a long time, then gently)*:   Is he doing it
for you?

Participant: I don't know.

Hellinger: He's doing it for you. There was a gleam in your eyes as you told about it. The resolution lies with you. *(Pause)* Does anyone else have a question?

Participant: I'd like to know more about something you said earlier. You told Ernest that he's too old to find a resolution. Was that a provocation? You opened something up.

Hellinger: He has already done what needed to be done. It doesn't matter how that happened. Look at him, how he's beaming at me.

Related Questions

Question: It seems to me that you ask a great deal from the clients. You said yourself that you go to the outermost limit. But I've also noticed that you suddenly stop at a certain point so that the work can continue on its own, so that it accumulates a certain power. Can you explain how you understand that process?

Hellinger: Together with the client, I survey the entire field of the consequences of his or her actions and fate. I don't limit it to what's easy and pleasant. I go with clients to the limits of their systems, to the boundaries where their systems stop. In effect, that means that we eventually meet death, and with them, I look at the possibility that they will die, or that something terrible will happen. I accompany them, I go with them to the outer limits, without fear, without hesitation. We look at everything that's there, up one side and down the other.

Once we've done that, we've seen the entire field of reality that's operating in their system. We've explored the whole field and we know where the limits are. Only by going to the outer limits can we know what's possible, the good as well as the bad. That gives clients strength, and with that strength, we can look for a resolution that's good for everyone.

Sometimes the resolution is that we must accept the inevitable, that we've reached the limit, and that nothing else is easier or possible. But usually there's another possible solution. When there is another possibility, it can be reached more easily after we've already been to the outer limits. The client can see the reality of the situation and can then choose the best and most appropriate path for himself or herself.

Question: Much of what you say sounds dogmatic. Yet, I'm surprised at how much inner tranquillity and centeredness you maintain in spite of the very heavy situations that people repeatedly bring and the rather hostile confrontations by people in the audience that sometimes arise. I see, too, a gentleness of spirit in you that touches me deeply. How do you maintain your centeredness and the clarity of your perception?

Hellinger: Tranquillity and clarity of perception are made possible by consenting to the world *as it is* without any intention to change it. That's fundamentally a religious attitude, because it aligns me with a greater whole without separating me from it. I don't pretend to know better or hope to achieve something better than what the inner forces already at work in the system would do by themselves. When I see something terrible, that, too, is an aspect of the world, and I consent to it. When I see something beautiful, I consent to that also. I call this attitude "humility"—consenting to the world as it is. Only this consent makes perception possible. Without it, wishes, fears, judgments—my constructs—interfere with my perception.

And there's another thing to consider. The Orders of Love aren't rigid structures. They're always changing; they're different from moment to moment. There's something richly varied in them, a profound abundance that we can glimpse for only a brief moment. That's the reason why every family constellation is different, even when the issues in the families are similar. When I recognize that an order is a certain way, then I say what I see. Some people who are accustomed to thinking in terms of "true and false" or "right and wrong" have a tendency to hear what I say as a statement about a general truth. It's not! It's only a recognition of the truth that could be glimpsed in a certain moment. It applies only to that moment, and in that moment, it has its full truth. If someone isolates what I've seen from its momentary context and makes a general principle out of it, then it appears to be dogmatic. But others do that with what I say—I don't.

CHAPTER THREE

Parents and Children

The love between parents and children, like love in other relationships, is constrained by bonding, by giving and taking, and by dividing functions appropriately. Unlike other love, parent–child love succeeds when a disparity of giving and taking is maintained. The first systemic Order of Love between parents and children is that parents give and children take.

The most valuable thing that children receive from their parents—no matter who their parents are or what they may have done—is the opportunity to live. Receiving life from their parents, children take their parents, and those parents are the only possible ones for them. Children can't add to, omit from, or reject anything in the life their parents give, and it's also impossible for parents to add or withhold anything when they give themselves as parents to their children.

This first giving and taking between parents and children is different from the giving and taking of gifts and favors. When children take life from their parents, they take what their parents previously have taken from their own parents. In a certain sense, children *are* their parents and grandparents. Love succeeds when children value the life they have been given—when they take their parents *as parents* as they are. Everything else that children need in order to thrive can be given by someone else, but only their parents can give them life.

I'm Glad You Had Me

During a workshop on family systems, a businessman told the group that his mother had given him away as a child so that she could live a free and unburdened life. He had grown up in a foster family and met his mother for the first time when he was 20 years old. At the time that he participated in the workshop, he was over 40 and had only seen his mother three or four times. The following day, he remembered that she lived not far from the course site, and that evening he visited her. He returned to the workshop the next day and related how he had gone to her house and had told her, "Mother, I'm glad you had me." The old woman beamed, and her heart knew peace.

Parents know deep satisfaction when they are taken by their children, when they see the quick flash in a child's eye, or hear the joyful laughter that says: "I'm glad you had me." Children know peace when they take their parents—like the man above did—as they are.

In addition to giving them life, parents also give their children other things. They care for them, and provide them with advantages, disadvantages, and opportunities for good or ill. Children are unable to balance out the great disparity of giving and taking in their relationship with their parents, even when they want to. And so an irreconcilable disparity of giving and taking is the second Order of Love with which children must contend.

The bonding love that young children feel for their natural parents is blind to the details of what the parents do or fail to do. Children act as if love could tolerate no difference—as if only being similar would bond them together and that being different must lead to separation and loss. Their actions bear witness to the magical thinking of the child's soul: "Like bonds to like."

This unconscious assumption about love gives rise to a child's instinctive urge to bond to the parents by being like them. This is easily seen in young children who openly imitate their parents, but this aspect of children's love continues to operate in the inner lives of adults as well, playing an important role in family relationships. Acting out of love, children follow their parents even in suffering, and although it's usually unconscious, they perpetuate their parents' misfortunes by copying them.

A Good Girl

A 35-year-old woman told the group that she was getting a divorce. She had been happily married and had three children. Although she could give no satisfactory reason for wanting to divorce, she was adamant and rejected out of hand all suggestions to reconsider. In a later session, the therapist asked her about her parents. Her father had died trying to rescue his companions on an aircraft carrier. The therapist asked how old her mother was at that time. She replied, "My mother lost my father when she was 35." The therapist then asked, "*Must* a good girl in your family lose her husband at 35?"

Motivated by blind love, the daughter did as her mother had done, sharing her loss as if a second separation could equalize the first, as if her divorce demonstrated loyalty. Children unconsciously aspire to equal their parents in suffering. Their bonding love is so deep that it blinds them, and they can't resist the temptation to try to care for their parents by taking on their parents' suffering. Although acting out of love and believing that they are doing good, they begin to function as their parents' parents, and they live out their parents' greatest fears by damaging themselves. Their blind love protects their bonding to their parents, but by functioning as parents and trying to give to their parents rather than take from them, they reverse the flow of giving and taking and they inadvertently perpetuate suffering. Love between parents and children obeys a hierarchy within the family that demands that they remain unequal partners, that parents give and children take. Thus, the third *Order of Love* is that love succeeds best when children are children and parents are parents—that is, when the hierarchy within the family according to time and function is respected.

GIVING AND TAKING
BETWEEN PARENTS AND CHILDREN

Both parents and children are tempted to give and take what damages love. Misunderstandings about what love allows are common, and the consequences are often painful. The fact that the giving and taking between parents and children can't be balanced by reciprocal giving demands that they look for other resolutions.

Three common patterns of giving and taking between parents and children are injurious to love:

1. Children refuse to take their parents as they are.

2. Parents try to give and children to take what is harmful.

3. Parents try to take from children and children try to give to parents.

Refusing to Take Parents as They Are

Instead of taking their parents as they are, children sometimes presume to evaluate them as if parents had to earn the right to be parents. They say, in effect, "I don't like this about you, so you're not my father." Or, "You didn't give me what I needed, so you can't be my mother." This is an absurd distortion of reality. Parents enter parenthood through the events of conception and birth, and these acts alone make them the child's parents. Children are absolutely powerless to change anything about this first giving and taking.

Children experience inner solidity and a clear sense of identity when they find resolution with their parents, when they take both parents and acknowledge them as they are. They feel incomplete and empty when they exclude one or both of their parents from their hearts. The consequence of demeaning or excluding a parent is always the same—children become passive and feel empty. This is a common cause of depression.

Children, even when they've been hurt by their parents, can still say: "Yes, you are my parents. Everything that was in you is in me too. I acknowledge that you are my parents, and I accept the consequences that has for me. I take the good from what you gave, and I trust you to deal with your fate as you see fit." Then they are free to set about the often difficult work of making the best out of what may be a very bad situation.

The Rest House

Cloaked in memory and loss, a man wanders the streets of the town where he was born. Many things that happened there remain hidden from him, and many doors are locked. He wishes he could put that past far behind him, but something holds him, as if he were wrestling with a demon whose blessing he must win before he can go. And so he feels caught between a desire to go forward and a need to stay, between leaving and remaining.

He comes to a park and sits down on a bench, leans back, breathes deeply. He closes his eyes. Trusting to an inner force, he allows his turmoil just to be and feels himself growing calm and supple like reeds in the wind, in harmony with all diversity and with the spaciousness of time.

He imagines himself as an open house, and whoever wishes to may enter. All who come bring something, stay a while, and then leave.

There's a perpetual coming in this house, a bringing, a staying, a leaving. Everyone newly come brings something, grows old in staying, and leaves when the time is ripe.

Many who have been excluded or long forgotten enter his house. They too bring something, stay a while, and leave. Even those who are unwelcome enter, and they too bring something, mingle with the others, stay a while, and leave.

Whoever enters meets those who came before and those who will come after, and because they are many, all must share. Everyone who has a place has limits. Whoever desires something must also give. Those who enter continue to grow as long as they stay. They came after others had left, and will go when others need to come. And so in this house of coming and going, there are time and space enough for everyone.

Sitting there in this way, the man feels comfortable in his house. He feels at ease with all who have come, are coming, and will come; with all they've brought, are bringing, and will bring; and with those who have stayed, are staying, or have left. It seems to him as if whatever had been incomplete is now complete. He feels a long struggle coming to an end, and leaving is now possible. He waits until he feels that the moment has come, opens his eyes, looks around, stands up, and goes.

Children contribute to their parents' feelings of guilt when they refuse to take them as they are. If children remain unhappy, caught in a cycle of failure and suffering because their parents' caretaking was deficient, then the parents are guilty of causing hurt to the children to whom they gave life. If children are able to overcome whatever they may have suffered in childhood and learn to live happy, satisfying lives, then their parents feel relieved. Because they have good lives, these children don't cling to their resentments against their parents. Rather, they take the life they've been given and live it as fully as they can. Still, many people prefer to remain unhappy rather than take life fully and aid their parents in putting old feelings of guilt to rest.

Refusing to Take Father as He Is: An Example

Participant: I have a question about children honoring their father. I've been working intensively with a family for some years. The parents are divorced and the father lives in another city. The children reject their father with an intense hatred because he repeatedly terrorized their mother. They watched him beat her on several occasions. The children also found out that their father had sexually molested young schoolboys. He's made a genuine effort to change and has repeatedly tried to establish contact with them, hoping that some form of reconciliation might be possible. He's written them letters and sent them presents, but they refuse to have anything to do with him. They even shredded the family photo album, tearing out all the pictures of him.

Hellinger: How old are the children?

Participant: Ages 10 to 18. They all live with their mother, and they say they don't ever want to see their father again.

Hellinger: Okay. The first thing is that the hate that the children feel toward their father is most likely their mother's, and not their own. It's just too intense to be merely children's hate. The fact of their taking on their mother's hate doesn't protect them from the consequences of the hate. That's very important to understand—whatever we do has consequences, and it has consequences for our children as well. Having a moral justification for doing something destructive doesn't exempt the action from its consequences, and neither do good intentions reduce the consequences of harmful actions.

It would be useful for the children to learn to allow their mother to deal with her own hate. One strategic intervention would be for them to tell their mother, "About all this hate for Dad, we'll take care of it for you." You can suggest that to them, but don't explain it. That would be a first step to getting everyone thinking about what's going on.

When people are caught in other people's feelings, it's usually better to work with them indirectly. So, after you offer the sentence to them, you could try a telling them a long story with a surprise ending. For example, here's a story about something that really happened.

Where Do You Stand with Mother?

Once my wife and I were invited by the director of a psychosomatic
hospital to work with some of the patients who were staying there. We
worked very intensively for 14 days. They all had a special program
every morning and Primal Group Therapy every afternoon.

One woman with whom I worked was extremely depressed. During a therapy session, she screamed with cold hatred that she wished
her father had died in the war. On the next day, I asked her what had
happened to her father. She explained that he had suffered a head
wound, and often had outbreaks and did crazy things that were very
difficult for her and her mother. They came to hate him, and to wish
that he had died. But judging by the way she talked, I suspected that
the daughter felt and expressed her mother's hate—not her own.

At our next meeting, I asked her if she had children. She said,
"I've got two sons." I said, "One of your sons will follow your father."
She looked at me, but didn't say anything. I asked her how her marriage was. She said that it wasn't very good. Her husband took good
care of her and the children, which was why she stayed with him, but
she didn't like him very much.

She was very depressed and agitated when I next saw her a few
days later. When I asked her what the matter was, she said that she
had received a letter from the home for disturbed children where
her youngest son lived. He'd had a suicidal episode there. Although
she confirmed what I had said a few days earlier, she didn't see the
connection, and I didn't say anything either. Then she said, "I love
him so much." But the way she said it didn't seem genuine. So I told
her that it didn't sound much like love, and that it upset me to hear
her speak about him like that. She became furious with me and sent
me away.

She was surprised when I checked on her the next day. I asked her
to experiment with imagining that her son was there and telling him,
"I hate your father, but I love you." After she did it, I asked her,
"How would your son respond if he heard you say that?" She said,
"I don't know." I asked, "Would he be able to react at all?" She
answered softly, "No." I said, "That's what's making him crazy."

In the same room was a young man whose mother had left him in
a hospital and disappeared. He'd been in a series of foster homes and
had suffered a great deal, but he accepted his fate openly. I said to
her, "Look at him. He's suffered a lot, but he didn't get psychotic. He
knows where he stands with his mother."

If you tell them a horrible story like that, perhaps they'll catch on
to the hidden dynamic. Becoming a father and being one have noth-

ing to do with whether the father's good or bad. Becoming a father or a mother is a process beyond good and evil. Conceiving a child fundamentally serves life, so it doesn't depend on moral judgments for its honor.

I'll give you another example. A doctor once told a group that his father had been a doctor for the SS and had supervised many human experiments in the concentration camps. After the war, he was found guilty and given the death penalty, but somehow was freed and he disappeared. The son's question was, "What shall I do about my father?" I said to him, "In the moment your father impregnated your mother, he wasn't acting as an SS officer. The two things are different, and you can and must keep them separate."

Like this doctor, it's possible for a child to acknowledge his or her father *as a father* without assuming responsibility for the father's actions. Children in such situations must not minimize or excuse their father's actions, but they can say, "What you did is your responsibility. Still, you are my father. Whatever you have done, we're related. I'm glad that you gave me life. Even when what you did was horrible, I'm your son, not your judge." What other option is open to a child in a situation like that?

This distinction is also very important for the children in your case. What their father did makes it necessary for them to separate from him for a while, but they won't manage to separate as long as the hate is so strong. The hate binds them to him. They'll be free when they honestly say, "What you did was very hard for us, and we're not going to see you for a while, but you're still our father, and we enjoy the life you gave us."

Maybe you can help the mother, as well. She's probably caught in an identification with someone in her own system, and the exaggeration of her hate comes from that identification. Perhaps she's taken on someone's hate in the same way that her children are taking on her hate. If she's entangled, it'll be difficult for her to think clearly about what's happening. It might help her if she can find out what was going on in her family. If she can find the person to whom the hate belongs, she may be able to give it back. Then she'll only have to deal with her own hate and whatever else actually belongs between her and her former husband.

There's a danger that her children will later copy their father's behavior and become like him. If she gets to the place where she's genuinely looking for a resolution, the systemic solution would be for her to say, "I married your father because I loved him, and when I see you, I still love him." If she could honestly say that, the children would be free. But you probably wouldn't dare to propose something like that, would you?

Participant: No, I wouldn't!

Hellinger: That would be an effective intervention. Of course, you'd have to offer it to her with conviction, with true compassion. You can't say something like that as a technique.

Participant: The courts are going to decide whether or not the children and the father can have contact with each other. The mother is contesting visitation rights.

Hellinger: I'd agree with her that there should be no contact for now. I'd tell the father that it's appropriate for him to give up his rights to visitation for the time being. If he were to do so, he would be accepting the consequences of his actions, and that would make it easier for the children to respect him. The courts decide according to legal criteria, but they often decide what's psychologically best anyway. I wouldn't encourage his protesting the decision.

Giving and Taking What Is Harmful

Among the things that parents must not give their children, and that children must not take, are debts, illnesses, obligations, burdens of circumstance, injustices suffered or committed, and any privileges gained by personal achievement. These are all things that parents have earned or suffered through personal effort or circumstance. They haven't been inherited from a previous generation in order to be passed to the next as a good bequest, so they remain the parents' responsibility. It's the parents' job to protect their children from the negative effect of such things, and children must trust their parents to deal with whatever fate has meted out—in whatever way the parents choose. When parents give what is harmful, or when children take it, love is injured.

There are negative consequences of a different kind when a younger person feels entitled to the rewards and privileges of an older person without having earned them.

A Better Lawyer

A young lawyer took over his father's highly successful law practice. Because he was less experienced, and perhaps less gifted than his father, many of the more important clients soon left. Rather than accepting this loss of income and reduced standard of living, he acted as if he had the right to the same success as his father—even though he had not earned it with his own efforts. He began to accept well-paid but illegal work.

His actions were soon exposed and he was barred from legal practice for some years.

My Mother the Actress

Fate smiled generously on a well-known actress, giving her both talent and luck. Fate was less generous with her daughter. However, the daughter felt entitled to the same success as her mother and became depressed and suicidal when she could not achieve it. She began to hate her mother, as if her mother could have given her luck and talent, as well as life.

Eventually, the daughter found a life of her own in a different profession, and enjoyed modest success, a happy family life, and a good friendship with her mother.

Children must differentiate themselves from their parents and recognize the limits of their rights and responsibilities. This too shows respect and love for their parents.

Children have advantages or disadvantages according to their parents' circumstances. From what they're given in this way, children create anew their own advantages and debts. But love is injured when children feel entitled and demand to take what their parents have acquired through personal efforts or suffering. For example, bitter quarrels that split families and destroy love may result when children expect or demand an inheritance.

An inheritance is a gift from parents to their children, and like any gift, it may be given however the giver wishes. Even if one child gets everything and the others nothing, resentment has no good effect. An inheritance is always unearned, and complaining about getting less than someone else is inappropriate. However, those who have received more may freely give a fair share to those who have been given less, and thereby assure peace and harmony in the system. Whenever those who have received less are dissatisfied and demand more—as if an inheritance were a right—turbulence develops in the flow of love.

Sometimes children take something harmful from their parents, and sometimes parents try to give to their children an obligation, resentment, or debt, as if that were a good inheritance. Fate brings advantage and misfortune in different measures. Individuals may be able to turn misfortune aside or escape its consequences, but sometimes they cannot and so must suffer the consequences of fortune's whimsy. Such unavoidable blows of fate, however, also give strength and wisdom to those who understand and surrender to them. The good qualities earned in this way may then be passed on to others without the price that's already been paid. Passing on wisdom earned through suffering is possible only if the other members of the system have the courage, respect, and wisdom not to interfere. For example, grandparents who have accepted with grace whatever unavoidable suffering and loss fate has given give freely to their grandchildren, and are loved by them. But whenever younger persons—even if motivated by love—take on burdens or obligations from older persons, they intrude into the most personal sphere of those older persons and rob them and their suffering of the power for good.

The order of giving and taking in a family is turned upside down when parents haven't taken enough from their own parents, or when they haven't taken and given enough to each other in their partnership. Then they want their emotional needs to be met by their children, and their children may feel responsible for meeting them. Parents then take like children, and children give as if they were parents. Instead of flowing from older to younger, the giving and taking run against the flow of gravity and time. Such giving can't reach its proper goal any more than a mountain stream can flow from the valley up to the peaks.

When Father Acts Like a Child

A young couple came to therapy with their six-year-old son seeking help in dealing with him, as he was very difficult. During an emotional outburst, the father held his son firmly, close to his body, and talked to him. The father spoke as if he were a child himself, talking about his own needs and feelings as if his son should understand him like a father, and the boy found no resolution.

The therapist sat behind the father and said, "Imagine that I'm your father. Lean against me and speak to your son as a father speaks." He did so, and a resolution established itself at once. In the end he sat with his son, holding hands, and his wife sat with their two daughters, facing them. Father and son were at peace together, as were the mother and daughters. It was a beautiful picture.

At the next session, the man lay on the floor playing with his son. They wrestled happily. Suddenly, the boy became angry and ran out of the room. The therapist, overhearing their conversation, noticed that the child had become angry when the father reverted to speaking as a child, and the order was disturbed again.

When parents have unmet emotional needs, it's appropriate for them to turn to each other or to their own parents. When they turn to their children with demands to be comforted or reassured, the roles and functions in the family are reversed. That's *parentification*—children assuming the position of a parent toward their own parents. Children can't protect themselves against this process. Everyone suffers when families are caught in the pattern of children feeling responsible for their parents and parents expecting their children to behave as adult partners. The children take on an exaggerated and inappropriate importance in the family, *and* they're doomed to fail, for no child can satisfy his or her parents' emotional needs and emptiness. And the parents can't protect themselves from doing to their children what they don't wish to do. Moral arguments and logical justifications don't count at all, only the actual experience of love. The flow of love can be felt, but not legislated: Children know whether or not they are open with their parents.

Questions and Answers from Seminars

Question: Is it parentification when a daughter feels as though she's the mother of her mother or the mother of her father?

Hellinger: My definition was more precise: Parentification is when a child assumes the position of the parent. That has more scope because we're not just looking at an individual child and what that child may feel, but at the dynamics of the family system as a whole, where you can see patterns across several generations. For example, one mother had strong irrational feelings of resentment toward her daughter. Looking into the family system, she remembered how she had resented her own mother, and she discovered that the resentment she had for her daughter felt exactly the same. The entangled love for her mother entangled the love with her daughter. That's parentification as a family dynamic. It's more than just an individual's feelings, so you've got to try to see what's going on in the whole family.

Do the children hold themselves responsible for a parent's inner condition? Do they try to give what a parent or partner may give, but what a child may not give? For example, do they think or feel, "If I do this, my mother will get ill," or, "If I don't do that, my father will leave us"? Parentification is immediately clear in the family constellations. Often the person representing such a child will start to feel nervous and fidgety. If the person with whom that person is identified is brought into the system—for instance, the missing grandmother or partner—the child immediately becomes calm.

Question: You said that children separate from their parents by taking them. It seems to me that children separate from their parents by drawing a clear boundary between them. Would you comment on that?

Hellinger: When a child complains to his or her parents, "What you gave me wasn't enough or it was the wrong thing, and you still owe me a lot," then the child can't separate from them. These demands bind children to their parents in such a way that they can't take anything. If they were to take their parents as they are, and also the good things that they gave, then their taking would dissolve their demand and make it seem foolish. As it is, they remain bound to their parents, and can neither take nor separate.

Taking one's parents has a strange effect—it separates. It's not something done against the parents, but something that completes and rounds out the relationship with them. Taking your parents means, "I take whatever you've given me. It's a lot and it's enough. Whatever else I need, I'll take care of myself or get from someone else, and now I'll leave you in peace." It means, "I take what I've been given, and although I may then leave my parents, I have my parents and my parents have me."

In a group, a very successful doctor asked, "What shall I do? My parents meddle in my business all the time." I told him, "Your parents have the right to butt into your life whenever they want to! And you have the right to go ahead and do whatever *you* think is right for yourself anyway."

Children who don't take their parents must try to compensate for the deficit. Often the search for self-realization and enlightenment is, in reality, the search for the not-yet-taken father and the not-yet-taken mother. The search for God often stops or becomes different when the father and mother are taken. Many people have discovered that their so-called "midlife crisis" was resolved as soon as they successfully took a previously rejected parent.

Question: As I understand what you've said, it's important for me to position myself next to my mother, to take her. To be honest, I have to admit that I haven't done that, not as a child, as an adolescent, or as a grown woman. Is there anything I can do now?

Hellinger: Yes, there is. Stand next to her and look at her with a daughter's love. Taking your mother is really an inner process.

Question: What if there's no current input from her? My mother has never managed to feel that she's worthy of being an equal partner to a man, so she's lived all her married life in my father's shadow. She's the perfect example of a woman who's always believed that a wife should be subservient to her husband. If I move into her sphere of influence, what then?

Hellinger: Our parents give us life, and they're the only ones who can do that. Others can give us what else we need in addition to that. Strictly speaking, we don't get life from our parents—it comes to us through them from far away. They're our connection with the source of life, with what is beyond whatever shortcomings they may have. When we connect to them, we access that deeper source, and it holds many surprises and mysteries. Something beautiful happens when people look at their parents and recognize the source of life. Love demands that the receiver honor both the gift and the giver. Whoever loves and honors life implicitly loves and honors the givers of life. Whoever disdains or devalues life, and doesn't respect it, dishonors the givers of life. When people take and honor both gift and giver, they hold the gift up to the light until it shines, and although the gift flows through them to those who follow, the giver is illuminated by its glow.

Additional Considerations

When we have the feeling that we're missing something from our mother or father, we have an image of what should have been. That's the image of the good parent. Taking our parents is a question of giving those good images a place in our hearts and letting them do some good work there. That's an option that remains open to most people even when they were hurt by their parents. Taking one's parents doesn't demand denying what was negative, but it permits children to touch the depths of all parents' hearts where they suffer bitterly when they see their children caught in the same pattern in which they were caught. When people succeed in seeing their parents in that depth, they're changed—and so are their parents.

Hellinger describes a possibility of looking at our parents so that we see them in the context of their fate. We see their failures, we see their suffering and disappointments, we trust them to deal with their fate as best they can, and we remember our own position as children in the family hierarchy. Beyond that, we see past them to the larger mystery of life that flows to us through them.

Obviously, it's easier if our actual father and mother displayed some of this goodness, and almost every parent does at times. In our therapy groups, participants are sometimes invited to do an experiment. They imagine that their own son or daughter has grown up and is suffering from family problems that have been passed on. This is invariably a painful image for people, even for persons who have no children. Then they're invited to imagine that their children manage to accept and to rise above the problem. They imagine that they succeeded in taking what was good and in leaving behind what was burdensome. That's a great relief for parents.

Hellinger is describing an actual movement, an action that real people do with other real people. This means taking the actual father and mother and seeing them through the eyes of an adult standing in the Order of Love, not through a distressed child's eyes. Many people have been able to put their relationships with their parents in order so that love returns to their family system in spite of terrible things that have happened to them. When they succeed, everyone in the system feels it—the parents, themselves, their children. [H.B.]

THE HIERARCHY
BETWEEN PARENTS AND CHILDREN

Healthy, happy children and loving parents can be found in all cultures, religions, and social classes. This means that there are many successful ways to rear children, and that they differ from, and may even contradict, one another. Nevertheless, love demands bonding, a balance of giving and taking, and appropriate social orders in all cultures, but it leaves us great latitude in how we achieve them.

Love flows smoothly when all members of a family system follow the hierarchy. As we've seen earlier, the family hierarchy must meet three criteria: time, weight, and function.

With respect to time, the family hierarchy flows down from above and from earlier to later. Like time, it can't be stopped or reversed in its direction—children always come after their parents, and the younger always follow the older. Konrad Ferdinand Meyer describes this movement from above to below in his poem "The Roman Fountain."

> *A gush of water rises,*
> *falling fills a marble bowl*
> *which veils itself in overflow*
> *into a second bowl below.*
>
> *The second floods its wealth*
> *into yet a third*
> *and each takes and gives,*
> *is still and lives.*

The relationship between father and mother exists before they become parents; there are adults without children, but no children without biological parents. Love succeeds when parents care well for their young children, but not the other way around. Thus, the relationship between husband and wife takes priority in a family.

The priority according to time also applies to siblings. Those who are closest to the beginning of life take from those who have lived longer. The older give to the younger, and the younger take from the older. The first child gives to the second and the third, the second takes from the first and gives to the third, and babies take from all of the others. The eldest child gives more, and the youngest child takes more. For this reason, the eldest often has compensating privileges and the youngest child often takes more responsibility for caring for their parents in their old age.

New relationship systems also have a systemic priority over older systems. This is the opposite of the dynamic of precedence within a system where the older members have precedence over those who come later. The couple's relationship takes priority over the relationship with the family of origin in the same way that a second marriage has precedence over the first. Relationships suffer when this principle isn't honored—when parents remain more important than partners and children, and first partners more important than new ones.

With respect to weight, the most important relationship in the family is that between the father and the mother; then come the parent–child relationships, the relationships with the extended family, and, finally, those with other, freely chosen groups. Certain individuals who carry an unusually heavy fate may have enough systemic weight so that the normal sequence according to time must be adjusted.

Putting Children Before Partners: Examples from Seminars

Louis: My mother once told me that she had stayed with my father because of me. I don't thii.k I've honored that enough.

Hellinger: Nor should you, at least not in that sense. When your mother says that you're the reason she stayed with your father, she's not telling you the whole the truth. If you think that she stayed with him because of you, you make yourself too important. She stayed with your father because she accepted the consequences of her actions. She did it for herself and for him. That's something completely different. You didn't participate in their decisions and agreements, so you can honor her for being willing to accept the consequences of her own actions, but not because she did it for you.

If you look at it as being something she did for you, you distort the truth. On the other hand, if you see that she willingly accepted the consequences of her actions, you honor both your mother and your father. By formulating it that way, you focus on the intimacy between your father and your mother. By saying it the other way, you focus on the intimacy between your mother and you.

The dynamic is the same when the parents marry because of a pregnancy. They don't get married for the child, but rather because they accept the consequences of their actions. The child had no active part in the agreement between the parents, but he or she often feels responsible, especially if the marriage is unhappy. Such children are completely without blame and there's no need for them to feel responsible. Nevertheless, many children do so anyway and they then feel too important.

How was your parents' marriage?

Louis: Partly, very close. I often saw my mother sitting on my father's lap, but apparently there were sexual difficulties. She refused him once, and then she complained to me later that he didn't want her sexually anymore.

Hellinger: I want to tell you something about being drawn into confidences between your mother and father. Whatever happened between your parents is none of your business! The correct therapeutic procedure is to forget whatever she told you as quickly as you can! Cleanse your heart and soul of the matter. Mastering the skill of forgetting is a healing resource. That kind of forgetting is a spiritual discipline. *(Louis immediately nods confirmation.)* That was too quick. A "too-quick" nod is a substitute for a real agreement.

Question: Is that true for a child of any age?

Hellinger: Yes, it's possible to get entangled in things that are none of your business at any age. A mother, for example, shouldn't tell a child the intimate details of her sexual life with the child's father. It's injurious when one parent speaks disparagingly about such intimacy to the children—or to others. Our sexual intimacy is a point on which we're all very vulnerable, and if that isn't respected between partners, that's the end of their relationship. The parents' intimate life is none of the children's business, and they shouldn't be drawn into it. They can't protect themselves against getting sucked in, but later on, they can forget what they've heard! Then it causes no harm. If they forget with good inner judgment and love, it can be truly forgotten.

Question: What about when my mother tells me intimate things about her relationship with her first husband?

Hellinger: It's exactly the same. You can tell her, "I only care about Papa. I don't want to know what happened between you and your first husband, and I don't want to know what happens between you and Papa either."

Question: What about telling a new partner about intimacies from a previous relationship?

Hellinger: That's also a violation of trust. What was private between you and your former partner should be protected and kept as a secret. If you expose the intimate details of your earlier relationship, your new partner will have difficulty trusting you.

Question: When parents have affairs, is that also none of the children's business?

Hellinger: That's right, none of their business at all!

Question: What if there are children from the second relationship?

Hellinger: In that case, it's not a secret, and it touches them directly. They're entitled to know about it.

Question: I know of parents who have allowed their children to read their old love letters.

Hellinger: If they were my parents, I wouldn't read them.

Question: I worked with a family in which the father brought his mistress home, and the mother was too weak to stop him. Could the sons intervene and tell him to leave his women outside their home?

Hellinger: I'm very cautious about answering speculative questions or making generalizations. Nevertheless, they probably would be well advised to assume that their mother is in agreement with the situation—at least, that she's choosing the least bad of the not-too-good options open to her. It would be reasonable and appropriate for the sons to leave home as soon as possible. It's always difficult when children become involved in their parents' relationship.

Question: My ex-wife constantly puts me down in front of our daughters. It's clear to me that I can't do anything about my ex-wife's behavior, but is there something I can do for my daughters?

Hellinger: Nothing, absolutely nothing. Perhaps someday you can tell them a story about how people learn to forget.

Systemic Entanglements

Whenever parents outwardly act against the best interests of their children, one may assume that they're caught in some earlier systemic violation of the Orders of Love. Parents naturally desire that their children be spared whatever they themselves have suffered, and they suffer when their children suffer; they know discouragement and defeat when their children know them. When parents' suffering is balanced out blindly by their children's suffering, it passes from person to person, from generation to generation, and knows no end. The work with family constellations frequently reveals repeating patterns of harm and suffering crossing generations within families.

Children are boundless in love but limited in life experience, so it's a great temptation for them to unite with their parents in suffering. If a mother is depressed, her children feel tempted to be depressed as well. If a father drinks too much, his children come under pressure to find some way to emulate his suffering, perhaps by failing to be successful in life. But maturing love demands that children gradually give up the blind love of childhood and learn to love as adults. Instead of repeating what is harmful, mature love demands that they free themselves from the family entanglements. Then they fulfill their parents' deeper expectations and hopes for their children. The better the children are, the better are the parents.

Children disentangle themselves from the negative effects of the blind love by recognizing and obeying their parents' true wishes— that the children be happy and fulfilled. It takes great courage for children to see their parents suffer and yet still obey the greater love, to see to it that they themselves succeed in life and fulfill the desires of their parents' hearts.

Even though children want to be like their parents, they also fear their fate. For this reason, children may outwardly reject their parents and strive to be different from them even while they secretly emulate them. Such children, although they make a great show of being different from their parents, still unconsciously do as their parents have done, and attract—or react to—life situations in which they experience approximately what their parents have experienced. When children say to their parents, "Under no circumstances will I ever be like you," they still love their parents blindly and are bound tightly to them. In spite of themselves, they commit themselves to following their parents' example, and they become exactly like them. When children fear becoming like their parents, they constantly watch their parents, because whatever they don't wish to be like they must continually observe. It's no wonder then that they become exactly like their parents.

A man brings the values and traditions of his family into a partnership, and a woman does the same. Yet their values and traditions are often quite different. Children outwardly follow the more dominant parent, but inwardly they follow the other parent. For example, if the father's values dominate, then the couple's children tend to follow his values outwardly while inwardly they adhere to the mother's values. It's more common for the mother's values to dominate and to be outwardly followed by the children, with the result that, although they outwardly reject their father, they secretly emulate him—usually without noticing what they're doing.

In deviating from one parent's values, a child is generally following the value system of the other parent. For this reason, disobedience to one parent is often a kind of loyalty and obedience to the other. If children get the direct or indirect message from one parent, "Don't become like your father/mother," then their loyalty demands of them that they become like the forbidden parent.

I'll Consent If You Become Like Your Father

A woman divorced her alcoholic husband and was awarded custody of their son. She was worried that he would become like her former husband. Her therapist told her that her son had the freedom to choose to follow his father, and that, if she wanted to relieve him of the systemic necessity to become like his father, she could say to her son, "You may take all that I give to you, and you may take all that your father gives you. You may become like me and you may become like your father." She objected, "But what if he becomes an alcoholic?" The therapist answered, "Exactly, even then! Then tell him. 'I will consent if you become like your father.' That's the test."

The effect of this kind of permission and respect for the diminished parent is that the son can then honor his love for his father by taking him as he is without also having to take his entanglements. If the mother had said, "Don't you dare become like your father," then the son would have come under systemic pressure to do so to honor his bond to his father, and he would have been unable to protect himself.

By maintaining loyalty to one parent outwardly and loyalty to the other parent inwardly, children are able to hold the family together, but the system doesn't achieve the kind of balance that members experience as natural and effortless love. For this reason, one parent can never really triumph over the other. For example, children secretly emulate the parent who comes out worse in a divorce, sometimes with destructive consequences.

In adoptions that don't turn out well, and when stepparents have difficulties with their stepchildren, it's frequently the case that the adoptive parents or stepparents wish to replace the natural parents rather than complement them. Then the loyalty to the natural parent puts the child under pressure to undermine the new family.

DIFFICULT ISSUES
IN PARENT–CHILD RELATIONSHIPS

Child Custody

Question: I do a lot of work for the courts, trying to determine who should get custody of the children. Sometimes the divorces get very ugly, and it's very difficult to make a recommendation. Can you say something about this problem?

Hellinger: The question of who gets custody of the children after a divorce is actually not as difficult to resolve as you might think. There are two systemic principles that can guide you in making the decision: (1) The children should go to the parent who most values the other parent in them, and (2) Whoever abandons the relationship shouldn't be rewarded with custody of the children.

In actual experience, most often it's the father who values the mother more in their children than the other way around. Even when that's the case, if the woman wants custody, she earns the right to have their children by learning to value the qualities of her former husband in them. Otherwise, she harms the children by wanting and valuing only half of them.

Question: How do you tell which parent values the other most in the children?

Hellinger: You see it immediately, and they also know it, if they are honest with themselves. You only have to look at the parents and you know right away which one it is.

Question: But couldn't it happen that they value each other equally?

Hellinger: That's a hypothetical objection. If they valued each other equally, they wouldn't need to divorce—or at least they wouldn't be fighting about child custody.

Question: There are two principles: "The parent who most values the other in the children should get custody" and "Whoever abandons the relationship shouldn't be rewarded with custody of the children." Are they the same?

Hellinger: What's important is to look closely at the actual people with whom you're working. Therapeutic principles have a healing effect when they serve the needs of your clients, but you mustn't reshape the people to fit the principles. The complexity of the issues can't be captured in two sentences; they're just helpful guidelines.

Ultimately, the parents must decide who gets custody of the children, not the therapist. Parents also decide whether to remarry or stay single. For example, if a divorced man has custody of his children and he wants to remarry, it's not appropriate for him to make his decision dependent on his children's agreement. He has to do what's right for him, and the children have to accept that. Children aren't equal partners and shouldn't be consulted in such things as if they were. However, they're certainly not obliged to love the new partner.

Question: But the courts ask the children about custody.

Hellinger: I know. Legal thinking and systemic thinking are sometimes different. I'm speaking here about psychological dynamics, about what's best for the children.

When the parents decide about custody amicably between themselves, then the children are spared the difficult decision of choosing one or the other. Parents often have the idea that the one who was given custody is taking the children away from the other. But that's impossible. Even if the children are living with only one parent, they will always remain the children of both parents. However the parents proceed, it must remain clear to the children that both parents remain their parents, even though they're no longer a couple.

Adoption

Question: I'm a social worker in an adoption agency. We're often called on to make recommendations about whether children should be adopted or placed in a foster home. And we're also confronted with adoptions that go wrong. Are there any systemic guidelines that might be of help to us?

Hellinger: When children can't be raised by their own parents, then the best alternative is probably the grandparents. They usually have the closest connection to the children. If they can take the children, the children are generally well taken care of—and the way back to the parents is easier if the situation should change. If there aren't any living grandparents, or if the grandparents can't take the children, then the next best choice is usually an aunt or an uncle. Adoption is a last resort and should be considered only if no one in the family is available.

Judging from my experience in working with families, the crucial factor is the adoptive parents' intentions. If they're truly acting in the best interests of the child, then the adoption has a good chance of turning out well. Adoptive parents often don't really consider the child's interests, but rather their own. Typically, they can't have a child and are rebelling against the limits nature has set for them. They're implicitly asking the child to protect them from their disappointment. When that's the case, then the fundamental flow of giving and taking and the order of the relationships are disturbed before they start, and the parents can expect to suffer the consequences of their actions, or that the child will suffer.

When partners adopt a child out of their own needs and not out of concern for the well-being of the child, they effectively take a child from his or her natural parents in order to meet their personal needs. It's the systemic equivalent of the theft of a child, so it has serious negative consequences within a family system. It doesn't really matter what motivated the natural parents to put the baby up for adoption; the adoptive parents very often pay with something of equal value. For example, it frequently happens that couples divorce after adopting a child for the wrong reasons. Sacrificing a partner is the compensation for robbing the natural parents of their child. In families with which I've worked, the consequences of adopting children for inappropriate reasons have included divorce, illness, abortion, and death. In its most destructive form, this dynamic has expressed itself in the illness or suicide of one of the couple's natural children.

It's also not uncommon for adopted children to resent their adoptive parents and not to appreciate what's been given to them. In such families, it's often the case that the adoptive parents secretly consider themselves superior to the biological parents, and the child, perhaps unconsciously, demonstrates a solidarity with his or her natural parents.

Sometimes the biological parents have given their child up for adoption when it wasn't absolutely necessary. Then the child feels legitimate resentment toward the parents, but it's the adoptive parents who become the targets. It's worse for them if they've assumed the position of the natural parents. If the adoptive parents are clear that they're only acting *in loco parentis* for the natural parents, then the negative feelings remain targeted on the natural parents, and the adoptive parents get the appreciation they deserve. That's a great relief for adoptive parents, and also for adopted children.

When adoptive parents or foster parents are acting in the interests of the child, then they have the inner sense that they're substitutes for or representatives of the biological parents and not their replacements—that they're helping the real parents by completing what those parents couldn't do. They have an important function, but as adoptive parents, they come after the biological parents, no matter who they are and what they have done. If this order is respected, then the child can accept and respect adoptive parents.

A man in a group had separated from his wife and was concerned about the custody of their adopted child. In the family constellation, he placed the child between himself and his wife. I asked "Who wanted the adoption?" He said that his wife had. I told him, "Yes, and she sacrificed her husband for it." The man representing the boy in the constellation suddenly felt weak and said that he felt like falling to his knees. I told him to do so, and he knelt while his natural mother was positioned behind him. As he then turned toward her, he said that he felt a great relief. I placed the representatives of the adoptive parents behind him so that they could look on as he knelt before his natural mother. As they watched, they felt themselves becoming a couple.

When children are adopted, it's helpful to make clear distinctions between the names of the parents. It's clearer for an adopted child to use different names for the natural and the adoptive parents, for example, "Father and Mother" and "Dad and Mom." Adoptive parents shouldn't identify an adopted child as "my son" or "my daughter." The message they communicate to the child should be more like, "This is the child we've been given to care for as representatives of the natural parents." This message has a very different quality.

There's no set solution for every situation. The main point is that the adoptive parents retain a deep respect for the natural parents, and that they make this respect clear to the children. In many cases, it's better for the adopted child to keep his or her original name so that it remains clear that this is an adoption.

Question: What if the child wants to take the name of the stepfather or of the adoptive parents?

Hellinger: I advise caution. Children feel intuitively what the adoptive parents want, and act as if they want it too. The adoptive parents must look very carefully to see what's good for the child and then do it, and not let themselves be distracted by their own needs. They also mustn't allow the child to be the voice of their needs, as if their needs were the child's own. When parents discover what's truly good for their child, then the child will naturally want that as well. The issue with a stepfather in a second marriage is clear: If the mother respects and honors the natural father, there will be no problem for the child. The same holds true for a stepmother.

Question: When one partner brings a child from a previous marriage into a new marriage, should the new partner adopt the child?

Hellinger: Generally, I advise against it. It isn't good because the child then has to deny his or her own father or mother. But look at the child, and you'll know what's best. It's very difficult for a child to have to deny a parent. I'll give you another example,

A woman called me in despair. Her adoptive father was dying and she was unable to resolve her ambivalence toward him. She wanted to be near him at his death, but she couldn't bring herself to approach him. She explained that her mother had divorced her father many years ago to marry this man, and that he had adopted her.

I suggested that she rescind the adoption. She hesitated, thanked me, and hung up. Some time later, she called again to say that she had done it. The situation had changed immediately, and she had been able to be with her adoptive father in his dying process. He had died shortly before the second phone call, and she was feeling at peace with him and the situation. It had become very clear to her, she said, that she had brought something back into order, and had regained her proper place in her family.

Question: I know of two children whose parents and grandparents were killed in an automobile accident. An uncle and an aunt each is willing to care for one of the children. Is it more important that the children stay with relatives, which means being separated, or that they stay together in a foster home?

Hellinger: That's difficult to say without knowing the children and the aunt and the uncle. We don't know why the aunt and the uncle each is prepared to care for only one of the children, but it suggests to me that they're not primarily interested in the children's well-being. Maybe they feel obligated. Otherwise, one or the other would do what is necessary to care for both of the children. Unless there are clearly extenuating circumstances, I suspect that the children might feel happier in a foster family where they can live together.

I've often observed that people who, as children, lived in a foster home (or who were adopted) have a desire to care for foster children or to adopt children. Children in need are well taken care of by such foster parents, because the foster parents are passing on what they themselves received. That's an excellent dynamic.

Thomas: A couple in the town where I live have no children of their own. They flew to a developing nation several times and paid huge amounts of money to adopt a child. As soon as they got the child home, the man had a nervous breakdown and was hospitalized for three months. As soon as he was released, they adopted a second child. I think what's happening there is really terrible.

Hellinger: Who knows? Look at the children and think, "They'll make it somehow."

Thomas: I have another question. Friends of mine . . .

Hellinger (*Interrupting*): No, no, no! What did I just say?

Thomas: The children will make it somehow.

Hellinger: Yes, but before that, I said, "Look at the children." Who were you looking at?

Thomas: You're right. I was looking at the parents.

Hellinger: They don't deserve any better than what they're getting. They're aware of their actions. It's amazing what people do.

Eighteen years or so ago, I worked with a man named Peter. When he was two years old, his mother had had a schizophrenic episode and had thrown him against a wall. His father took them to a doctor. After they determined that Peter's injuries weren't serious, the parents and the doctor disappeared into the next room and left him alone in the waiting room. After a while, the door opened, and the doctor looked in. Peter said that he still remembered that doctor's look. It was as if the look had said, "You'll make it." That was all. That was the anchor that he had used to hold himself steady throughout his life. You see, the doctor did just the right thing. He looked at the child.

Question: My nephew, my brother's son, was adopted by his stepfather. He now has his stepfather's name, and the new family has broken off all contact with my brother and our family. Is there is anything I can do for the boy?

Hellinger: Not really. When you consider what you can do for him, there's love in your heart. If you allow that feeling to work in your heart, and at the same time resist the temptation to do something until a good opportunity arises, then you're doing something good for the boy. It may take years for a good opportunity to present itself.

Raising Children

Question: In our clinic, we work with many families that are having trouble with their children. Each of the parents tells the children something different, and the children are really confused about the right thing to do.

Hellinger: When parents are having trouble raising their children, it's often the case that they don't have a harmonized system of values, goals, and priorities. The solution in such cases is for them to agree on a common system in which the values of both of their families of origin are represented fairly. This mutual system is more inclusive than either of the original systems, and, in a certain sense, both partners have to relinquish their former family values. This is difficult to do because both then feel guilty regarding their own families. The belief that one value system is right and the other wrong makes the process much more difficult. When parents are united in one value system, they have a sense of solidarity with each other when they face their children, and the children feel secure in their common value system and follow it willingly. When parents aren't united, their children must live in two different belief systems or value systems at the same time and in the same house. That's confusing.

A father and a mother asked me what they should do about their daughter's behavior. The mother felt responsible for setting limits for the girl, but didn't feel supported in this by her husband.

I suggested three principles to consider when raising children:

1. A father and a mother have different ideas about what's good for their children according to whatever they experienced as important or missing in their own families.

2. A child accepts as right and follows whatever *both* parents believe is either important or missing.

3.   When one parent overrules the values of the other in raising the children, the children automatically ally themselves with the one who was overruled.

I then asked them to notice where and how their daughter loved them. They looked at each other, and their faces lit up. I suggested to the father that he might occasionally let his daughter know how good it made him feel when she was good to her mother.

Illegitimacy

Question: You said that parents should not tell their children about intimate details of their lives. I work with several parents who haven't told their children that they were conceived out of wedlock, or that they are illegitimate. I can't believe that's really good for the children.

Hellinger: There's a tendency in society to make moral judgments about such things, and when there's a negative judgment, the reluctance to speak about it is also understandable. When you look at such a situation without moral judgment, as we do here, you often see that things turn out fine just the way they are. Quite often, something very good comes out of our sins, and that's beyond the grasp of the moralists. You can't talk about deep issues in the presence of someone who judges you and looks to see if what you do is right or wrong.

Thomas: I'm an illegitimate child and I grew up with my mother. Five years ago, I found my father, but I don't know his other sons, and my father is reluctant to tell them about me.

Hellinger: A woman in a previous workshop was in a similar situation. She was illegitimate, and her father had also married and had sons, and was reluctant to show her to them. I couldn't see any reason why she shouldn't look the sons up and introduce herself as their sister.

Later, she called to tell me how things had worked out. She said that she had been invited to a party and that her father was there, as well as her half brothers. At the end of the party, it happened that everyone had left except for her, her father, and the boys, and they were able to talk.

If I were you, Thomas, I'd look them up. But if you do it, there's a danger that you'll give up your profession as a pastor.

Thomas: Why is that?

Hellinger: A common motivation for the search for God is that the searcher doesn't have a father and is looking for him. If the father is found, the search for God isn't so important anymore—or it's different. The whole thing started with Jesus. As far as we know, he, too, grew up without a father.

I'll share a poem with you.

The Way

A son went to his aged father and asked,
"Father, bless me before you go."
His father answered:
"My blessing is that
I will accompany you a while
along the path to knowledge."

They met at sunrise
at the appointed place,
climbed the mountain
up out of the shadows
of their narrow valley.

As they reached the top,
although it was the end of day,
they could see in all directions
stretching to the sky
—the land bathed in light.

The sun sank,
taking with it
its radiant glow.
It was night,
yet in the darkness of the night
they saw, revealed,
a multitude of
—twinkling, distant stars.

Caring for Elderly Parents

Question: My parents are getting older, and more and more they'll be needing me to take care of them. I've also got a family and a job. How do I balance the responsibility to give to my wife and children and my responsibility to them?

Hellinger: Children have a responsibility to care for their elderly parents. Nevertheless, many children fear what awaits them as their parents grow old. That's because they imagine that they must care for their parents in whatever way their parents wish. When they feel so compelled, their worry is justified. The solution is for children to tell their parents, "We will do what's right by you." That's a completely different situation, but what's truly right may be different from what either the parents or children first imagine.

There's a specific dynamic behind this problem: Children can't see their parents as they are. Regardless of their actual age, as soon as they meet their parents, children have a strong tendency to feel and act like five- or six-year-olds. And parents see their children as five- or six-year-olds, regardless of their children's actual ages, and treat them accordingly.

The only exception to this general rule I've ever come across was a psychiatrist in a seminar who insisted that she and her daughter were truly equals. Later, over coffee, she kept talking about her "little Snookie," until someone asked her who Snookie was. She answered, "My daughter!" Snookie was about 35 years old. *(Laughter)* So that's the only exception I've found.

Whatever is truly needed can usually be arranged.

During a workshop, a very successful businesswoman said she needed to call her mother, who was hospitalized. The mother very much wanted her daughter to take her into her home and care for her. The woman felt she couldn't do it because of her business obligations. I said to her, "Your mother has priority. First care for your mother and then for your business." She protested that it was impossible. I told her, "Just sit with it a while. You know it has priority and you know what's important. Just let it work in you."

As is so often the case when someone is prepared to do the right thing, the solution was unexpected. She got a call from a highly skilled practical nurse who was looking for a job caring for an older person. The nurse was expensive, but the woman had adequate money and was more than happy to pay. That was the solution.

When children freely accept this responsibility right from the beginning, parents find it easier to let them go because they know they will be there for them when they need them—and children feel freer to separate when they know they're not abandoning their parents. Children feel relief when at last it's appropriate for them to give something to their elderly parents.

Incest

Question: You've said that problems in families are usually attempts to love that have gone wrong. Is that true of incest as well? Can you say something about how you view incest?

Hellinger: Incest is complex, and it comes in many different forms, so we need to be careful about generalizations. Sometimes the violence and abuse are so damaging that the sexual aspect becomes secondary. Then it's altogether different from incest that's primarily sexual. But yes, I've seen that incest is often an attempt to love that's gone wrong.

In the usual way of looking at incest, therapists don't see the family as a whole. Rather, they see two individuals: the perpetrator, who is usually a man, and the victim, usually his daughter or stepdaughter. Some therapists tend to see the perpetrator as an inhuman beast who forced the victim to meet his or her uncontrollable sexual desires or emotional needs. They don't see the larger context of the family system. I ask, "Does the victim–perpetrator model of looking at incest really help the child?" That's the crucial question. In the vast majority of cases with which I've worked, it doesn't seem to help at all.

The fundamental principle of systemic psychotherapy is that we always look at the children and listen to them in the context of the whole family relationship system. We ask: What's going on in this family, and what's best for the child? What does she or he need to find peace? If we're not careful, our images of perpetrator and victim prevent us from seeing the individuals involved, and they also may prevent us from seeing the whole family context. The solution for each child is different, so therapists need to stay alert. It's always better to sacrifice a preconceived belief than a child.

If you look at the family as a whole, you usually see that the parents have a problem, and that the child was recruited to help them solve it. Incest, more often than not, is a family problem, and is possible only when the parents collaborate. I'll say it in that provocative way; that is, both parents participate—the man in the foreground and the mother in the background—and they share the responsibility. When incest *is* a family problem, resolution becomes possible only when the complexity of the family situation as a whole is clearly seen. In those situations, children need to have the courage to hold both parents responsible.

In one common form, incest is an attempt to compensate an imbalance of giving and taking in the family—usually, but not always, between the parents. When that's the case, the perpetrator has been denied something; for example, what the person does for the family isn't sufficiently appreciated. In this form, the incest is an attempt to correct the imbalance of giving and taking in the family. Of course, there are many other forms of incest, but one common pattern is that a mother with a daughter marries a man who has no children. Although her new husband provides for her and her daughter and concerns himself with their welfare, his efforts and needs are discounted, unappreciated, ignored, and sometimes even belittled or ridiculed. An imbalance of giving and taking develops between the partners in which the man gives more and the woman takes more. A woman in that situation might still be able to balance the giving and taking if she were to communicate genuine gratitude to her new husband, "Yes, it's true that you give and I take, and I deeply appreciate what you do." Then correcting the imbalance might not have to descend to such a destructive level.

However, when there's an additional deficit in the exchange between the partners—for example, in their sexuality or their emotional needs—an imbalance develops in the whole system. The woman attempts to balance the sexual deficit in those situations by offering her daughter to the man (I've worked with families in which the mother even did so consciously), or by abandoning her daughter to him in such a way that he is actually drawn into a compensatory relationship with her. I've even worked with a few families in which the daughter offered herself to her father or stepfather in order to help her mother and to keep him from leaving. A less common form of incest involves the boy who helps to redress an imbalance in the family.

Question: Everything in me resists the idea that the mother should take the blame.

Hellinger: That's especially true as long as you're more interested in your ideals than in the people involved. You're looking for the one to blame. I'm not interested in blaming anyone. I'm looking for a solution. In order to find a solution, I need to see the people in their situation, and I need to understand the dynamics of the family.

My goals are always very specific: I look for a solution for the person who's come to me, and I resist the temptation to go beyond that. The solutions are different for every member of the family. Everyone in the family—the man, the woman, and the child—knows, at least unconsciously, that the family has a problem, so we need to look for a solution that allows everyone in the system to accept his or her share of the responsibility and to maintain dignity.

For a child who has been induced to help with an imbalance of giving and taking, and some other forms of incest as well, the solution is to get to the place where she honestly can say, "Mama, I consent to do this for you," and to her father, "Daddy, I did it for Mama." Sometimes, when the man is actually present, I've had the child say, "I'm doing it for Mama, and I agree to do it for her." Some people object to the word "agree," but the victims confirm that it's important.

These sentences name the dynamic *already operating* in the family, *and they bring the child's love to light.* A child who authentically speaks these sentences gives voice to the archaic beauty and power of her innocent love for her parents. She reveals a depth of the soul where children willingly, although often unconsciously, make the most painful and destructive sacrifices for their parents. Systemically viewed, the child is sacrificed to redress an imbalance in the family, and, at least unconsciously, she agrees out of love. The solution for her is to speak the truth, to name the system dynamic and to declare her love openly. By openly naming the mother's part in the incest dynamic, the child extracts herself from her unconscious agreement to help solve her parents' problem. The sentence names her mother's complicity in what happened, but it doesn't release her father from his guilt.

The effect of having this intimate love seen and acknowledged is healing. The sentences remind children that they were trying to do something good, even if it went wrong. When they consciously feel their love and we confirm it, they *know* that they're good. That's a great relief. When victims manage to say the words authentically, they're released from their entanglement in their parents' problem. They don't have to wait for their parents to change before they can do this. They're free to go on their way regardless of what their parents do, whether or not they admit responsibility and feel remorse.

Question: But that's not the way the girl feels. She feels as though she's doing it unwillingly, like she's the victim, and she'd resist saying those sentences.

Hellinger: A victim by definition is a person who couldn't prevent what happened. If victims want to change anything, they've got to get in touch with their authentic power. Children's power is their love. That's what the sentences do: They reveal the child's love. They make clear to everyone in the system what the child has done to try to solve the family's problem.

When you offer sentences like these, you must listen very sensitively to hear the sentences the child's soul is *already speaking.* When you've found them, you cautiously offer her a gift, words that express what she's secretly been feeling but couldn't articulate. If you listen deeply enough and find the words that are just right, her soul understands the message: "You acted out of love. You did the best you could, but now it's okay to give the problem back to the adults. It's their problem, and they can handle it." The message is usually something like that. It requires courage, but many girls have found release by saying aloud what they've secretly been feeling all along.

The proof as to whether or not you've found the right sentences is their effectiveness. If you've found the right formulation, a girl, or an adult woman, experiments with the sentences, and all at once she feels a change in her body and knows herself to be good. It's really a dramatic and beautiful process to see. She feels relieved because the sentences demonstrate her love and her dependence, and therefore, her innocence. It's of absolute importance that the child be helped to find a way back to self-worth and dignity, and that her love be acknowledged and affirmed.

Question: But what happens if you're working with a 15-year-old girl, for example, who's still in the situation?

Hellinger: The sentences are most effective then. A child is in the weakest position in a family, so she's limited as to what she can do to get the incest to stop. Her best chance of getting it to stop is when we name the hidden dynamic operating in the family and bring everyone's responsibility into the open.

Question: What do the sentences do to the father? In this formulation, he's reduced to a passive participant. He's also a person who acted, who violated his fatherhood and misused his own child. What can he do?

Hellinger: If he's seriously interested in doing something to restore some order to the system, there are some general principles he must follow, but the details will vary.

First, he's got to accept fully the consequences of his actions. If he was charged and convicted, he must feel agreement with the verdict and the penalty. Then he has to face his daughter and really see her, see the consequences for her of what he has done. He must genuinely tell her that he carries the full responsibility and bears the full consequences for his actions, and that he'll withdraw from her and leave her in peace.

Since there's no way to undo what's been done, he must see to it that something good comes out of it. Guilt gradually fades away when it accomplishes its purpose—change for the better. One stepfather underwent intensive personal psychotherapy, and then did training and became a therapist working with other men. His relationship with his stepdaughter is distant, but cordial. She can respect him, and it's easier for her to respect herself.

Question: I've always wondered why court decisions against the perpetrator in these cases so seldom bring a solution for the child.

Hellinger: Punishing the perpetrator isn't enough to bring resolution for the child. There's an important law of systemic behavior that needs to be respected: A system is disrupted when one of its members is rejected or excluded from the system. Resolution requires that the wholeness of the system be respected, that the excluded person be taken back into the system, and that everyone accept his or her appropriate share of the responsibility.

When you work systemically, even though you're working to find a resolution for the client, you must serve and protect the wholeness of the system. Therefore, you have to connect yourself to those who are excluded. Unless you are able to give the perpetrators a place in your heart, you can't work with the whole system. You gradually come to view what happens in the context of larger systemic dynamics, and that larger perspective opens more options for healing. That's why I regularly ally myself with the excluded and the hated.

Question: Are you saying that everyone in the system participates in what happens—the mother, the stepfather, and the child? That they're all acting under the pressure of systemic dynamics, and that a therapist who polarizes the victim and the perpetrator actually contributes to the problem?

Hellinger: Everyone is involved when the incest is an attempt to solve a systemic problem. It's a common pitfall for the therapist to join the mother in a battle against the father; the wrong he has done is easy to see. Therapists sometimes get pretty emotional about his perversity, but that only splits the family more. I wonder where all this affect in therapists comes from. Why not stay calm and study the phenomenology until we find a good resolution for the child? Such intensity of affect in therapists makes me wary. Something's going on or else the therapist's feelings wouldn't be so strong. Something's being given too much importance. Therapists who ally themselves with the victim help to exclude the perpetrator from the system, overlook the mother's share of the responsibility, and don't acknowledge the depth of the child's love for and loyalty to *both* parents. That makes the situation worse for the victim.

I'll tell you how I came to understand this.

Standing by the Villain

In a group, a psychiatrist told about a client who'd been raped by her own father. The psychiatrist was horrified by the wrong done to her client and emphasized what a base creature the father was. I invited her to do a constellation of the situation and then to take her place in the family as therapist. She stood next to her client. Everyone in the constellation was immediately angry with her, including the representative of her client. The whole system was restless, and nobody trusted her. Then I moved her to a position next to the father, and everyone immediately became calm and trusting. Since then I've often observed that standing next to the villain is a very good position for a therapist.

Victim and perpetrator are systemically connected, but often you don't know in what way. When the connection becomes clear, then you can understand what needs to happen to bring the system back into balance. When I work with a perpetrator, I confront him with his guilt. That goes without saying. But people often make the assumption that something will change for the victim if the perpetrator accepts his guilt or is punished. In actual practice, nothing changes. Once they're out of the situation, incest victims can act on their own to free themselves of the entanglements independently of the actions of the perpetrators, but they do need to be willing to give up the idea of revenge.

Question: Does that mean that incest victims should be encouraged to forgive their parents?

Hellinger: I've seen that it's inappropriate and impossible for a child to forgive her parents for incest. She can say, "What you did was bad for me and I'm leaving *you* with the consequences. I'll make something out of my life in spite of what happened." Or she can say, "You've done me a great wrong and I must not forgive it. I have no right to do that." She can confront both of her parents at the same time and tell them, "*You're* at fault, not I. And *you* must take the consequences, not I." In doing this, she shifts the guilt back to her parents where it belongs and distances herself from their responsibility. It isn't necessary for the child to make massive accusations against her parents. It's enough if there's a clarity between them that sets her free.

Similarly, a father can't ask his daughter for forgiveness after he's committed incest with her. If he does, he asks her for something that goes beyond her right and duty to give. By asking *her* to limit the consequences of *his* actions, he effectively misuses her again. He can say something like "I regret what I did" or "I acknowledge that I've wronged you." But he still must keep the full responsibility for his actions, and suffer the full consequences. However, he must not go beyond that, or he imposes an additional burden on the child.

Question: That means that when children are brought to us and we discover that sexual abuse is going on, we can protect the children, perhaps help them get away from the parents, but we shouldn't initiate proceedings against the parents.

Hellinger: As far as the solution for the child is concerned, that's my experience. You shouldn't even talk disparagingly about the parents in front of the child, although you must help the child to see the parents' responsibility and to feel innocent of any wrongdoing. There may be cases in which it's necessary to initiate proceedings against the parents; nevertheless, my experience has been that children's suffering increases when they must testify against their parents.

Question: In a systemic problem, there's a circle of cause and effect, yet you often choose the woman as the starting point. Whatever the man did to cause the woman to act as she did doesn't seem to interest you much.

Hellinger: Yes, I often do that. There are several reasons. One reason is to redress a bias right at the beginning. Remember, in systemic work, we're not making moral judgments about people. We're looking for ways to help the family come back into balance so that the victims—the children—are free to live healthy, fulfilling lives, and so are freed of the systemic pressure to do unto others what was done unto them. Systemic balance can only be achieved when we can identify everyone's part in the dynamic. Since the perpetrator is generally a man, his responsibility is usually already clear. What's usually not so clear is the woman's part in the whole thing. So I often start by looking for that. I'm not blaming the woman, but to understand the family as a whole, I need to find out what was going on in the background.

Question: But the child, especially a very young child, is left with a deep wound. At least I can't imagine any other possibility.

Hellinger: You need to guard against overdramatization. When we really *see* the victims, they describe a variety of experiences. Sometimes the experience was violent and humiliating and sometimes it was a more tender, perhaps even loving, relationship. In some cases, it was the kind of incest in which sexual contact never actually occurs, but which causes stubborn difficulties in later relationships. That kind of incest isn't even recognized by law.

It is often the case that incest *victims* feel guilty for what happened. I'll give you an example.

A Guilty Victim

A woman in a workshop had been abused by her father and her uncle. She'd been seriously disturbed for many years, was filled with self-hatred, and had made multiple suicide attempts. She had the delusion that when she was in a group, everyone could see that she was evil, and that they wanted to kill her.

I asked her to explore the feeling of being evil, which she did. She sat in the group, looking down, feeling evil. She suddenly remembered her uncle, and imagined him lying at her feet. She remembered that he had committed suicide. As she continued to look at him in her imagination, her face became hard and old. It took on an expression that wasn't her own, so I asked her, "Who looks down at him so hatefully and triumphant?" She answered that it was her mother. As the work continued, she gradually pieced together her memories, and it emerged that her mother had become pregnant during an affair with her husband's brother. So the man she had thought was her uncle was in fact her father, and the man she had thought was her father was her uncle.

Her mother had felt relieved when the child's biological father committed suicide, but the child felt responsible for his death, as if he had killed himself because of her, as if she were his murderer. Her self-hatred and suicide attempts were expressions of her feelings of guilt.

Because of such guilty feelings, many sexually abused girls subsequently take up a victim profession. Many prostitutes were abused as children, continuing as adults what they experienced as children. I've met nuns who were victims of incest and abuse, apparently entering the cloisters as an attempt to atone for the wrong they felt they had done. Other victims become mentally ill, paying for what they already suffered with more symptoms and suffering. Some commit suicide. Some defend the perpetrators to the end, continuing to allow themselves to be abused in various ways, as if to say, "You don't need to have a guilty conscience for what happened, because I really am a worthless person." Some become perpetrators themselves.

There's an additional problem for the child: The first sexual experience, even an incestuous one, normally establishes an especially intensive bonding. Children who have bonded to someone through an early sexual encounter have difficulty in later sexual relationships unless they become aware of the bonding and deal with it by acknowledging the love involved.

Paying My Mother's Debt

A woman in a workshop told of her sexual difficulty. She had been married for almost 30 years, had adult children, and was still in love with her husband. Try as she might, she was unable to surrender to sexual passion with him as she wanted to.

As she explored her experience, she remembered her early sexual experiences with an adult friend of the family. In a family constellation, she remembered that he had entered the army at the age of 17 in order to impress her mother, to whom he was engaged; had survived seven years of heavy combat; and had spent an additional six years in a prisoner-of-war camp under terrible conditions. While he was in prison, her mother had abandoned him to marry her father. Her mother later sent her to live with the man during summer vacations.

As she stood before his representative in the constellation, she was critical and hateful toward him. She remembered that her mother later charged the man with child abuse and that he had gone to jail. Then she suddenly burst into tears and threw her arms around his representative, weeping freely. She was flooded with memories of how much she had loved him; how he was the only person who had understood her, talking to her for hours; and how deeply she had been touched by his loneliness and pain.

She recognized that she had willingly given her body to him even though she was very young; that she had enjoyed his gentleness and was proud of her ability to soothe his pain. She felt in her body a deep connection to him, and needed assurance from the group that her feelings were normal. She radiated freshness and joy as she remembered this first love, and still she was able to tell him lovingly that she had been too young for such an experience.

After several months, she wrote a letter to the therapist telling how she felt released to give her husband and herself the passion and the pleasure they both had waited for so patiently.

Question: Can children really experience pleasure in incest?

Hellinger: I know that many people think that's terrible, but some children have found their incest experiences pleasurable, even beautiful. Children in such situations must be allowed to admit that they also experienced pleasure. People often tell them that something bad happened, and they need assurance that they're innocent—especially if the experience was pleasurable. In such cases, children must be allowed to acknowledge their experience—that sexuality can be fascinating—in spite of what others may think.

It's completely appropriate for a child to be curious about sex and to want to experience something she finds fascinating. If the child's curiosity isn't recognized as being normal and healthy, her sexuality is put in a terrible light. At the risk of saying something else that's controversial, sexuality isn't evil or dirty—even when it's incest. When the child can hear that, she feels relieved.

Question: I've understood you to say that perhaps the child was being seductive, and that it's very important for her to understand that that doesn't make her guilty.

Hellinger: It's perfectly normal for a child to be seductive at times. That mustn't be a criticism of her. Why shouldn't she be allowed to be seductive? If she's being seductive with her father, it doesn't mean that she wants sex like an adult; she's just practicing and learning about being a woman. It's his responsibility to understand that difference and to keep the boundaries clear. It's his job to provide her with protection. It's not hers to meet his needs.

Question: I feel very ambivalent about your statement that children enjoy incest. We saw a film last week in the clinic where I work and the girls in the film described it very differently.

Hellinger: If we're going to communicate with one another, you must resist the temptation to change what I said into what you think I said. I did not say that "children enjoy incest"—and neither do you get the objective truth about what goes on in a family from a film. Every film has a point to make. You mustn't assume that your client experienced the same thing as the girls in the film did.

Question: I know that, but it's not a good idea to make assumptions about the child's enjoying it.

Hellinger: That's exactly my point. Look carefully at the child, and listen to her! Then you'll know. Don't decide about your client on the basis of what you saw in a film or read in a book. Every child is different. The child must be allowed to acknowledge that it was pleasurable, *if it was pleasurable.* And *if it was,* you've got to be willing to see that, too. Then you can reassure her that she's innocent, even if she was fascinated by the sex or curious about it. If it was painful or humiliating, she must be allowed to acknowledge that as well. It's absolutely clear that the responsibility for incest lies completely with the adults, but it's the child who pays the price. That's how family systems work.

Question: Does it make a difference if the perpetrator was violent?

Hellinger: Violence dramatically increases the consequences for both the child and the perpetrator. Still, I guard against anything that inhibits my ability to help the victim and the perpetrator. The power of the soul to affirm life after tragedy is miraculous, so even in cases of great damage, there's still hope.

Transcript

LESLIE: A CHILD GIVEN UP FOR ADOPTION

Leslie was a participant in a large workshop for adopted children, adoptive parents, and parents who had given a child up for adoption. Her work makes clear some of the unexpected complexities that adoption presents and points the way toward good resolutions for difficult situations.

Hellinger: How may we be of help to you?

Leslie: I have difficulties in relationships and I get sick all the time. I have the feeling that's connected to my constant longing to feel like I'm at home somewhere. I was picked up from the hospital by my adoptive parents when I was 14 days old. I guess I'm still trying to find that original contact.

Hellinger: What kind of illnesses do you have?

Leslie: As a child, I constantly had tonsillitis. Now I've got various psychosomatic illnesses that I call "losing myself".

Hellinger: What would you like me to do?

Leslie: I read your book, and as I put it down, I thought, "That's it! That's what I want to do." So now I'm sitting here with high hopes that I can get clear about this, or at least get a new perspective.

Hellinger: Are you married?

Leslie: Yes, but I'm separated from my husband.

Hellinger: Do you have children?

Leslie: We have a 13-year-old son.

Hellinger: Who is he living with?

Leslie: Half and half. It depends.

Hellinger: What do you know about your biological parents?

Leslie: Absolutely nothing. I know their names. It probably would have been possible for me to have found out their addresses, but I didn't want to do that.

Hellinger: What were you told about the adoption? Who put you up for adoption?

Leslie: As far as my adoptive parents know, it was my mother who did, because of her poverty.

Hellinger: And your father?

Leslie: I don't know. That's just what I've been told.

Hellinger: We'll just go ahead and set up this system: your father, your mother, you, and your adoptive parents. Have you seen how it's done?

Leslie: Sort of. I'm pretty confused just now.

Hellinger: You choose people—anyone you want—to represent your father, your mother, yourself, and your adoptive parents. By the way, did your adoptive parents have their own children?

Leslie: No, they couldn't have any. *(She chooses representatives.)*

Hellinger *(to Leslie):* Okay, now take the representatives by the shoulders and put them in their places in relation to one another. Collect yourself and do it with the feeling of being completely collected. The constellation will emerge all by itself as you begin to move the representatives. *(To representatives):* And you stay collected in yourselves as well, and pay attention to how your feelings and sensations change as she moves you around.

Hellinger *(to representatives):* Now, I'll ask you what's happening for you, and you tell me as exactly as you can what your experience is. What's happening for the mother?

Mother: I feel the father moving out of the constellation and I'm being pulled to follow. I first thought the daughter would come closer, but she stopped.

Hellinger: And the father?

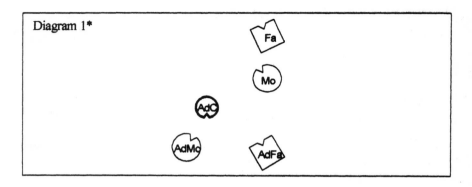

Father: I feel extremely sad. I've got a huge knot in my stomach. I feel lost here and very sad.

Hellinger *(to Leslie's representative):*   What's happening for the child?

Leslie's Representative: I feel much better since the adoptive parents came in. I'm still very confused.

Hellinger: What's happening for the adoptive mother?

Adoptive Mother: My heart was thumping before I was placed here. I feel secure here and that I can see the child. I also feel the distance between us. I'm uneasy that the adoptive father is also here, although I can't see him. I can't see him at all just now.

Hellinger: You mean your husband?

Adoptive Mother: Yes.

Hellinger: What's happening for the adoptive father?

Adoptive Father: I feel a bit alone here, and a little sad as well. I don't have much contact with my family. I'm in a corner, which gives me a little sense of security, but I'm alone. *(Hellinger moves the adoptive mother next to her husband.)*

---

*Legend: Fa—natural father; Mo—natural mother; AdFa—adoptive father; AdMo—adoptive mother; AdC—adopted child

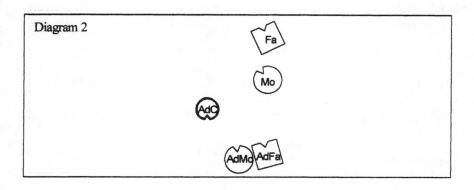

Hellinger: How's that?

Adoptive Mother: That's better.

Adoptive Father: The unpleasant feeling of isolation and lone-liness is gone. It's better now. I feel something like help or support.

Hellinger *(to Leslie's representative):* What's changed for you?

Leslie's Representative: It's more difficult now. There was so much emptiness to my left and to my right. That was better after the adoptive parents came, but now it's empty again. *(Hellinger turns her to face everyone)*

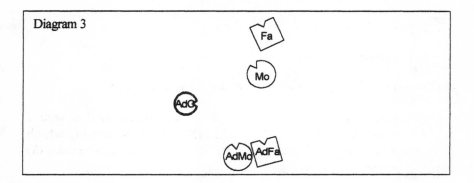

Hellinger: How's that now?

Leslie's Representative: That's better. I didn't feel anything at all for my parents, but now I can see them at least.

Hellinger *(to mother):*   What changed for the mother?

Mother: The longer I stand here, the more I notice that I want to turn to face the child, and look at her. She's more in view now, but farther away. I want to move closer to her, and I want to turn around.

Hellinger: Turn around so that it feels right for you.
(To father):   How's that for the father?

Father: I feel a huge heaviness and I feel like everyone has left me.

Hellinger: Turn around and stand next to the mother.

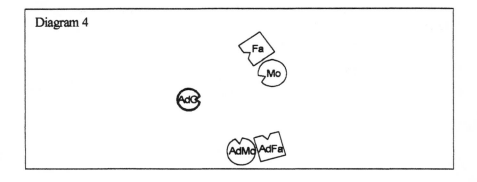

Diagram 4

Hellinger *(to Leslie's representative):*   How's that?

Leslie's Representative *(deeply moved):*   I want to go to her.

Hellinger: Go ahead. *(Leslie's representative goes to the mother, embraces her, and sobs deeply.)*

Hellinger *(waits for them to finish embrace):*   I'll put Leslie in her place now. *(To Leslie):* Go to your mother. *(Leslie quickly goes to the mother and holds her tightly.) (To the father as the mother and Leslie embrace):* What's happening for you?

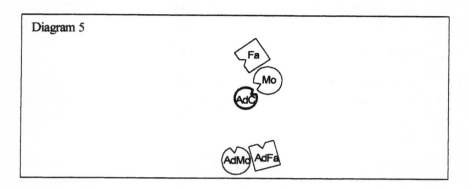

Father: I still feel alone and lost. The best would be for me to go. I don't feel as if I belong here.

Hellinger: Then turn away and move a step away.

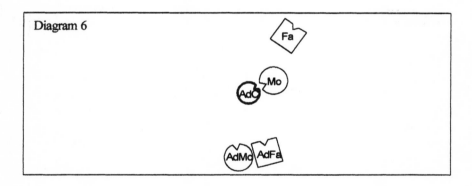

Hellinger *(to the father):* How's that?

Father: I feel lighter here.

Hellinger *(to Leslie as she slowly moves back from the mother):* Look your mother in the eyes and call her "Mama".

Leslie *(choking back tears):* Mama.

Hellinger: "Mama, please."

Leslie: Mama, please.

Hellinger: What's happening for the mother?

Mother: I don't understand anything. It's all happening so fast, but I can let her in. I'm overwhelmed.

Hellinger: Tell her, "I'm sorry."

Mother: I'm sorry.

Hellinger *(to Leslie):*   Say to her, "Please look on me as your daughter."

Leslie: Please look on me as your daughter.

Hellinger: "Please, Mama."

Leslie: Please, Mama. *(Mother and daughter embrace tightly. Leslie sobs loudly.)*

Hellinger: "Please, Mama, please."

Leslie: Please.

Hellinger *(to Leslie as she becomes calmer):*   Breathe deeply. It's like taking your mother into your heart. Deeply and calmly. *(To adoptive mother):* How's that for the adoptive mother?

Adoptive Mother: At first I felt as though I wanted to take my adoptive daughter in my arms and hold her. I felt so pulled toward her, but I couldn't move because she was standing at another place. At the same time, I felt my husband's light touch. That was very reassuring. Then I realized that my adoptive daughter had really found her natural mother and I saw how happy that made her. That made me very happy too.

Hellinger: And the adoptive father?

Adoptive Father: It's gratifying to see that something's slipped into place. That touches me deeply. I'm also feeling something toward her father that's not clear. I feel as if I'm carrying something, some responsibility, that's not mine.

Hellinger: How's the mother doing now?

Mother: I'm doing great.

Hellinger *(to Leslie as she releases her mother):*   Look at her and tell her, "I take you as my mother."

Leslie: I take you as my mother. *(Mother and daughter embrace again, naturally and simply.)*

Hellinger *(to mother):*   Now you can take her by the hand and lead her to the adoptive parents. Bow down in front of them, however you feel is right for you, and tell them, "Thank you."

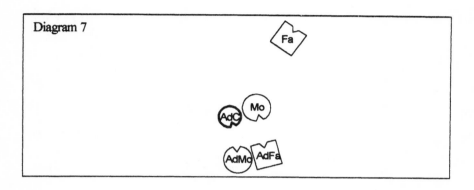

Mother *(bowing deeply):*   Thank you.

Hellinger: "Thank you for taking care of my daughter."

Mother: Thank you for taking in my daughter.

Hellinger: "And for giving her what she needed."

Mother: And for giving her what she needed.

Hellinger: "I hold you in high regard for doing that."

Mother: I hold you in high regard for that.

Hellinger *(to Leslie):*   How's that for you?

Leslie: Wonderful. They really gave me a lot.

Hellinger: Look at them, and tell them "thanks" too.

Leslie *(spontaneously bowing deeply before her adoptive parents):* Thank you.

Hellinger *(to adoptive mother):*   How's that for you?

Adoptive Mother: Good. But I still want to take my adoptive daughter in my arms and hug her.

Hellinger: I can't think of anything that's standing in the way. *(Leslie and the adoptive mother hold one another tenderly. Leslie then also embraces the adoptive father.)*

Hellinger *(to father as Leslie embraces the adoptive father):* How are you doing?

Father: I'm not doing so good. I still feel a tremendous weight on my shoulders, and that knot in my stomach. I don't have any connection to the others.

Hellinger: Turn around and face them. *(Hellinger places Leslie next to her adoptive mother and places her mother at a distance to the left.)*

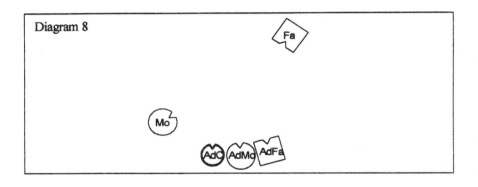

Diagram 8

Hellinger *(to Leslie):* Look at your father and try telling him, "I take you as my father."

Leslie: That doesn't feel right.

Hellinger: It's a first step. Give it a try. Look at him, and tell him, "I take you as my father." *(The adoptive mother strokes her back to show encouragement.)*

Leslie *(choking back tears, as the father bows his head):* I take you as my father.

Hellinger: "Please give me your blessing as your daughter."

Leslie: Please give me your blessing.

Hellinger: How is that for the father?

Father: I want to run away. I can't stand it.

Hellinger *(to Leslie):* Try repeating it one more time, "I take you as my father."

Leslie: I take you as my father.

Hellinger: "And I hold in honor what I have from you."

Leslie: And I hold in honor what I have from you.

Hellinger: "And I let you go your way with love."

Leslie: And I let you go your way with love.
(Leslie begins to weep; the father hangs his head and cries as well.)

Hellinger: Go to him.
(Leslie goes to her father, and they hold one another. The father sobs.)

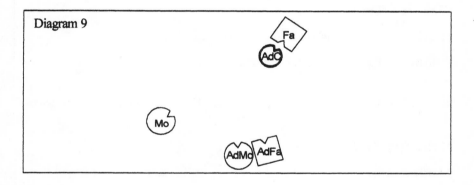

Hellinger *(To father):* Breathe deeply and the pain can flow away. Breathe in and out, deeply.
(To Leslie): How do you feel with your father?

Leslie: I feel as if I have to be the stronger one here.

Hellinger: Yes. That's the way it is. Go back to your place by your adoptive mother. *(She moves beside the adoptive mother and they hold hands.)*

Hellinger *(to father):* Take Leslie's mother by the hand, then go with her to the adoptive parents and stand facing them. *(To biologi-*

cal parents): Bow down before them, and thank them. *(Both bow
with respect, and then look at adoptive parents.)*

Diagram 10

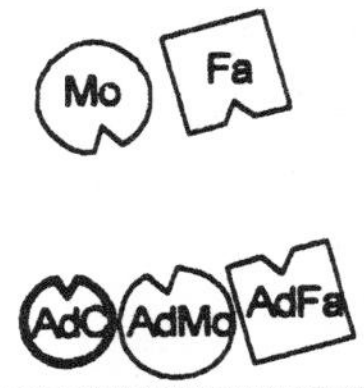

Mother: Thank you.

Father: Thank you.

Hellinger: How is that for the adoptive parents?

Adoptive Father: That's better for me. I can accept their gratitude.

Adoptive Mother: It's good for me too. I'm glad that my adoptive daughter is close to me.

Hellinger *(to Leslie):*   How are you doing now?

Leslie: I'm looking for my brothers and sisters.

Hellinger: That's the next step. You can look for them, and all the
others who belong to your family—your grandparents, for instance.
Do you think that your adoptive mother would support you if you
did that?

Leslie: Not completely, but she'd try.

Hellinger *(to adoptive mother):*   Tell her, "You're allowed to do it."

Adoptive Mother: You're allowed to do it.

Hellinger: "And I'll help you."

Adoptive Mother: And I'll help you do it.

Hellinger *(to group):* A child can't do something like that without permission. The child needs the permission and support of the adoptive parents. *(Leslie and representatives take seats.)*

Hellinger: In that constellation, we could clearly see the power of the love operating in families, and how hidden it sometimes is. You could see what kind of resolutions are possible and what healing energy is set free when that love is brought to light—and how easy it can be is to bring that love to light.

If we look at a family like this one, who shall we blame? Who would dare to blame any of the five? They're all entangled in some way. In listening to the feedback from the representatives, it seems that the initiative for putting the child up for adoption came from the father. He was the one who felt most guilty, and who most wanted to leave as compensation. That's why it was easier for the child to move toward her mother. We saw that clearly.

When someone sets up a constellation with such concentration as Leslie did, it seems safe to me to assume that the representatives' reactions are giving us information about the actual situation in the family. The representatives seem actually to feel what the people felt. Obviously, that's not something that can be verified scientifically, but we could clearly see how the representatives' reactions led the way toward a good resolution. Leslie now has a very different image of her natural parents that she carries with her, as well as of her adoptive parents and of herself. Because she now has that new image of them in her heart, she is a changed person. And there's a very strange thing: If she meets any of those people, she will see that her adoptive parents, and her natural parents (if she finds them), will be changed as well. It's a family system, and when we change one part to become more loving, the whole thing changes. Other members of the system are affected.

Question: Could you explain the role of the biological father? I couldn't hear all that was said, and things happened so fast anyway. I didn't understand.

Hellinger: In watching the reaction of the father's representative in the constellation, I had the impression that he didn't want to be involved at all; I suppose it was because he felt guilty. That's why he kept wanting to get away. Wanting to have nothing to do with the child had serious consequences for his position in the constellation.

To be honest, I had already given up on him, as if he had thrown away his rights as a father.

When a person gives a child away, the person usually also gives up any rights as a father or a mother. But even then, there's sometimes a resolution. Even the mother had difficulty in facing the child, because she felt guilty as well.

Participant: That went so fast.

Hellinger: In situations like this, it can't go fast enough. It was only when the child said, "I take you as my mother," that the mother felt acknowledged as a mother and could overcome her guilty feelings to face her daughter.

I didn't think it was going to work with the father, but when she asked for his blessing, his heart melted and the contact was possible. Whenever love flows, the destructive power of guilt is dissolved. Then she could go to him, and he could move toward her. That's the dynamic behind what we saw.

Question: I have another question concerning the father. You said that he may have turned away because of his guilty feelings about having given the child up for adoption. But isn't it also possible that he turned away because he felt bonded to his family of origin, and that the child must accept that fact? Isn't it more nearly the reality of the situation, that in the end he would turn away? Doesn't the child actually deny the reality when he stands by her rather than seeing that he is involved in other things and wants to leave?

Hellinger: I only look at what's in the foreground. Regardless of whatever entanglements and involvements he might have had, he must carry the consequences of his actions. Entanglements do not release his actions from their consequences. His other involvement may help us to understand his actions, but they cannot remove the results of what he did. In a situation like this, we mustn't act as if he couldn't face the consequences of his actions. That would demean him. He already was acting enough like a child, even though he had managed to impregnate the woman. His feelings were the feelings of a child. Nevertheless, he is the child's father and reality is not served if we pretend otherwise in order to go easy on him.

If he were the client, then, of course, we could explore his entanglement, but if we'd done that today, we would have been distracted from Leslie, who was the main person. He would have taken center stage, and the child who was looking for a resolution would have been pushed to the sidelines. We have to be clear about who's working, and maintain that hierarchy.

Participant: I didn't mean to suggest that we work with his family of origin here, because he obviously wasn't the client. It just seems more realistic to accept the fact that he turned away because he couldn't fulfill his role and carry his responsibility as father. That seems more realistic than bringing him into the picture as a good force, as you did.

Hellinger: Let me ask you a question in return. Who has the better place in your heart—the father or the daughter? That's an important question. It's important for the therapy that persons who are most affected by a situation have a good place in my heart. And that's usually the children. I give the children a place in my heart, and I hold the adults accountable for their actions. I trust the father to act as a father in spite of his entanglement, and I trust the mother to act as a mother in spite of her entanglement.

Therapists and social workers sometimes are very concerned about the adults. They ask, "Who is the poor mother? How can we help her? The poor mother, how can she possibly raise the child?" Then they treat the mother as if she were a child, and the child as if he or she were an object to be disposed of.

I go about it differently. I stand by the child and hold everyone else accountable for the responsibility he or she has as a result of his or her actions. I'm looking for a solution that puts the responsibility back on the adults and relieves the child. Too often, it's the children who have to carry the consequences of what adults have done.

Participant: The point you're making is clear. Perhaps I didn't express myself clearly. I'm also concerned about the child. To reformulate my question: Wouldn't it be better for the child to see the reality that her father turned away from her and to accept that as fact? That's the reality with which she has to live.

Hellinger: No. That turns the child into a parent. Then the child must understand and must act like the bigger person, and the father gets to act like a child, as if his actions had no consequences. We all saw what can happen when we trust parents to act like parents.

C H A P T E R   F O U R

The Conscience of the Family Group

In addition to being children, partners, and perhaps parents, we also share a common destiny with our more distant relations—whatever is done by or happens to a member of our family group, whether for good or for ill, touches us, and also all the others. Together with our family, we form a fellowship sharing a common fate.

The Wind of Fate

In a group, a man told how, as a boy, he had sat on a high hill and watched his village being attacked and destroyed by neighbors who belonged to another religion. He described his hatred toward those men, some of whom he had known and liked. He told how a thought had come unbidden as he watched: What would I feel if I had been born into one of those families? What if a wind had blown my soul a few hundred meters off course, and I had entered the belly of one of those mothers, instead of my own mother? Then I would feel victory and pride, as they do, and not grief and rage, as I do—and I would hate us and love them.

The course of this boy's life was influenced by the winds of fate, not because of anything he had done or failed to do, but merely by virtue of his belonging to one family and not to another.

The bonds connecting the members of a family group also extend through time and across distances, so that members of the family are linked to other members long deceased or far away.

I Release My Grandmother

A 42-year-old woman told how she had been abandoned by her mother and raised by her grandparents. As a result of her work in the group, she felt a deep inner connection to her mother for the first time in her life. That night after the group met, her mother called to tell her that her grandmother had died unexpectedly at about the same time as she had worked in the group. The woman was convinced that establishing an inner connection to her own mother released her grandmother to die peacefully.

Systemic psychotherapy abounds with similar anecdotes of events related in time—even when the mechanisms connecting them elude our explanation.

I'm Your Son

A young father lost his wife and child in a tragic accident. Some years later, a second woman became pregnant by him, and in a panic that something similar might happen to her and the child, he abandoned them. Eleven years later, working in a group, he said that he felt deep remorse and the desire to contact his child. The group leader counseled patience, and he took no overt action.

A week later, the man received a letter: "Dear Ray, My name is Daniel. I'm your son. I'm 11 years old. I like skateboarding and football. I'd like to meet you soon."

The systemic orders that allow love to thrive in families are very difficult to define precisely. They have far greater flexibility than social or moral laws that have been invented by societies or individuals and that must be obeyed to the letter. They are also different from the rules of a game that can be modified to suit the circumstances or according to whim. The orders are simply there. Love requires what it requires, and it's immune to individuals' wishing that its requirements were different. You can't break the order as you break a law, but the Orders of Love can, and do, break individuals who insist on ignoring them. If you don't act as love requires, it simply withers and dies, but it often demands restitution for such neglect.

It is an act of humility to submit to the Orders of Love in a relationship. Contrary to being a limitation, this submission supports freedom and life. It's like swimming in a river that carries you along: If you swim with the current, you're free to maneuver from side to side.

Regardless of whether or not they are still alive, the following belong to a family system.

- the children

- the parents and their siblings

- the grandparents, and sometimes one or more of the great-grandparents

- any others who have moved aside to make a place for someone in the system; for example, a former partner or lover of a parent or grandparent—even if separated, divorced, or deceased—or someone from whom a family member gained some advantage by loss, misfortune, departure, or death

The Grocery Store

A woman was having difficulties getting her life in order. In the family constellation, it emerged that her parents had bought a small grocery store from an older couple. The older couple had wanted to give the store to their son, but he had been killed. Even though he was unrelated to the woman, he belonged to her family system since she indirectly gained from his death. Although she had never met him, she was beholden to him. When he was included in the constellation, she became calm. Acknowledging the importance of his death had a positive effect on her, and she soon began to make some of the changes in her life she had long desired.

THE ORGANIZATION OF FAMILY GROUPS

As we have seen, love succeeds in our relationships when belonging, a balance of giving and taking, and a good order can be maintained. This is also true for the extended family, but five additional dynamics constrain the success of love in family systems: (1) honoring the right to membership, (2) maintaining the completeness of the system, (3) protecting the hierarchy according to time, (4) following the order of precedence between systems, and (5) accepting the limitations of time.

Honoring the Right to Membership

Individuals may continue to affect the other members even when they are shunned by their family, excluded from participation, and perhaps even forgotten. As long as they have an influence on any other member of the group, even unconsciously, they are members of the family system, and anyone who has no visible or hidden effect on any other member is no longer a member of the system. Membership doesn't depend on the family's decisions or beliefs, only on effect.

Everyone in the system has an equal right to belong, and no member can deny another his or her place. A family system is disrupted when one member communicates to another, "I have the right to belong, but you don't." This happens, for example, when members shut out of memory someone who suffered, or was sacrificed, or did some wrong—perhaps a sister who died in childhood or an uncle who became insane. Members of a family are naturally tempted to exclude those who have committed a crime, brought shame on the family, or violated the family values, but the exclusion of any member is destructive for those who come later in the system, no matter what the original justification was.

The family constellations of people with serious psychological and physical illnesses often reveal such acts of exclusion. Although those suffering such illnesses are unaware of the connections, they reenact in their own lives the fate of the excluded or forgotten person. Members may forget those who have been excluded, but the system "re-members" its own. Exclusion of persons who have a right to membership is the most common dynamic disrupting a family system.

Maintaining Completeness

Members of an extended family experience themselves as whole and complete when everyone belonging to the family circle has an honored and respected place in their hearts. Persons who are concerned only with themselves and with their personal happiness don't feel whole. Whenever a member of the family succeeds in "re-membering" an excluded member in his or her heart, the difference is immediately felt. The internal images of family and self become more complete, and he or she actually *feels* more whole.

My Mother's Lover

All of the representatives reported discomfort and irritation when a woman set up the constellation of her family. Her mother's first lover, who had died very young, then was added to the constellation, as well as her father's first wife, whom he had left when he began an affair with the woman's mother. With the addition of these two persons, the representatives immediately became calm. As the woman took her place in the constellation, she described a sensation of "opening" in her chest and a deep and profound sense of "rightness." In the days that followed, she described a shift in her experience of herself, as if she were becoming larger and more at peace.

Her sensation of "opening" in the body is typical of people who are "re-membering" persons previously excluded from the family circle. Our sense-of-self changes when excluded members of the system are brought back into awareness. Systems are wholes, and individuals in a relationship system only feel whole when the whole system is represented in them.

Protecting the Hierarchy Within a System

The self-evident and natural laws of being and time also apply to family systems. Being is qualified by time: Earlier occurs before later. Time gives being sequence and structure. In relationship systems, this means that whoever enters the system first has a certain precedence over those who come later. Parents enter the family before their children, the firstborn before the second, and so on. Time establishes a natural hierarchy within the family that must be respected.

In dysfunctional families, a younger person often disrupts the hierarchy of the family by assuming the responsibility, function, privilege, or guilt that belongs to an older person. An example is a son who is suffering for his father's wrongdoings, or is trying to be a better husband for his mother than his father is. Younger persons who injure the hierarchy of time by assuming the functions and responsibilities of earlier persons often unconsciously react with a tendency to self-destruction and failure. Because violations of the order of precedence are motivated by love, those caught in this dynamic don't recognize their guilt. Such violations are often important contributing factors when events in a family turn out tragically—for example, in cases of suicide or psychogenic mental illness, or when a later person turns to crime.

The orders of precedence according to time that support love in a family are more complicated when two existing families are combined. When partners bring children from their previous marriages into a new relationship, their love for each other doesn't precede their love for their children. In these families, successful love usually requires that the earlier bonding between the partners and their children take precedence over their younger love for each other; next comes their togetherness as man and woman in a partnership of equals; and, finally, the bonding to any children they have together.

One must not apply this as rigid dogma, but many problems in second marriages occur when one of the new partners feels jealous of the other partner's earlier children; that is, when he or she wishes that the new love would have priority over the earlier love between the children and their parent.

I Love You for Being Faithful to Your Daughter

A couple decided to divorce and their daughter stayed with her mother. The man didn't want any more children, and subsequently married a woman who also did not want children. After some years, the man's first wife died suddenly, and the child came to live with her father and stepmother.

The child and her stepmother were not fond of one another. Both felt a claim on the man's love and constantly competed for precedence. The man felt torn between his love for his child and that for his wife.

One day, after a quarrel in which the couple considered separation, the woman visited a friend who helped her to understand the systemic implications of the situation. That evening, she said to her husband, "When I see your love for your daughter and your first wife, I see how faithful you are. I love you more for that."

A woman with a child said about beginning a second relationship, "I couldn't love a man who didn't respect my love for my child."

Maintaining Precedence Between Different Systems

The order of precedence between two relationship systems is different from the order of precedence within a relationship system. Here the new system has priority over the old system. For example, when a couple starts a family, the new family system takes precedence over their families of origin, just as a second marriage assumes precedence over a first.

. Experience shows that when families don't follow the order of precedence between systems, they encounter difficulties. For example, if a young couple's love for their parents continues to take priority over their love for each other, there's a disturbance in the order of precedence that must be dealt with if their relationship is to succeed.

Second partnerships present special complications. The new system must have precedence over the first in order for the new family to succeed, but if one of the new partners brings a child from a previous relationship into the new one, then the bonding to and love for the child must maintain precedence over the bonding to and love for the new partner. Couples have problems when the new partner demands precedence over a child from a previous partnership, or when the new partner demands from the child the love that belongs to the child's natural parent.

When a person has a child during a partnership with someone other than his or her partner, the partnership is usually over. That means that if a woman has a child with another man during her marriage, she forms a new system with him. As a rule, she must leave her first family and go to her new partner. If she chooses to stay with her husband, the only safe place for the child is with the natural father.

The precedence of a new system over a previous one also requires that a man who has a child with another woman during his marriage leave his family and go to the new woman and child. Nevertheless, he must continue to support his first wife and child. In situations like this, the former partners and children pay a very heavy price, but experience shows that all other solutions result in greater pain for all concerned.

Family systems react profoundly to the birth of a child.

Accepting the Limitations of Time

Although it's necessary for all members of a family to have their places and to be "re-membered," families must be allowed to forget what is past after an appropriate time.

The Polar Bear

A polar bear lived in a circus. He lived in a very small cage and couldn't even turn around—he could only walk two steps forward, and then two steps back.

The owner of the circus gave him to a zoo, where the polar bear had an open space in which to roam. Still, he walked two steps forward and then two steps back.

One of the other bears asked him, "Why do you do that?"

He answered, "Because I had to live in a cage for so long."

Death and life are inseparable, as are remembering and forgetting and past and future. The recognition that all life sooner or later comes to an end helps members of a family to recognize what must and must not be done in every situation.

There is a strong tendency in families to try to hold on to things that are past—memories of both good and hurtful experiences. When members of a family group hold on to something that should be over, the past holds them captive and continues to work inappropriately in the present. Because the old then cannot fade away, the new has difficulty in establishing itself. It requires great discipline to extract yourself from such systemic entanglements, and to release everything that deserves to be finished. All members of a family group must let go of things, both positive and negative, as soon as their effect for good is past.

How a Widow Made Her Children Curious

A woman was widowed while she was still young. She had loved her husband and could not allow him to rest in peace. She decided not to seek a new partnership, but did not enjoy life after her husband died.

She lived with her children until they left home, and then withdrew into the house she had shared with her husband and thought about him day and night. She became bitter and depressed.

Apart from her children, she had no life of her own. Her children found no joy when visiting her, but they felt guilty when they didn't. Caught between the joylessness of visiting her and the guilt of leaving her alone, they came to resent her and began to stay away. Her loneliness and bitterness increased.

With the help of a friend, she came to understand that her holding on to the past was damaging the love between herself and her children. She entered a retirement community, found new friends and interests, and increasingly allowed her past to become past. For a while, she almost forgot about her adult children.

They grew curious about her life, and soon were unable to resist their curiosity and the pull to visit.

There is grace in letting bygones be bygones and allowing the future to come as it will. All the leaves on a tree are shaped according to the same pattern, but each leaf is different. Every autumn, they turn yellow, red, or gold, and then fall. Every spring, different leaves shaped with the same basic pattern emerge in vibrant, tender shades of green. That's the secret of this systemic dynamic. Change is constant; individual leaves wither and die, yet the tree remains. The tree also dies, yet the forest remains. Holding tight to withered leaves may soothe memory, but it doesn't help the tree. So, too, members of families are born and die, and holding on to what was once good or bad inhibits the natural flow of life.

The Man Who Didn't Realize the War Was Over

In the terrible years after the Thirty Years' War, people slowly came out of the forests where they had hidden, and began to rebuild their farms and homes. They planted their fields again and cared for the few animals that had survived. A year later, they had their first harvest in peace—the animals had multiplied, and the people celebrated.

At the edge of the village, there was a house that was boarded up. Sometimes, when the people passed by, they thought that they heard something inside, but they had so much to do that they didn't care to look into it.

One night, a little injured dog sat whimpering by the front door of the closed-up house. A piece of the mortar fell away and a stone fell out. A hand reached through the small hole, picked up the little dog, and lifted it inside. There really was someone inside who had not yet realized that peace had returned to the outside world. The person held the little dog and felt flooded by its soothing warmth. The little dog fell asleep. The person peeked out at the world through the small opening, saw the distant stars in the heavens, and breathed the fresh night air.

Soon the first light of day began to glow on the eastern horizon, a rooster crowed, and the little dog awoke. The person saw that the little dog belonged with its companions, let it crawl out through the opening in the wall, and watched it run home.

As the sun rose in the sky, some children came by, one of them holding a juicy red apple. They saw the opening and, peering in, saw the man sleeping peacefully.

For him, one glimpse of freedom had been enough.

Just as holding on to the past can limit freedom, so, too, can trying to control the future. We can intuitively sense how the larger systemic orders function, but the resolutions are often surprising and different from what we contrive or wish. For this reason, as members of families, we delude ourselves when we think that we can determine the course of fate. No matter what we may believe to the contrary, we must submit to the future as it comes, for although we sometimes can influence it, we cannot determine it.

The Verdict

A wealthy man died and knocked on the pearly gates. Saint Peter opened the door and asked him what he desired. The rich man said, "I would like a first-class room with a good view of the earth, my favorite foods every day, and also the daily paper."

Saint Peter hesitated, but the rich man was adamant. Saint Peter shrugged his shoulders and gave him a first-class room with a good view of the earth, and brought him his favorite foods and the daily paper. He said, "Well, here's what you wanted. I'll be back in a thousand years." Then he left and locked the door.

After the thousand years had passed, he returned and looked into the room through the peephole. "There you are at last," cried the rich man. "This heaven is terrible."

Saint Peter shook his head sadly. "You're mistaken," he said. "You've chosen hell."

ENTANGLEMENTS IN FAMILY GROUPS

Family members don't experience injuries to the hidden orders of the family group as guilty feelings in their personal conscience. Injuries become obvious only in the suffering they bring, especially to children, who often suffer the consequences of things they themselves didn't do. The dynamics of a family bind all members in full participation. One bird in flight may turn in many directions, yet we watch the flock turn as a whole. Every bird submits to the greater whole of the flock, and through this submission, maintains its membership in the group.

In a similar way, the family whole binds each member so firmly that the obligations and sufferings of one member are experienced by other members as debts and obligations. In this way, any family member can become blindly entangled in other members' debts and privileges; in their thoughts, cares, and feelings; and in their conflicts or goals. Individual happiness and suffering are limited in the interests of the family, just as a whole constrains its parts.

How Can We Know Peace?

In a television documentary, a young man was filmed beside a cave. Many thousands of bodies had been found in the cave, lying in three layers. The bodies in the first layer were those of adherents to a particular political persuasion who had been murdered by adherents to another group in retribution for injustices done. The bodies in the second layer were those of members of the second party murdered in retribution some years later by members of the first. The tide of power in that country had shifted again, and the third layer again contained bodies of members of the first party murdered, in retribution, by their enemies.

The young man, whose relatives were among the bodies in the middle layer killed almost 50 years previously, was asked if there would be an end to the killing. He replied, "When we hear the cries of our mothers, and see their tears for their murdered sons, how can we know peace? We must avenge their loss."

The man in this documentary believed he was acting freely, but he was not. Because he loved blindly, he was caught in a web of tragedy that had begun long before he was born, demanded his obedience, and, tragically, will not end until long after his death.

When the love that binds together the individual members of a family operates blindly, it demands blind obedience, and unless individual members gain insight into its dynamic and transform it, they unknowingly submit to the laws of blind systemic justice—an eye for eye and a tooth for a tooth. Then the damage is passed from one generation to the next, and the extended family finds no peace.

The systemic laws operating within the family don't respond to a child's love. The drive for balance working in the family group is more fundamental than love, and it readily sacrifices individual love and happiness to maintain the larger family equilibrium. The struggle of love against the dynamics of family systems is the beginning and the end of the greatest tragedies. Extracting oneself from this battlefield requires insight into the Orders of Love, and a willingness to follow them with love. Insight into Love's Hidden Symmetry is wisdom; following it with love is humility. That requires giving up an inflated sense of self-importance and returning to one's designated place in the family order, while those who have come before regain their higher place in the hierarchy.

The young man standing at the mouth of the cave loves, but his love is a child's love, and it seduces him into assuming a responsibility inappropriate to his position. His child love seeks balance in revenge blindly, as if more deaths could heal the emptiness left by past deaths. Peace will not return to his family clan until he manages to listen to the "cries of our mothers," to see their tears, and to say to them with love, "Yours is a great loss. I pay homage to your suffering. Because I love you, I will not take up this sword, and I do you the greatest honor by entrusting your suffering to you. With you, your suffering is in better hands than with me." In her heart, every grandmother prefers that her grandchildren live in peace. Then the deaths of those who have gone before have a good effect on those who come after. That is the greater love.

Recognizing Entanglement

Question: How do you recognize when systemic entanglement is operating? Are there characteristic signs or signals, anything we can get a grip on?

Hellinger: Unfinished situations from the past express themselves in later relationships in the form of impulsive inappropriate actions and inappropriately intense feelings. An identification with another person has the feeling quality of "not being quite myself," or "something just got into me." Whenever a person displays unusually intense emotions or behaviors that aren't understandable in terms of the current situation, you can suspect that there's a systemic entanglement of some kind. This also is true when one person has unexplained difficulty in talking with another, or reacts in an inexplicable way—as if he or she were influenced by invisible conflicts and anxieties. People who are fanatic about being right are often entangled. When they "fight" with exaggerated bitterness and vehemence, they may well be representing someone else in the system. If there's a scapegoat in the present family, it's often the case that there was a scapegoat in a previous generation, and it's useful to look for it carefully. Any reaction or emotion that seems exaggerated, or inappropriate, or amplified may be an identification.

You develop a sense for the cues that hint at entanglements. Your sense will improve with practice, just as your ear for music develops with practice. As a beginner, you only hear the most blatant differences, but with experience, the subtle nuances begin to be detectable. Let me give you an example.

Hitting the Wrong Target in the Family

A young man had strong suicidal compulsions that he couldn't understand. In other respects, his life seemed to him to be okay. Exploring these urges, he told a group that, as a little child, he had said to his mother's father, "When will you die and go?" His grandfather had laughed, but the question continued to bother the little boy. This sentence was loose in the system. I said, "This sentence belongs to someone else in the system, but it comes out of the mouth of the weakest member of the system and it hit the wrong target. We need to find the real sender and the real target."

We then found out that the little boy's other grandfather had had a long affair with his secretary, and that during this time, his wife had contracted tuberculosis. The sentence belonged to the paternal grandfather. It was easy to imagine how he must have felt toward his wife: "Why don't you die and make room for somebody else?" The grandfather's wish was fulfilled and his wife died.

But then the next generations innocently took upon themselves the task of atoning for his guilt. First, one of his sons prevented the grandfather from enjoying the benefits of his wife's death—he eloped with the secretary. Then the grandson (the client) took up that ominous sentence, but spoke it to his other grandfather, and then turned it against himself. That was his suicidal compulsion.

Question: Are there indicators in a constellation as to when emotions have been taken on from someone else and when they actually belong to the individuals themselves?

Hellinger: No, not always. Sometimes they emerge during the constellation. Perhaps someone feels something at the beginning that doesn't make sense in the situation. It might be possible that it's a transferred feeling. Then I send up a test balloon to test the hypothesis. The reactions of the representatives are usually a reliable indication as to whether there's some identification.

Identification.

One important aspect of resolving entanglements is to find out who's missing from the family, who has been excluded, and then to bring that person into awareness and so complete the family unit. As a rule, an excluded person is someone who has suffered or has been the victim of some injustice. In the eyes of the other family members, that person was often seen as bad, and was excluded from the family system with moral justification or righteousness. Those remaining then feel morally superior. The central dynamic is that someone in the system uses a moral justification to claim a systemically unjustified privilege, to say, "I have more right to belong than you do."

The pressure of a group to "re-member" all of its members, to maintain its wholeness, demands that a later person then represent the excluded person. The wholeness of the group is frequently maintained by *identification*—a younger person unconsciously assumes the roles, the functions, and often the feelings of an earlier, excluded person.

Question: About a year ago, I found out that I have a half sister. The news came out after my father died. It had been a family secret between my parents. I was shocked at the reactions of the others in the family. I was the only one who called her. I didn't meet her though, and now I've lost contact with her.

Hellinger: You seem to be identified with her. You've got her feelings—for example, the feeling of not being entitled to belong. *(The questioner suddenly begins to cry bitterly.)* Yes, that's her feeling.

Question: Do you mean that the feeling isn't mine?

Hellinger: Well, it's yours when you feel it, but it seems as though you're feeling something that's connected to what your sister must have felt. You can change it by imagining yourself sitting next to her and telling her: "You're my sister, and I'm your sister." Your grief honors her. *(Her mood shifts immediately. She beams through her tears.)*

The family group "re-members" the excluded, the ignored, the forgotten, the unrecognized, the dead. When a legitimate member of the group is shut out, someone in a later generation must compensate for this injustice by suffering a similar injustice. The persons drafted for this service don't choose their fate. In fact, they usually don't even notice what's happening and can't defend themselves against it. They relive the fate of the excluded person, and recreate that person's experience, complete with the guilt, the innocence, and all of the other feelings that belong to that experience.

Cross-Gender Identification with a Missing Person

Carla came into the group with the complaint that she felt unable to make use of her knowledge and life experience. She had the belief that she was forbidden to know or understand what was going on in her family. This excerpt from the work begins during a constellation. Here, a possible identification with a missing person is sought.

Hellinger: Was someone excluded from your family system?

Carla: My mother had a fiancé.

Hellinger: He may be an excluded person. Let's put him in. *(When a representative for the mother's fiancé is placed in the constellation, the improvement for the others is seen immediately.)*

Carla: I just remembered—my mother gave me all of the paintings he had painted for her. I've kept them all. I haven't thought about them for a while, but I've always loved them. They're special for me.

Hellinger: Carla, you seem to be identified with your mother's former fiancé. If that's true, then it would have been difficult for you to have a good relationship with your father, since you were representing his rival. The bonding to your mother would also have been difficult since you not only were the daughter, but also represented her lover for her. In addition, it would have been difficult for you to develop a clear sense of yourself as a woman, since you were identified with a man. The solution would be for you to say to your mother's ex-fiancé while pointing to your father, "He is the right one for me." And then to say to your father, "You are the right one for me, and I'll have nothing more to do with that other man." Then you could return to the position of a child with two parents, and you could separate from the fiancé, and then the pressure to relive his fate could dissolve. *(This was then done in the constellation.)*

Carla *(after the constellation)*: But what can I do to be able to learn? That was my question.

Hellinger: Give yourself a little time. It can take as long as a year or two for internal images to complete their transformation and fully take effect. There's also a loss to be dealt with in giving up your identification with a man your mother seems to have loved very much. It's a very decisive step to return to the more appropriate, but less important, position in the system.

Carla *(relieved)*: Yes, I am the child!

Hellinger: Exactly! That's the first new learning.

Identification is a strange, almost uncanny phenomenon. The systemic dynamic of completeness in the family group defends the rights of any earlier person who has been excluded, and it isn't concerned with the rights of those who come later. There's a crude justice for the earlier person at the price of injustice for the others, and the injustice is passed on from generation to generation.

Unquenchable Yearning

A young woman suffered from an unquenchable yearning that she couldn't explain. In exploring this strange feeling in a family constellation, it became clear to her that what she was feeling wasn't her own longing, but something that seemed to belong to her older half sister. Her father had divorced his first wife and remarried, but his daughter from his first marriage wasn't allowed to see him again. The client traced the half sister to Australia, made contact with her, and sent her a ticket to visit the client in Germany. But destiny wasn't to be changed. On her way to the airport, the half sister disappeared and couldn't be traced again.

Identification is like a systemic repetition compulsion. It attempts to recreate and reproduce the past in order to bring justice to an excluded person. But such justice is primitive and blind, and it brings no resolution. In this dynamic, later persons become entangled in the destiny of an earlier person. Even if their actions are motivated by love, they take upon themselves an inappropriate responsibility. A later person can't set something in order for an earlier person after the fact. Such a retroactive justice only continues the systemic imbalance indefinitely.

Whom Is She Trying to Wash?

A therapist told her supervision group about a woman with a hand-washing compulsion. The supervisor asked her, "Which woman in her system is she trying to wash?" That became clear when the therapist asked her client. After the war, her father's sister had turned to prostitution to earn money to feed the family, and she contracted syphilis. Although she had acted to help the family and had significantly contributed to their well-being, she was rejected by them and died alone.

Another's guilt and tragedy often appear easier to master than one's own, but taking on someone else's tragedy creates no life-affirming energy. If misfortune is to be useful in developing strength, it must be returned to the person to whom it belongs, and he or she must be trusted to endure it.

Question: How do the people who are identified with excluded persons get their information? What are the channels?

Hellinger: I don't know how it works. It's just a phenomenon that can be observed in the family constellations and in families. I don't understand it, but, fortunately, it isn't necessary to know how it works to find a solution. I try to avoid theoretical explanations. The things I say are what I've observed, and I'm not making any other claim. I like to keep things small.

Question: When someone in the system is identified with an excluded person, will that continue into later generations?

Hellinger: There seems to be a time limit. The effect of the identifications diminishes as time goes on, and after a while, they no longer have any effect. For example, if a grandchild is identified with the grandfather—for whatever reason—and that grandchild has children of his or her own, the children aren't likely to have an identification with the great-grandfather. At least, I've rarely seen it.

Question: Can there be an identification with the siblings of a grandparent?

Hellinger: That's rare, and it seems to occur only in cases of extreme tragedy. I've seen it perhaps two or three times.

Question: In systemic therapy and hypnotherapy, the *here* and *now* are very important. How do you understand the importance of the past in your work?

Hellinger: It seems to me that the present and the past form a polarity that can't be separated, so I work with both.

Question: Would you explain what you mean when you use the term "double shift"?

Hellinger: Whatever has been repressed in a family tends to reappear in those who possess the least ability to defend themselves. In a family, that's the children and grandchildren. The *double shift* is a subtype of identification. The first shift occurs when a later person takes on the feelings of an earlier person via identification. The second shift occurs when the feelings from the excluded person are expressed, not to a guilty party, but, through a further shift, to an innocent person. A great many problems in relationships exhibit this dynamic, including situations in which the victim was so weak that he or she couldn't take appropriate action. Problems like that don't belong to the individuals alone, but to the whole family, and anyone in the family can be called on to compensate for the wrongdoing of someone else in the family.

The Murderer in My Family

A 40-year-old man came to psychotherapy because he was afraid that he might become violent and strangle someone, or that he himself could be strangled. No explanation could be found in the analysis of his character or behavior. He was asked: "Is there a murderer in your family?"

Further exploration revealed that his uncle, his mother's brother, was a murderer. He had had an employee who was also his lover. One day, he showed her a picture of a woman and told her to get her hair cut and dyed to look exactly like the woman in the picture. After his lover had worn her hair that way for a while, the man traveled abroad with her, murdered her, and returned with the woman in the picture, who became his new employee and lover. He was caught, however, and is still serving a life sentence in prison.

The therapist asked for additional information about the uncle's family, especially the grandparents, and questioned where the drive for such an act might have come from. The patient knew nothing about the grandfather, but the grandmother was said to be a pious and respected woman. He later inquired into the family history and discovered the following. During the Third Reich, this pious woman, acting with the help of her brother, had accused her husband of being a homosexual. As a result, he had been arrested and put into a concentration camp, where he was murdered.

The pious grandmother was the real murderer, and the impulse toward violence stemmed from her—at least as far as we could trace it. The client's uncle was recruited by the conscience of the family system to act on his deceased father's behalf. The uncle spared his mother and unconsciously compensated for the injustice done to his father by murdering a woman he loved. He repeated what both his parents had done and demonstrated his solidarity with both of them: with his mother through the murder and with his father through the imprisonment. The client himself felt the systemic turbulence of this chain of injustice as a fear of committing violence.

The double shift also works in the positive. Here is an example.

Strange Love

Among the attendees at a workshop were a man and a woman who had three children, the youngest of whom was a three-year-old daughter. The man had such a deep feeling for his daughter that it didn't seem like a father–daughter connection. There was something so intimate and sweet between them that it was touching to see, but their intimacy somehow wasn't appropriate. It wasn't incestuous, but it just didn't seem like the normal feeling between a father and daughter. Something wasn't right.

What emerged was that the man's father—the child's grandfather—had a twin sister who had died very young. The man's feelings for his daughter reflected those of his father toward his twin sister. The feelings had been transferred.

The man wrote a letter about a month after the workshop ended. He said that they were all very happy. He had the clear feeling that he was exactly the right father for his daughter. He said that it had suddenly dawned on him that although his daughter's name was Claudia, they had always called her Deedee. Deedee was the name of the deceased twin, but no one had noticed.

That was an entanglement, but not as destructive as many. It was also a solution.

Question: If I'm identified with someone, how do I get out?

Hellinger: An identification can be resolved when younger persons who are repeating the fate of earlier persons realize what the problem is. Then they can look at the shut-out person, or stand by that person and give him or her a loving place in their hearts. This love creates a relationship and then the excluded person becomes a friend, a guardian angel, a source of support. An identification is, after all, the opposite of a relationship. When I'm identified with someone, I feel and act as that person does, but I can't love the person because I don't experience him or her as different from me. I can only love someone I experience as separate from me. When I love a person as separate from me, my love dissolves any identification I might have. The identified person can then return to his or her appropriate place in the family, and the equilibrium of the system is reestablished.

Because identifications aren't experienced consciously, following feelings doesn't provide helpful guidelines for their resolution, and learning to express feelings doesn't resolve the identification either. That means that when the problem is related to an identification or imbalance in the family, the therapist can't expect the client to be able to find a resolution on his or her own; such resolutions can only be found through conscious insight into the group dynamics.

There is a parallel phenomenon in the physical body. There are many dangerous conditions of which we're not aware, but they still do damage outside of awareness—atomic radiation, for example. In spite of the misleading feeling that everything is going well, tragic things often happen in relationship systems. It's up to the therapist to understand the systemic processes that might help the client find a solution. A solution brings with it a feeling of being unburdened, of peace and contentment. In a family constellation, one can actually see a family system change and the family find tranquillity when an excluded member is returned to a respected place in the family, and order and full membership are achieved.

However, you must also be wary of relying on theoretical knowledge about family systems, because there are always new and novel variations on the common themes, and each family is different. The work is always trial and error; you've got to experiment with various possibilities until you find one that works. If there's no relief, you haven't found the solution, regardless of what your theory tells you.

The tendency of a family to balance itself by matching tragedy at one point with tragedy at another can be avoided when members are willing to seek balance at a higher level—for example, by honoring the excluded members instead of repeating their mistakes. This is possible if the younger members take from earlier members what they give, and if they respect the earlier members, regardless of their actions. At some point, the past, whether good or tragic, must be allowed to be past in order for the system to find peace. Excluded members become a source of blessing rather than intimidation when they're reinstated as guests in the soul. When everyone who belongs to the system has a proper place in the hearts of the other members, all of those in the system feel whole and at peace.

Here's a story that creates what it describes—if you let it.

The Return

Here is an invitation to go on a journey into the past, to visit a place where things happened many years ago, like old soldiers years after the truce walking across the battlefields on which they were tested. Now all danger is past and all difficulties overcome. The scars of the earth are hidden. Grass has long since grown again, meadow flowers bloom, raspberry bushes are heavy and their fruit scents the air. It may even be difficult to recognize this place; it looks so different from what we remember, and we need help to find our way.

It's curious as to the many different ways in which we cope with danger. A child freezes in terror at the sight of a large dog. Mother comes, picks the child up, and holds him or her in her arms. The tension goes, sobs break loose. And soon, from the safety of that lofty perch, the child looks back calmly at the dog. Sometimes we can't stand the sight of our own blood, but if we look away, we scarcely feel the pain. What a relief to look away—each sense working independently of the others, no longer all focused on that one event. Then we no longer feel overwhelmed and we can see what is, and hear what is, and feel what is, and know what is independent of our fears.

This journey allows each of us, according to individual desire, to see all, but not all at once; to experience all, but not without protection. That way, what's important can be distinguished from what is not. And whoever prefers may send another in his or her stead, like a dreamer sitting comfortably at home in a favorite chair, watching with closed eyes. The dreamer makes the journey, and can meet all that needs to be resolved, and still be safe at home asleep.

The journey takes us to a city that was once rich and famous and is now a ghost town filled with emptiness. The shafts where gold was mined are in ruins, empty houses are standing still intact, the opera house in good repair, waiting for the audience. But everything has been abandoned and there's nothing left but memories.

Whoever travels there seeks and finds a guide, and following this lead, reaches the place where memories awaken. This is the place where, long ago, painful things occurred. But now the sun is shining, warming the abandoned town. The streets, which once buzzed with life, are calm.

The traveler wanders up and down the streets and finds the remembered house, but hesitates to enter. The guide enters the house alone to see if it's safe, and to determine what has been left from what was there before.

Waiting outside, the traveler looks around the empty street, remembering neighbors and old friends, remembering the times of laughter, the lighthearted mischief of a child bursting with the joy of life, curious to try new things, pushing toward adventure into the great unknown, toward the thrill of fear defied. Thus time passes.

The guide waves. The traveler goes into the entry of the house and knows which people could have helped that child to overcome the difficulties of that past time—people who were strong, and loving, and knowing. It's as if those people were now present, as if their voices could be heard, their supporting strength felt. The guide takes the traveler by the hand, and together they move on.

Holding tightly to the guiding hand, the traveler looks calmly at the room, seeing first one thing, then another, and finally everything exactly as it happened. Strange how different it all seems when looked at from a centered place, in the company of the guide. Memories long shut out return safely, and many fragments find their place within the whole. The traveler waits patiently until he understands.

With the memories, old emotions well up, and with the pain, one feels one's love. It's like returning home, knowing what endures beyond revenge and right or wrong, trusting destiny to take its course, humility to heal, and gentleness of spirit to bring peace. The traveler breathes deeply, releasing tensions long held that now flow away like water into the desert sand.

The guide then turns and says, "Perhaps you carried something away from here that didn't belong to you. Perhaps a guilt from someone, or an illness, or a belief, or a feeling that isn't yours. Perhaps it's a decision you then made that caused you harm. All these you must leave here where they belong."

The words take effect. Letting out a great sigh, the traveler feels relief, at last laying down a heavy burden. The guide speaks once again: "Maybe then you abandoned something that you should have taken with you. It may have been some ability or desire, some guilt or innocence, perhaps some memory or hope, or the courage to engage life fully. Gather up what you lost, or left, and take it with you into your future."

These words, too, take their effect. Reviewing what was given away and reclaiming what longs to be reclaimed, the traveler feels the earth underfoot and the swelling weight of personal substance.

The guide leads the traveler still further, until they reach a hidden door. They open it, and at last find what reconciles.

Now there is nothing more to be resolved in this old place. Feeling ready, the traveler thanks the guide, turns, and begins the journey back. At home again, he takes the time he needs to come to terms with this newly found freedom and strength. But secretly he already plans the next journey—this time into some new and unknown land.

Transcript

BONDING IN THE FAMILY OF ORIGIN I

The following case is transcribed from a video of a training workshop for professional systemic therapists. More than 20 people with life-threatening illnesses, together with their physicians or psychotherapists, were invited to participate in the inner circle, while a larger group of mental health professionals observed the work. The presence of each patient's physician or psychotherapist provided continuity to the treatment. The following family constellation was the first of the two-day seminar. A brief introduction and four short conversations with "mini-interventions' have been omitted from this transcript. Irene is in her mid-30s.

Hellinger: Hello. What's your name, and what brings you here?

Irene: I'm Irene. I have cancer.

Hellinger: What kind of cancer?

Irene: Cancer of the lymph glands.

Hellinger: How long have you had it?

Irene: About a year. Before that, I had bladder cancer. I had to have my bladder removed, and now I've got metastases to the lymph glands.

Hellinger: Come over here and sit next to me. I'll ask you a couple of questions about your family, and then we'll set up your family constellation. Are you married?

Irene: Yes.

Hellinger: Do you have children?

Irene: Yes, two boys.

Hellinger: Have either you or your husband been in another significant relationship?

Irene: No.

Hellinger: Has a child in either of your families died?

Irene: Yes, in my family.

Hellinger: Who?

Irene: My brother. He was 14 months old.

Hellinger: Of what did he die?

Irene: He had three-day measles and didn't survive.

Hellinger: Was your brother older or younger than you?

Irene: He was a year younger than I.

Hellinger: We'll set up your family of origin first. That includes your father, your mother, you, and your brother. Is there anyone else who belongs there?

Irene: I have two other brothers. They're still living.

Hellinger: Have you ever done a family constellation before? Do you know how it works?

Irene: Yes.

Hellinger: Okay, go ahead. Choose someone to represent your father. *(Irene hesitates)* Go ahead, it isn't too important whom you choose. Then choose representatives for the other members of the family. We'll leave your deceased brother out at first. Just get them collected here in the middle of the circle. *(Irene assembles the representatives in the center of the circle.)* Okay, now position them in relation to one another—without talking. Take them by the hand, one at a time, and lead them to their places. Do it the way you feel it. Thinking about it doesn't help. *(To representatives)*: And you needn't talk either. Just stay centered and pay attention to how your sensations change as she guides you to your places. *(To Irene, after she is finished)*: Now, go around the outside. Stay very centered and collected and check that your constellation is right, and change anything that needs to be changed. Slowly. Now choose someone to

represent your deceased brother and place him in the constellation.
Then take a seat where you can see.

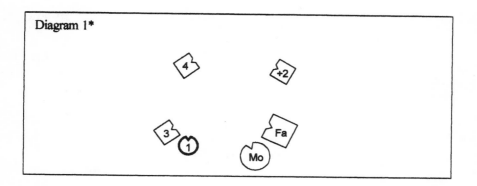

Diagram 1*

Hellinger: How is the father feeling?

Father: Good, very relaxed.

Hellinger: Strange, you don't look it. *(To Mother):* How do you
feel?

Mother: My heart's pounding. The children are so far apart. I
don't feel good.

Hellinger *(to Irene's representative):*   How are you feeling?

Irene's Representative: I'm very distant from my mother and I
feel good next to my brother.

Third Child: That goes for me too. I'm glad that my sister is
there. I've no idea what my other brother is doing.

Hellinger *(to fourth child):*   How do you feel?

Fourth Child: I don't have any connection to my family. The
only one I can even see is my dead brother, and I want to get out of
here. I've got a headache.

Hellinger *(to deceased brother):*   And how are you feeling?

---

*Legend: Fa—Father; Mo—Mother; 1—Irene's representative; +2—2nd child,
boy, died at 14 months; 3—third child, a boy; 4—fourth child, a boy.

Deceased Brother: I've no idea who these other people are. I'm facing in the opposite direction. I don't feel particularly good *(laughs)*.

Hellinger: I can well imagine. *(To Irene):* What happened in your father's family that might be significant?

Irene: His father died early, when my father was in the fourth grade. He really suffered from his father's death. He wasn't able to learn a profession as he had wanted to because his mother was a very weak person and never managed to get it together again.

Hellinger: That doesn't help us. It's a description of someone's character. What's useful are things that actually happened. For example, it's useful to know that his father died early. Choose someone to represent your father's father and put him into the constellation. *(To Irene as she places paternal grandfather):* Irene, be careful! You weren't respectful enough when you first set up the constellation. I almost had to break off the work because you weren't taking it seriously enough. You weren't gathered in yourself. You know, that happens quite often with people who have cancer; they aren't collected within themselves. Sometimes they actually try to avoid finding a resolution. They unconsciously believe it's easier for them to die. I let you continue even though you weren't placing the representatives with the appropriate respect because I know people with cancer have that difficulty. So where does your father's father belong? Go on and put him in.

Irene: The problem is that I can't feel where I should put him.

Hellinger: Yes, you're cut off from your own soul—that's the part of you that senses what's right for you. *(To father's representative):* When you imagine where your father would stand, where would that be? *(To group):* Did you notice? He immediately showed me with his gaze where his father should stand. He would stand here *(moves the grandfather)*.

Hellinger *(to deceased brother):*   How do you feel with your grandfather standing there?

Deceased Brother: A bit better than before.

Hellinger: Yes, I can see it in your face. *(To group):* The therapist always watches the effect that any moves have on the constellation.

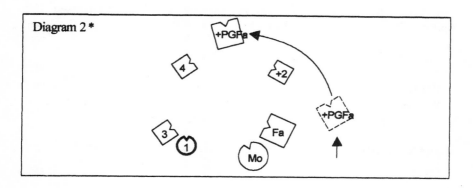

Diagram 2 *

The representatives' spontaneous reactions give the most useful information. *(To youngest brother):* How are you doing?

Fourth Child: Much better.

Hellinger *(to father):* And you?

Father: Better.

Hellinger *(to group):* I have a hypothesis about the dynamic in this family. My suspicion is that the father in this family wants to follow his own father . . . I'll show you. *(Places the father behind the grandfather.) (To Irene's brothers 2 and 4, deceased brother and youngest brother):* Now you two, turn around and face your family.

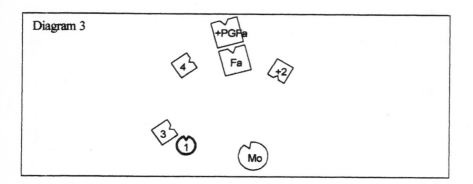

Diagram 3

---

*Legend addition: +PGFa—paternal grandfather, died when Irene's father was 10 years old

Hellinger *(to group)*:   Ah, did you notice the mother's immediate reaction? *(To mother)*: How are you feeling now?

Mother: I feel better *(deep sigh of relief)*.

Hellinger *(to youngest brother, whose face has begun to shine)*:   Yes, that's clear. *(To deceased brother, whose face also is beaming)*: You too! *(To Irene's representative)*: So, how are you feeling now?

Irene's Representative: A bit funny when I look at my dead brother.

Hellinger: How's the relationship with your father?

Irene's Representative: It doesn't bother me when he's there.

Hellinger *(to Irene)*:   So what shall we do with this family?

Irene: Bring them together so that everyone isn't facing in different directions.

Hellinger: Do you really believe it's as simple as that? That we can just push them around however we want and expect it to have a positive effect? Come here and take your place in the constellation so that I can work with you directly. *(To Irene's representative)*: You can sit down now. Thank you very much. *(Irene assumes the position)*.

Hellinger: How's the grandfather feeling?

Paternal Grandfather: Not very well. I don't know what happened to the people behind me after I died.

Hellinger *(to father)*:   How are you feeling, better or worse?

Father: Somewhat better, but I can't see my father's face.

Hellinger: I'll turn him around now and put you beside him.

Hellinger *(to father's father)*:   How's that for you?

Paternal Grandfather: Finally, I've got an overview of the whole situation. It's a mess!

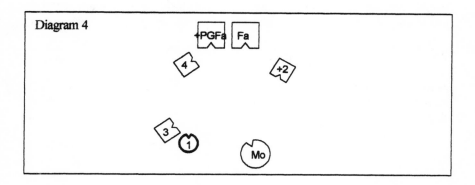

Diagram 4

Father: I'm feeling better than before. My angle of vision is larger.

Hellinger *(to mother):* Now you can see your husband again. How's that for you?

Mother: It's good.

Hellinger: Go and stand next to him.

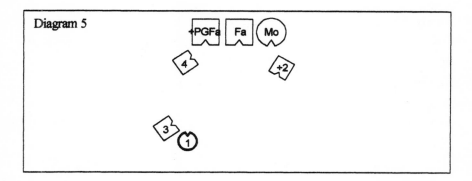

Diagram 5

Mother: That's better!

Hellinger *(to group):* That's essentially the same position as before *(she's again standing next to her husband)*, but now the deceased grandfather is present. You can see what a difference it makes when someone who died early is returned to the system. *(To Irene):* How are you doing now?

Irene: Before I had the feeling that everyone was just watching out for themselves, but now it's a little better. I feel a special togetherness.

Hellinger: How was it with your deceased brother? Was he remembered in the family, or forgotten?

Irene: No, he was remembered. Not too often, but we thought about him every now and again.

(Hellinger places the grandfather a little to one side and the children across from the parents, in birth order.)

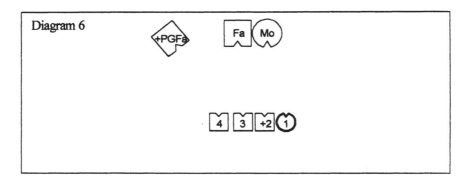

Hellinger *(to Irene):* How's that for you here?

Irene: Quite good. I can't really feel much. My feelings are a bit cut off.

Hellinger: Try turning around. *(Hellinger turns her away from family and a little to one side.)*

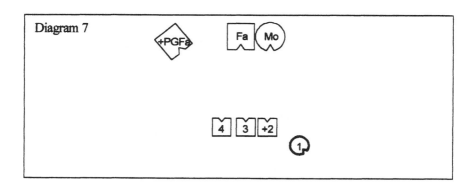

Hellinger *(to father):* What changes for you with her standing there? Is it better or worse?

Father: Not as good.

Mother: Worse.

Hellinger *(to deceased brother):* For you?

Deceased Brother: Also worse.

Third Child: For me too.

Fourth Child: Worse.

Hellinger *(to Irene):* How's that for you?

Irene: I feel good here by myself. *(Surprised murmur in group.)*

Hellinger *(to deceased brother):* I want to do a little experiment with you. Come over here and stand in front of your sister and look at her.

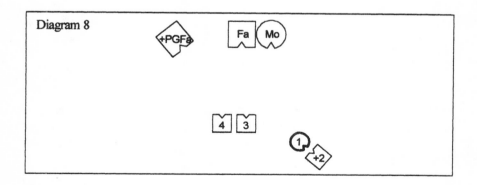

Diagram 8

Hellinger *(to Irene after a long pause):* What's happening?

Irene: I almost have to cry. I don't understand why.

Hellinger *(to deceased brother):* How do you feel?

Deceased Brother: I don't know exactly. I can feel how moved she is.

Hellinger: How do you feel when she's so moved, better or worse?

Deceased Brother: Better or worse? Better, I suppose.

Hellinger: What's really happening?

Deceased Brother *(laughing):* Actually, I'm also very moved, but I can't answer "better" or "worse."

Hellinger *(to Irene):* Go back to your previous place now. *(To deceased brother):* And you can take a place in front of your parents with your back leaning against them. *(To parents):* Lay a hand on his shoulder, very tenderly.

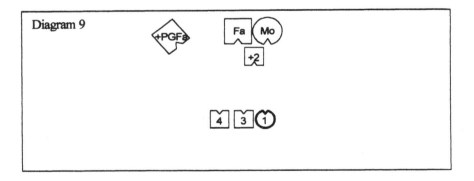

Diagram 9

Hellinger *(to group):* This child is shut out of the family. Can you see that? Do you see how deeply touched he is when he's permitted to move to his parents? His parents must have shut him out. *(To Irene):* What's happening with you now?

Irene: My feelings are cut off again, so cut off that I can't even tell what's happening. I can't even think. It's like I'm in an empty room.

Hellinger *(to group):* Those are, in a manner of speaking, the feelings of a dead person. And who's dead in the family? The brother.

Deceased Brother: I was really emotional before.

Hellinger *(to group):* I don't know what's appropriate to do with them. From the last constellation and from what we've experimented with, I assume that Irene is unconsciously trying to follow her brother into death, and that's one of the factors in her illness—she wants to follow him, to be with him. *(Long pause)* I don't believe there's anything I can do to stop her. *(To Irene):* Who could stop you?

Irene: Myself?

Hellinger: Do you really think its possible to lift yourself by pulling on your own hair?

Irene: I don't know. Who?

Hellinger: I know someone.

Irene: Yes? *(Begins to sob.)*

Hellinger: Breathe, open your eyes. *(Very gently)* Come with me. *(Takes her by the arm and leads her in front of her deceased brother.)*

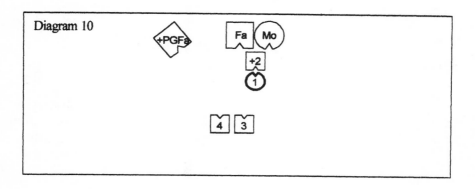

Hellinger *(to Irene):* Put your arms around him. *(Brother's representative hesitates.)* Go ahead and hold her, it's okay. *(To Irene, who is still sobbing deeply):* Breathe deeply, keep your mouth open. What was your brother's name?

Irene: Peter.

Hellinger: Say to him, "Dear Peter."

Irene: Dear Peter.

Hellinger: Tell him, "I'm coming too." *(Irene hesitates. To her, gently)* It's okay to tell him that.

Irene: I'm coming too.

Hellinger: Breathe. Mouth open. Say, "I'm coming too."

Irene *(Breathes deeply, and then between sobs)*:   I'm coming too. I'm coming too.

Hellinger: Breathe deeply and allow it to flow freely: "I'm coming too."

Irene: I'm coming too. *(Sobs for a long time, gradually becoming calm. Brother's representative is tenderly holding her.)*

Hellinger *(to deceased brother)*:   How do you feel when she says that?

Deceased Brother: I want to comfort her.

Hellinger: Of course. Tell her, "Irene, stay."

Deceased Brother: Irene, stay.

Hellinger: Tell her, "It's enough if you come later."

Deceased Brother: It's enough if you come later. *(Irene begins to weep again.)*

Hellinger *(After a long pause, Irene is calm.)*:   Irene, I think that's enough for now. Is that okay? *(She nods confirmation.)* Good. *(To representatives)*: Thank you for your help. You can sit down now. *(To group)*: Serious illnesses, suicides or suicide attempts, or accidents are some of the things we often see in psychotherapy that are motivated by love—the love of a small child. Small children love according to a magical belief system. For the small child, love means:

"Wherever you lead, I will follow. Whatever you do, I'll do," or "I love you so much that I want to be with you always." That is: "I'll follow you in your illness" and "I'll follow you in your death." Whenever someone loves in this way, he or she naturally is vulnerable to becoming seriously ill.

But how must the person feel who's loved in this way? How must he or she feel upon seeing that his or her illness or death is causing a child to become ill? *(To representative of deceased brother)*: How must they feel? Bad, right? Exactly! You showed that clearly in your reactions. *(To group):* In the constellations, we invariably observe that the deceased, the ill, and those who have suffered a difficult fate wish the survivors well. One death or misfortune is sufficient. The dead are well disposed toward the living. It's not only the child who loves, but also those who've suffered or died. In order for the systemic healing to succeed, Irene must recognize her deceased brother's love and honor his fate. *(To Irene):* Your brother's good wishes for you could heal you. That would be a resolution. Is that okay with you?

Irene: More than okay.

Hellinger: Good. You've done very well. Take him into your soul—the power of his love. Okay?

Irene: Yes.

Hellinger: Good! *(To group):* Well, that was our first constellation. You could see how it's sometimes possible to bring a hidden family dynamic to light—a dynamic that may be the cause, or at least a contributing cause, of an illness. But you could also see how the family dynamic suggests a direction in which to look for resolutions that have a good effect. Are there questions?

Irene: I'm not clear what you mean when you say, "recognize his love and honor his fate."

Hellinger: When a child dies, the other members of the family tend to become afraid—in part because they also, perhaps unconsciously, feel the kind of love that makes them want to follow the child. In order to contain their fear, they deaden their feelings. They effectively shut the child out of their hearts and souls. They may talk about the child, but they've cut off their feelings. Then, even though the child is dead, he or she is still having a deadening effect on the family system, a deadening of feeling. For love to succeed, the child must have a place in the family, just as if he or she were living. The surviving members of the family must live their feelings for the child and their grief. They might put up a picture of the child, or plant a tree in the child's memory. But the most important thing is that the survivors take the deceased with them into life, and allow their love for the child to live. *(To Irene):* You could show your children to your deceased brother, for example. *(To group):* A lot of people act as if the dead were gone. But where can they go? Obviously, they're physically absent, but they're also present in their continuing effect on the living. When they have their appropriate place in the family, deceased persons have a friendly effect. Otherwise, they cause anxiety. When they get their proper place, they support the living in living instead of supporting them in the illusion that they should die.

Related Questions

Question: When I was in the role, I felt feelings and had thoughts that really were foreign to me. It was as if I were someone else, as if I really had become the person I was representing. Why does that happen? Can you say something about this phenomenon?

Hellinger: Dramatic isn't it? I don't know why it happens. I just see that it is so, and I use it. Observers sometimes can't believe the power of the phenomenon until they actually have had a chance to be representatives themselves. When the representatives are especially willing to surrender themselves to the role, the information that becomes available can border on the uncanny.

Once a woman, a doctor, was representing a mother in a constellation, and she suddenly felt a sharp pain in her chest and left arm and broke out in a cold sweat. She briefly became concerned that she might be having a heart attack. It turned out that the mother she was representing had suffered a massive heart attack six weeks previously. Another representative began to have the symptoms of an epileptic seizure and we found out that the man he was representing was an epileptic. Things like that happen all the time. I can't explain them, and I don't even try. I like to stick to what I actually can see, so I avoid speculation, but I've learned through experience to trust whatever emerges in the constellations. The representatives' spontaneous body reactions provide useful information about the effect the system is having on its members.

Question: But don't the representatives project their own material into the role? How do you know that what they say has to do with the role?

Hellinger: Yes, sometimes it becomes clear that representatives are bringing their own material into the constellation, and then the therapist must take them out and put in someone else. Sometimes the roles are so bad that the representatives can't be left in them very long, as when they represent a murderer or a child abuser or someone like that. Then the negative effect of the role can be too strong. But with these exceptions, I always treat what comes as being a function of the role, and of the role alone. This orientation maintains hygiene in the work. If working on your personal material is mixed with your experience in the role, you can become very confused, and therapists lose their overview.

I sometimes have had the feeling that people were projecting their own material into a role and I've taken them out, only to have the replacement person react in exactly the same way. My experience is that it's almost always safe to trust the representatives, to trust that they're providing useful information about the system.

Question: Sometimes when you moved people just the slightest amount, I felt a dramatic change in my body. Then, at the end, there was a feeling in my body of complete relaxation, a physical sense of "now it's right." Can you say something about that feeling of rightness and relaxation?

Hellinger: When that relaxation occurs for everyone in a constellation, I assume that the system is approaching balance, and that everyone in the system has his or her appropriate place and function. I call the systemic laws operating in those constellations that support the bodily sensation of relaxation and rightness "Love's Hidden Symmetry."

Love's Hidden Symmetry is whatever is required to allow the bodily feeling of "rightness" you describe. It supports healing and communication in a family. Learning how to help families find it is the whole task of this workshop. You could see how easily and how profoundly love flows as a system approaches its order. Even the representatives feel touched by what they experience. The physical sense of "that's right" is what makes this approach phenomenological and not merely another theory about how families function. We experiment and observe carefully until we see that reaction. In this work, we're always looking for resolutions, for the systemic contingencies that support the free flow of love and meaning.

Question: You say her brother's love could heal her, but he was an infant when he died. What was set up here isn't how it really was for her in her family. How do we know a baby really loves his sister at all?

Hellinger *(to group):*   I only deal with what I can actually see happening. At the end of this constellation, everyone present felt and saw something very powerful happen as Irene confronted her brother. We all felt the goodness and love. What we saw and felt was the effect of her brother's love. That's a descriptive metaphor for what she felt standing in front of her brother's representative—for what we all felt. It's a name for the good dynamic we all witnessed. That good dynamic is what's real at this moment. It brings hope. Whatever the outcome for her, it will be better for her if she has more of this good dynamic and less of whatever was operating in her family before.

Question: We could all see that there was an amazing movement, and I think everyone here was profoundly touched, but what does the work mean in terms of the outcome that Irene can expect? Is her cancer cured? Is there any research about the long-term effects of such work?

Hellinger: I won't answer your question directly. It's inappropriate at this time. I'll explain. As you said, we all felt a powerful dynamic unfolding, and the final outcome is not under our control. Any benefit that comes will come from what I called "her brother's love." That's a new dynamic in her system, and we must resist every temptation that distracts her (or us) from feeling that dynamic. If you're paying close attention to the dynamic of love working in you, you're in a different state of mind than when you think about outcome. If you start thinking about outcome, you'll quickly distract yourself and stop the good effect of the love.

That's the reason why, when I'm working as therapist, I never think about outcome. I don't even want to know. If I start to think about the outcome, I can't see what's happening with the people standing in front of me. My attention wanders into the future, and I try to make things happen that are in my interest, but not necessarily in the client's. Then the kind of love we saw and felt just now can't happen. In a situation like this, any healing that occurs does so exclusively through the love within the family system, and the outcome is none of my business. I may be permitted to help the family find a resolution that allows members' love to become visible and to flow, but then my service is finished, and I must withdraw and trust the good effect of their love.

After work like this, I forget the people involved, so that they are left in peace to finish their work in whatever way they find appropriate. I trust to the good power of their love, and because of that trust, I must leave their freedom intact—I leave them in the freedom either to change or not to change. More cannot be done without violating or disrespecting love.

I make no claims that these experiences are any more than what you saw happen here, and I'm certainly not claiming to cure cancer. I'm doing a smaller thing—simpler and more modest: I'm just trying to help people find good dynamics in their family systems, "to help them on their way." If there's a surprising cure, I'll be very happy for them, but I don't want to know about it. For me, the love we all could feel working is enough.

Additional Considerations

Irene's therapist reported that she was free of symptoms for seven months following this constellation. Her life with her family was serene and filled with joy. She then entered the hospital because she wasn't feeling well. Her doctors found no further metastases, and she was released after a few days without further treatment. She spent the next three months peacefully at home with her family and died a few days after entering the hospital one final time [H.B.].

CHAPTER FIVE

Love and
the Greater Soul

In addition to our personal relationships and the social systems to which we belong, we are also members of larger relationship systems. The various Orders of Love that support us in our intimate relationships are not applicable to other relationship systems. If we are dealing with larger wholes and meta-systems, for example, with God—or whatever we name the mystery behind the world—or fate, or with the wholeness of the world, then those same orders and principles no longer apply. Attempts to apply them lead to absurd consequences.

Remembering our experiences as children, we may reach out to God, or the mystery behind the world, like children reaching out to their parents, and seek a good father or a good mother. Then we believe like children, hope like children, trust like children, love like children—and, like children, we may fear what is beyond our experience.

Or remembering our experiences as members of our extended family, we may relate to fate or the mystery behind the world as we do to members of our families, as if we were blood brothers in a company of saints. But then, as in a family, we may be selected or rejected according to a rigid law we neither can know nor influence.

Or remembering our experience as members of freely chosen groups, we may relate to the mystery of the world as if we were its business associates, behaving like its representatives or spokespersons, making covenants and agreements, as if life would allow us to regulate mutual giving and taking and to control our mutual benefits and loss.

Or we may approach the mystery behind the world as if we were entering an intimate relationship in which there are a lover and a beloved, a bride and a bridegroom.

Or we may relate to the mystery like parents to their children, daring to tell it what we consider wrong with its world and demanding improvements. And not being satisfied with this world as it is, we attempt to save ourselves and others from it.

But there is another way. When we relate to the mystery of the world, we can forget what applied to the relationships we know, just as when we are swimming in the ocean, we forget the rivers flowing into it, and when we are at our goal, we forget the path.

Absence and Presence

A monk, out seeking the Absolute,
approached a merchant in the marketplace
and asked for sustenance.

The merchant glanced at him and paused.
As he handed him what he could spare,
he addressed him with a question.

"What can it mean that you request of me
what you require for your sustenance
and yet feel free to think of me and of my trade
as something low
compared with you and yours?"

The monk replied:
"Matched with the Absolute that I pursue,
the rest seems low indeed."

The merchant was not satisfied
and tried him with a second question.

"If such an Absolute exists,
it extends beyond our reach.
So how can anyone presume to seek it
as if it could be found
lying at the end of some long road?
How can anyone take possession of it
or claim a greater share of it than others?
And how, conversely, if this Absolute exists,
can anyone stray far from it
and be excluded from its will and care?"

The monk replied:
"Only those prepared to leave
all that is closest to them now
and willingly forego what is chained
to Here and Now
will ever reach the Absolute."

Still unconvinced,
the merchant tested him with yet another thought.

"Assuming that an Absolute exists,
it must be close to everyone,
although concealed in the apparent and enduring,
just as Absence is concealed in Presence,
and Past and Future in the Here and Now.

"Compared with what is Present
and appears to us as limited and fleeting,
the Absent seems unlimited in space and time,
as do the Past and Future
compared with the Here and Now.

"Yet what is Absent is revealed to us only in the Present
just as the Past and Future are revealed
only in the Here and Now.

Like night and death
the Absent holds, unknown to us,
something that is yet to come.

But there are moments when,
in the twinkling of an eye,
the Absloute suddenly illuminates the Present,
as a flash of lightning illuminates the night.

"Thus, too, the Absolute draws close to us
at present Here
and illuminates the Now."

The monk then addressed the merchant
with a question of his own.

"If what you say is true,
what, then, remains
for me
and you?"

The merchant said:
"To us there still remains,
but for a little while,
the Earth."

LEAVING A LESSER FAITH FOR A GREATER ONE

The father of a group participant was a former priest who had left the religious order, started a family, and had several children with his wife. In the constellation, he wound up standing between the religious order and his family.

Hellinger: When you look at this constellation, you can see that it would have been easier for the father to have stayed in the monastery. That's often the case, and that's why I mention it. When someone has once belonged to God, or should have, and then leaves the church or religious order, it's very common for him or her to live an even more restricted life than if he or she had stayed. That's more pronounced with Catholics than with Protestants because the restrictions are greater (celibacy). They succeed in leaving the church only when they go the whole way; that means leaving behind a lesser faith, and stretching out toward a greater one.

Faith is destructive when it teaches that you can belong to God in a special way, and that God is angry and vengeful when you act in a way that's in harmony with creation. Belief and disbelief, like guilt and innocence, are inextricably bound together in the soul, and just as we continually swing between guilt and innocence, so do we swing between belief and disbelief.

There's a kind of religious belief that teaches us that the world is evil. If I follow that belief, I must divorce myself from creation *as it is* and, implicitly, from its Creator. In order to do that, I must turn away from everything I see and experience, and I must turn toward another god about whom I've only heard what others report they believe he revealed to them. That's all I know about that god. I have no personal experience of him, only what others have said. So the belief in that god, actually, is a belief in some other person's report, whose witness then is binding for me. If I wish to worship and to follow that god, I must forsake and deny what I experience and see, and I must believe what others claim has been revealed to them.

That kind of religion is passed on by culture and family tradition. People follow that kind of religion primarily because their family follows it. For them, renouncing such a faith means renouncing their family. This explains why everyone who turns away from religions of this kind have identical feelings of guilt, whether Muslim, Catholic, Jew, Protestant, or Buddhist. This kind of faith, therefore, is quite independent of the content of the Catholic faith, the Protestant faith, Islam, or Buddhism. It's a matter of loyalty or disloyalty to their families—not actual experience of God or of the Greater Soul.

Religion and faith based on consenting to the world as it is unites humankind, whereas the faith of a particular confession or group builds walls between people. The religious experience that encompasses and loves the world as it is recognizes no borders.

Those who accept and love the earth as it is can't remain within the confines of a single group. They go beyond the limits of their particular group and embrace the wholeness of the world as it is. This love of the earth and the movement such lovers make—reaching beyond their group toward the larger wholeness of the world—have a quality that is very different from the belief that fears and hates and divides. This love embraces, holds, and cherishes the diversity in the unity of life.

The Disciples

A man is born into his country, into his culture, into his family. Even as a child, stories enchant him about the one who was their prophet and lord, and he deeply longs to become like his ideal. He enters a long period of training until he is fully identified with his ideal, until he thinks and speaks and acts like him.

But one last thing, he thinks, is missing. And so he sets out on a long journey into the most secluded loneliness where he hopes to cross the final barrier. On his way, he passes old gardens, long abandoned. Wild roses still bloom unseen, and the fruit that tall trees bear each year falls unnoticed to the earth. No one is there to gather it.

He walks on.

He reaches the edge of the desert.

Soon he is surrounded by an unknown emptiness. He realizes that in this desert he could choose any direction he might wish—the emptiness remains the same. He sees that the great loneliness of this place has emptied all illusions in his mind's eye that would have led him onto any particular path.

And so he wanders on just where chance takes him, until one day, long after he has stopped trusting his senses, he is surprised to see water bubbling out of the earth in front of him. He watches the desert sands quietly soak it up again, but as far as the water reaches, the desert blooms like Paradise.

Still deep in wonder, he looks around and sees afar two strangers drawing near. They too have done what he has done. Each of them had followed his prophet and lord until he had become almost identical with him. They too set out as he had done into the desert wastes, hoping to cross the final barrier. And they, too, at last had reached that spring.

Then the three of them bend down together to drink the same water, and each feels his goal to be within his reach. Then they reveal their names: "I have become one with my Lord, Gautama, the Buddha." "I have become one with my Lord, Jesus, the Christ." "I have become one with my Lord, Mohammed, the Prophet."

At last, the night descends upon them. They see the heavens fill with shining stars unmoving, silent, and utterly remote. They fall into awe-filled silence beneath the vastness of this eternity, and one of them senses for a moment how his lord must have felt as he came to know this same impotence, to know the ultimate irrelevance of human design and to submit to that immensity—and he senses, too, how he must have felt as he understood the inescapability of guilt.

He knows that he has gone too far. So he waits for dawn, turns homeward, and at last escapes the desert. Once again, he passes the abandoned gardens, until at last he stops before the garden that he knows to be his own. An old man is standing by the gate, as if awaiting him. He says, "If someone has found his way home from as far away as you have done, he loves the moist and fertile earth. He knows that all that grows will die, and in dying nourish what lives"

The wanderer replies, "Now I submit to earth." Then he begins to husband his garden with tender care.

Transcript

GRACE: "IN MY HEART YOU ARE ALIVE"

Grace: I am a child of Holocaust survivors and I think this marks my life. The second thing that marks my life is that I grew up in Germany after the war.

Hellinger: You grew up in Germany after the war?

Grace: Yes. The way I see it working in my life is in the total absence of relationships.

Hellinger: How did your parents survive?

Grace: My parents were Polish Jews who escaped to Asia. I was born at the end of the war. After the war, they just got stuck as displaced persons in Germany, and I ended up becoming a German by chance.

Hellinger: Any relatives who died?

Grace: All of them practically, except my parents and a sister of my father's.

Hellinger: Now just name those who died.

Grace: I should name them? I couldn't. I don't know their names.

Hellinger: I mean your grandfather, grandparents.

Grace: All the grandparents.

Hellinger: The four grandparents died?

Grace: Yes.

Hellinger: Who else?

Grace: Everyone. My mother had four sisters and a brother, and they all perished. My father was one of seven children, and he saved his sister but everyone else perished. Both of my parents were the youngest in their families, which means that the rest of their family members already had children. My parents weren't married when the war broke out. It's just huge. I can't distinguish anymore.

Hellinger: I will select the representatives.

Grace: Maybe I should say one more thing. My father always told me, both of my parents told me, that I look like one of his sisters.

Hellinger: You should, actually. We'll choose representatives for your grandparents and for all your uncles and aunts who perished. Have you brothers and sisters?

Grace: I have a sister and two brothers, but one brother died when he was just a day old. I'm the first, but I shouldn't be the first one. Actually, I'm the second one.

Hellinger: The first one died?

Grace: Yes.

Hellinger: We need him too. Choose representatives for all those who perished, your father's family and your mother's family.
(Grace chooses representatives.)

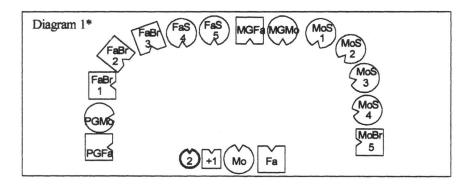

Diagram 1*

---

*Legend: †1—First child, a son, deceased; 2—Second child (Grace's representative); Mo—Mother; Fa—Father; MGFa—maternal grandfather; PGMo—paternal grandmother; MGMo—maternal grandmother; PGFa—paternal grandfather; MoS1—mother's first sister; FaBr1—father's first brother; MoS2—mother's second sister; FaBr2—father's second brother; MoS3—mother's third sister; FaBr3—father's third brother; MoS4—mother's fourth sister; FaS4—father's first sister; MoBr5—mother's brother; FaS5—father's second sister.

Hellinger *(to Grace):* Now look at them, at each one of them. *(To father):* Now you take her by the hand and go with her to everybody in your family, and bow in respect to each.
(Grace and father bow deeply in front of paternal grandfather.)

Hellinger *(to Grace):* There's no hurry, take the necessary time. *(Long silence)* Look at him and say, "Dear Grandpa . . ." *(Grace begins to weep.)*

Grace: Dear Grandpa . . .

Hellinger: "Look at me . . ."

Grace *(Still weeping):* Look at me. . .

Hellinger: "Friendly."

Grace: Friendly.

Hellinger: "I'm still alive."

Grace: I'm still alive.

Hellinger: And tell him, "I take my life as a special gift."

Grace: I take my life as a special gift.

Hellinger: "In my heart, you are alive."

Grace: In my heart, you are alive. *(Grace and paternal grandfather embrace.)*

Hellinger *(to Grace):* Breathe deeply. *(long pause)* *(to father):* Then take her to her grandmother and do the same.
(Grace and father bow deeply in front of paternal grandmother.)

Hellinger: Say, "Dear Grandmother . . ."

Grace: Dear Grandmother . . . *(weeping)*

Hellinger: "I honor you."

Grace: I honor you.

Hellinger: "Please be friendly while I'm alive and you are dead."

Grace: Please be friendly while I'm alive and you are dead.

Hellinger: Go to her. *(Grace and paternal grandmother embrace.)* Then bow in front of each of them with respect and love. *(Grace*

and her father bow deeply in front of each paternal uncle and aunt.) (To mother): Now you take her by the hand and go to your parents and brothers and sisters. Just bow deeply.
(Grace and her mother bow deeply in front of the maternal grandfather. Grace and her grandfather embrace.)
(To Grace): Ask him for his blessing.

Grace *(Sobbing quietly):*   Please bless me.

Hellinger: Say, "In my heart you have a place."

Grace: In my heart you have a place.

Hellinger: "In me you are still alive."

Grace: In me you are still alive.

Hellinger *(to Grace):*   Now move on to your grandmother.
(Grace and her maternal grandmother embrace, then Grace and the mother bow in front of, and embrace, each maternal aunt and uncle.)
Now embrace your brother.
(She embraces her deceased brother.)
Now I'll place you between your parents.

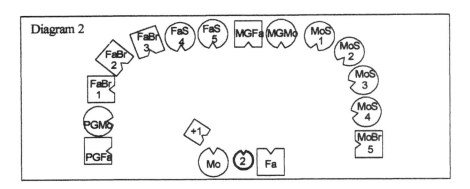

Hellinger: Look at your father and look at your mother. How are you feeling?

Grace: I feel secure now. I feel safe. I wanted to say something to my brother.

Hellinger: Yes, do.

Grace *(to brother):* You took the easy way out.

Hellinger *(to Grace):* Tell him, "I missed you."

Grace *(Tearfully):* I missed you.

Hellinger: "You are my big brother."

Grace: You are my big brother.

Hellinger: "I'm your small sister."

Grace: I'm your small sister.

Hellinger *(to representatives):* I just want to ask you what your experience was.

Paternal Grandfather: Very sad and moved and yet very happy and glad that she is alive.

Paternal Grandmother: I was very happy and felt, "You silly girl, go and live your life and don't worry about us."

Father's Eldest Brother: I felt very sad and moved and very warm toward her and wish her well.

Father's Second Brother: I felt very sad and I felt my heart open to you.

Father's Third Brother: I felt very sad and a lot of shivering all over, an engine moving. *(Pause)* There was a point where it felt like standing in front of a firing squad as well.

Father's Eldest Sister: I felt deeply moved and very glad to have the opportunity to meet you, and to know that you are alive.

Father's Second Sister: I felt very sad and wanted you to live.

Maternal Grandfather: Very moved, joy and sorrow simultaneously, and proud.

Maternal Grandmother: I felt very sad and then very proud, and then very hot when we hugged.

Mother's Eldest Sister: I felt very shivery, tingly, full of excitement at meeting you.

Mother's Second Sister: My heart really hurt, and then I was very glad to embrace you.

Mother's Third Sister: I felt very full-hearted and full of love and of hope for you to be truly alive.

Mother's Fourth Sister: I felt sad and I wanted to hold you.

Mother's Brother: I felt very sad not knowing whether you knew where and when exactly I died, but very glad that I could come back and see you and for you to see me.

Hellinger: How does the father feel?

Father: I felt very full of love for my daughter and gratitude that she was able to meet my parents, my brothers and sisters, and that I could introduce her to them properly for the first time. It meant a lot to me.

Hellinger: And the mother?

Mother: I felt, most especially in these last few minutes, the light in my daughter, and my heart has been aching to embrace that light because I lost so many people and I thought she was alive, this one.

Hellinger: Her brother?

Deceased Brother: At first I felt very detached, and then I felt acknowledged and needed, and then I felt very brotherly and protective.

Hellinger: All the best to you and peace. Thank you all. *(To audience, after a long silence):* In Germany, we are told by many people that we shouldn't forget—we should remember what happened. Very often, we are told accusingly, by people who feel superior, and that has a bad effect in the soul. The proper way of remembering is what we did here, mourning with the dead together—just being one with them. That has a healing effect on the soul; anything else has the opposite effect. *(Long silence.)* I need a little time just to recollect myself. I hope you understand *(long silence)*.

PART TWO

Psychotherapeutic
Considerations

C H A P T E R   S I X

The Therapeutic Posture

The most important element in successful work with systems is the therapist's posture. More important than learning techniques and procedures, those wishing to work systemically must understand the basic orientation and the values that guide the work. Therapists working in this way prefer to work with resources rather than with weaknesses, with solutions rather than with problems, and with the smallest interventions necessary for change. Above all, they look at whatever is actually visible, rather than allow themselves to be guided by theory, belief, or ideology.

SEEING

Question: You often talk about *seeing* a person. Can you say more about what you mean?

Hellinger: I make a distinction between "observing" and "seeing." The word "observing" means observing individual details at the cost of the perception of the whole. When I observe someone's behavior, I observe what he or she does, but the person as a whole escapes me. When I see persons, I take them in as a whole. Then, although many of the details of what they do escape me, I grasp with immediacy (apprehend) what's essential about them, and I do this in service of that person as "Other."

Seeing another person in this way is only possible when I turn toward him or her without ulterior motives. Seeing a person in this way creates relationship. It calls a specific intimacy into being that nevertheless requires profound respect for individual differences, and that requires maintaining a certain distance. In seeing, each person is treated as unique and no norms are established that later must be overcome. Judging right or wrong has no place in seeing, but only serving love and the quest for resolutions.

Seeing another person also places me under an imperative to serve. I may imagine that I'm free to do whatever I want, but as soon as I *see* someone in his or her situation and see what he or she needs, I'm compelled to adapt myself to *be* as the situation demands of me.

In a therapeutic context, only seeing can serve the quest for resolution, and *seeing* is useful only toward that end. Seeing doesn't help to make a diagnosis, or to make empirical observations, unless the diagnosis and the observations themselves serve some resolution. Seeing finds resolution and completion, not objective truth. It always has to do with the questions: "What does the client's situation demand of me now?" and "What does it permit me?" As a therapist, I ask myself these questions and I offer myself in service of the other person. When a person tells me something, I ask myself, "What is appropriate for *him or her*?" If I succeed in truly seeing the client, then I'm in contact with something greater than either of us alone. My immediate goal can't even be to help, but only to see the client in the context of a larger order. That's how seeing works, and it allows therapeutic interventions to remain respectful and loving, while at the same time being a force for healing.

It's strange how people change when I tell them what I see. Seeing is a creative process that has an effect on those who are seen as well as on the one who sees. There are secrets to seeing that I don't understand, but they too can be seen and used.

When you have an idea about what's going on with a client and are wondering if you should say it or not, try to *see* the person. If you succeed, you'll see whether your idea will help or will weaken. Seeing isn't something that you can make happen. When I open myself to someone, I'm often totally surprised by what I see. Often I see things that I never could have thought up. I often have a sense of fear and trembling about seeing, but if I shy away from what I see, if I hold back—even out of the fear of hurting someone—something closes down in my soul, as if I'd abused something precious.

Question: Isn't seeing the same as intuition?

Hellinger: I experience intuition differently, and seeing is more than intuition. I experience intuition as a flash of understanding that shows me where to go, that orients me toward the future. Intuition comes without my doing anything, instantly. Seeing is different. Seeing means that I open myself completely to complex connections and allow them to work in me, to affect me.

That's how I came to understand conscience. For a long time, I couldn't understand what happens when people claim to be acting according to their conscience, or acting conscientiously. That's a huge phenomenon, and I still don't understand it completely. But because I couldn't understand it, I tried to see what was happening. I just let it work on me, holding it in my attention, opening myself to it, but not actively trying to understand it. It took years, but all at once, I saw what conscience really is and how it works. Conscience is a perceptual organ for systemic balance that helps us to know whether or not we're in harmony with our reference system. It warns us if what we're about to do carries the consequence of being excluded from the system or assures our continued belonging to the system. I saw that a clear conscience only means that I feel entitled to continue to belong to my group. And a guilty conscience means only that I need to worry about whether I'll still be allowed to continue to belong.

Suddenly, out of a complexity of phenomena, the essence of the thing was clear. That clarity had an enormous effect on everything I did. I call this process the phenomenological method. It works only when I'm not intending to achieve something—to confirm a belief, for example, or to glorify a tradition. It's a very humble, simple, basic method of knowing.

Here is a poem that presents what I'm describing. It does so indirectly, but it points the way. The poem is an outline of a psychotherapeutic epistemology.

A Double Measure

An observer of detail asked a Seer:
"How does a part

recognize its place
within the whole?

"And how is knowledge of the part
different from knowing the
fullness of the Greater Whole?"

The Seer answered:
"The scattered parts become a whole
by yielding
to their center's pull,
by allowing it
to gather them.

"Their wholeness makes them
beautiful and real.
Yet, for us, their wholeness
is so obvious,
a gentle nothing,
an urge
to join together
hidden within enduring.

"To know the whole,
its many parts need not
be known,
or spoken,
or grasped,
or done,
or shown.

"I reach all that is in the city,
by entering a single gate.
I strike the gong,
its one tone reverberates and
sets the lesser bells achime.
I pick one apple.
I hold it in my hand.
Though I know no details
of its origin, I eat."

The Scholar objected:
"Whoever desires the whole Truth
must know all its parts as well."

The Wise Man answered:
"Only from what is past
can all the parts be known.
Truth springs out of the Void
into Being.
It is always new,
concealing its goal within itself,
as the seed conceals the tree.

"Therefore, whoever hesitates to act,
waiting to know more,
misses what works,
as if Becoming condoned temerity.
He mistakes the coin
for merchandise
and manages only firewood
from living trees."

The Scholar thought:
"There must be more
to the answer of the Whole,"
and asked
for what he thought
still failed.

The Seer said,
"The Whole is like a keg of fresh cider,
sweet and cloudy.
It needs time to ferment
and to clear.
Then those foolish enough to drink,
not sip,
get drunk."

PARTNERS IN DIALOG

Question: There's a particular atmosphere in your groups, a mixture of openness, critical alertness, and trust. There's a strong sense of community, and yet everyone is here for himself or herself. I'm also surprised at how frankly people sometimes respond with their criticisms and doubts.

Hellinger: There's much that can be said only in an atmosphere in which people are alert, critical, and respectful. When people hang on my every word, I must be very careful of what I say. On the other hand, when I'm certain that the participants will carefully check everything I say against their own inner experience and not just swallow it uncritically, then I can risk a lot. When the *other* is my partner in investigating experience, a dialog between equals can emerge. My freedom to take risks is a function of my trust in the other, and it brings us both great rewards.

Community in groups occurs only when the individual members are collected in themselves and centered. If the members of a group aren't centered in themselves, their unconscious minds are defenseless against group dynamics that can alienate them from themselves. The psychological mechanisms that allow individual members to center in themselves and the group dynamics that connect them to the larger group are largely unconscious. The process of gathering or collecting in yourself and centering allows all of the individuals in a group to become parts of the larger whole without losing their individuality. Gathering and centering are the foundation of a community of individuals.

Whenever therapy takes place in a group of people who are centered in themselves and connected to one another at the same time, both the client and the therapist feel the support of the larger group, and they feel safe to allow the work to reach an intensity that would be frightening in individual therapy.

HOLISTIC THINKING BEYOND GOOD AND EVIL

Question: We've been hearing about people's experiences, and some of what has happened to them seems to me to be just plain evil. I mean when people abuse their children and things like that, yet you don't seem to judge at all.

Hellinger: When I *see* people, I see them in the contexts in which they live, in the context of larger wholes, in the groups and subcultures to which they belong. All relationship systems are such wholes. When you see people in their larger contexts, your perceptions of freedom of choice, personal responsibility, and good and evil change. You see that most, perhaps all, evil isn't done because people are personally evil, but because they're caught in something on a larger scale. Evil is mostly a function of systemic entanglements; it's not really personal.

Good and evil are systemically bound to one another. If you want to work with people systemically, you must find a position beyond moral judgment, a position that allows you to see larger systemic phenomena and their effect on individuals.

For instance, when one member of a system assumes a position of moral superiority, he or she claims more right to belong to the system than the one judged and challenges the other's right to belong to the system. That always has disastrous results. It makes no sense philosophically or theologically to think that people no longer belong to the larger order of the universe because of their behavior. Individuals don't choose the roles fate gives them to play, but their roles do have consequences for the greater whole.

For example, the students who were part of the White Rose* belonged to a very tightly knit group that was different from the mainstream group, and they were able to do what they did because of their bonding to their group. Their membership in their group helped them to overcome the intimidation of the fear of death, and it made it possible for them to do what they did. If we compare the students of the White Rose with the Nazis, it's clear that the two groups valued different things, and that what they demanded from their members and considered good behavior was very different. Nevertheless, the systemic dynamics constraining membership in the two groups are similar: If you do as the others do, you can belong, and if you don't, you're out. The groups to which we belong determine how we act, and, in most cases, we don't choose those groups.

---

*The White Rose was a group of students in Munich, Germany, who actively opposed the Nazi regime. Most of them were arrested and executed for their activities.

Systemically viewed, the major difference in individual beliefs about good and evil is arbitrary. No group knows what's good for other, larger groups. If the Nazis had won, we would probably consider the members of the White Rose to be criminals, but we're free to view them as heroes because the Nazis were defeated. Most people's beliefs about good and evil are determined solely by the norms of the groups to which they belong, and it's very difficult for anyone to go beyond that limitation. Going beyond the limitations of one group's morality requires identifying with a larger systemic order. That's a truly moral movement, and you need to be willing and able to endure the feeling of guilt and alienation that comes when you violate what your friends and family hold to be good.

In systemic psychotherapy, it's simpler and more useful to avoid moralistic judgments altogether, to take the position that everyone is basically good, and that they do bad things when they're entangled. That way, you remain free to see them and to try to understand how they're entangled, and what needs to happen for them to get untangled. Because you're not caught up in feeling morally superior to them, you can also pay attention to how they affect you as you work with them. Thus, everyone maintains equality and human dignity. It's good in any psychotherapy to keep your distance from the idea of personal evil.

Nevertheless, what we do has consequences, and we all carry the guilt and pay the consequences for whatever harm we do to others, even when we act because of an entanglement, or because of what our group believes.

Question: That's something I like very much about your work, your respect. You respect individual differences that we usually think of as being good or bad.

Hellinger: I'll tell you how I do it: I'm always thinking about what a good resolution could be. There's a saying in the Bible that you know the tree by its fruit and the day by its end. The important thing is how it turns out. If you really *see*, then you see that those who claim innocence don't really accomplish much good.

Reality contradicts our expectations constantly. There's a rule of thumb in systemic therapy with respect to good and evil: It's usually the opposite of what people tell you. I've seldom seen an exception. In the constellations in which the father is presented as the bad one, you automatically look for the mother's destructivity and entanglement. When the mother is presented as being the bad one, you immediately begin to look at the father.

Question: In Germany, during the Nazi period, the people were completely without critical judgment and suspicion. They just went along like sheep. I'm not saying that I would have done any better under the same circumstances, but that's just what makes it so hard for me: How do I decide when to trust some authority and to go along, and when to doubt and resist?

Hellinger: I think there's a basic error in Western thinking. We think that individuals have the power to choose and shape their fates, but there are many powerful forces influencing us that we can't control, forces that impinge on our individual freedom of choice—historical forces, for example. Think about the changes in the Eastern bloc countries. No single individual made that happen, not even Gorbachev. It was a powerful historical process that swept up millions of people, and it changed their lives regardless of whether they supported it or opposed it.

What we understand to be destructive or evil is also such a force, catching people up and sweeping them along. Evil serves something beyond our grasp and control.

Question: But what about personal responsibility? Does the force of destiny remove our personal responsibility?

Hellinger: Are you asking psychotherapeutically or morally? When you judge someone to be personally responsible, you imply that the person should or could have done something different, and that if he or she had, things would have turned out better. You imply that you know what the person should have done. That's a morally superior stance that has no therapeutic value. If you ask the question therapeutically, then it's better to help people find a resolution that heals, or to put right what's gone wrong. If you ask the moralistic question, you focus your attention on the past, where there's no freedom of choice at all. The therapeutic question focuses attention on the present, where some corrective action may still be possible.

Question: So that means that we're controlled by fate and have no free choice and no responsibility at all.

Hellinger: You argue a very extreme position. Has that been your actual experience, or are you raising a hypothetical red herring?

Obviously, we can influence how things turn out, and we *are* responsible for what we do, even when we're caught up in something we can't control. Still, we have freedom of choice only in the smaller things. The consequences of our actions for our relationship systems and the larger whole remain our responsibility. That's the responsibility that really matters. Those consequences remain whether or not we feel personal guilt. The question is only whether or not we have the courage to look honestly at what we do and at what the consequences really are.

Question: I think that responsibility can only be personally defined, that only an individual can be responsible. You can't make history or societies responsible for what individuals do.

Hellinger: Yes, an individual is personally responsible when he or she is free. But when individuals are caught up in a great flow of events, they aren't free. Individuals are personally responsible in the sense that what they do has consequences—perhaps more for others than for themselves—but free choice is often very limited. You carry the systemic responsibility for the consequences of what you do even if you didn't freely choose your actions.

ACTIONS HAVE CONSEQUENCES

Question: So you wouldn't condemn the concentration camp guards—or officers, for that matter—who sent thousands of Jews to the gas chambers?

Hellinger: On the contrary! I do condemn them. They committed terrible crimes against humanity, and they must accept the consequences of their actions. Nevertheless, they were entangled, caught up in something larger than they were. Holding them responsible for their actions, and, at the same time, seeing that they were caught up in a far greater evil, is different from morally judging them to be evil persons—and feeling morally superior to them. You must decide whether you are thinking morally, legally, or systemically. All deeds of great evil are done by people who think that they're better than the others in some way—and because those who judge them also think that they themselves are better, they, too, are in danger of doing evil. For example, the secret police in the former East Germany did terrible things. Now they're being judged by their victims, but the people who are denouncing them are in great danger of becoming like them. The spying continues, and the snooping and fear. It's just that other people are doing it now. The previous victims are now the perpetrators, and they now think they know better—just like the secret police did earlier. The evil continues unabated.

Assuming any position of moral righteousness and acting as if we know what's right for others always causes injury to the larger systemic orders.

Question: When you worked with Beno, you said that his father was a murderer because he sent Beno's retarded brother to an institution during the Third Reich. If we follow what you're saying, it seems to me that Beno's father wasn't a murderer. He didn't kill the boy, the Nazis did. He was a victim of circumstance—just like the child. What I mean is, in a certain historical situation, he was caught up in and went along with the cultural morals and put his son in a home. That's different from the way you described it—as murder. It seems inconsistent to call it murder.

Hellinger *(to the group):* Pay attention to how this question affects you. It's a weakening intervention, because it robs the situation of its seriousness. He's inviting us to debate ethical issues. When I described the man as a murderer, I was describing the effect his actions had on his family system. I wasn't judging him to be personally evil. Obviously, he was caught up in the times, but it makes no difference for our work what his motivation was. The child is dead. That's what we're concerned with, the effect of his death on Beno. It's a matter of life and death. It has weight. The boy was asked to give up his life in the interests of the family. That's a great sacrifice. When an injustice of that magnitude happens, there's a pressure in the family for someone else to compensate. That's what Beno was doing without knowing it.

When a father kills one of his children, even if there are extenuating circumstances, the child is still dead. Both he and the other members of the family have to live with that fact and with its consequences. Recognizing the father's entanglements doesn't change the consequences. If that were the case, the victim would have to carry all of the consequences of the entanglement and the perpetrator none. That's crazy! Holding people responsible for their actions is not the same as judging them to be good or bad people.

UNDERSTANDING THE PRINCIPLES OF HELPING

Question: When someone raises a large issue, sometimes you answer with a single sentence and then move on to someone else. And then you may come back to the same theme a couple of days later.

Hellinger: Giving up wanting to help or to rescue people is essential if you sincerely respect them. There's an important ancient discovery that helps us in this: One can act through deliberate "nonacting." Actively being present without intentionally acting creates a collected force acting through nonaction. Nonaction isn't withdrawal or holding yourself back. Holding back doesn't bring anything good at all. Lao-tzu described the principle of nonaction beautifully in "Tao te Ching."

The Teacher

> *Resting in action, not acting,*
> *Teaching, not talking,*
> *Before him, all beings are present.*
> *Not withholding, he gives himself to those who come,*
> *Not possessing them, he convinces,*
> *Not holding them, he touches them.*
> *Not remaining after his work is finished,*
> *He leaves them free.*
> *Not clinging to them,*
> *He is not abandoned.*

When the therapist actively holds what he *sees* within himself without saying it, then what the therapist sees will often occur to the client. Sometimes it's easier for a client to find resolution when the therapist actively does nothing. Nonaction is very difficult to carry out actively, but it leaves the client free to discover. In any case, therapists have no control over what clients do with their interventions.

I once got to thinking about the story of the rich young man who went away after talking to Jesus, and I came to the conclusion that it's a good model for therapy. The therapist must respect the client's freedom to leave without being changed. It's a matter of having a fundamental respect for individual freedom—including the freedom to fail and the freedom to stay stuck. Good therapy has the quality of being present in relationships without intention and without specific goals. That is, up to a certain point, we must relinquish all our attempts to influence the client. That kind of presence creates the empty space in which healing can occur. Everything beyond the minimum necessary to get change moving weakens the client. In therapy, less is usually more.

Petra: Sometimes I feel like I can do therapy until I drop dead, and nothing really happens.

Hellinger: . . . until you drop dead?

Petra: Yes, and nothing really happens . . .

Hellinger *(Gently):* You're stuck in your self-importance.

Petra: It's very important to me to help when people are in pain.

Hellinger: I'll tell you a little story that exposes what's behind your feeling. But I need to warn you that the story has very serious consequences if you really understand it.

Belief

A man told how he had overheard two people discussing how Jesus would have reacted if, after he told the sick man, "Rise up, take your bed and go home," the sick man had answered, "But I don't want to."

One of the two then said, "Jesus probably would have been silent a while, then he would have turned to his disciples and said to them, 'He does God a greater honor than I do.'"

Question: My brother's children are all adopted. They all come from different families and one of the children is not doing well at all. How can I help them?

Hellinger: At the moment, you can help most if you leave the problem where it is. They'll find their own resolutions without your becoming involved.

Question: Can't I mediate, I mean, if the timing's right?

Hellinger: A therapist in one of my workshops had a daughter who married a schizophrenic man in spite of her family's objections, and the couple now have a number of children. At one time, the mother and her daughter were in constant conflict with each other, which is an especially difficult situation for a therapist. I suggested to her, "No contact for two years. Leave your daughter in peace for two years." I received a letter from this therapist two years later. She had just visited her daughter for the first time in two years, and they got along very well.

Question: I haven't said anything to my brother about the children yet.

Hellinger: Some people just can't be stopped from throwing the torch of good deeds into the haystack of the world *(laughter)*. A man told me a story of two friends. One became ill, and his friend kept watch the whole night long. In the morning, the one who was ill had recovered, but one who was watching died.

If your brother's children need your help, they'll come to you, or they'll let you know in some way what they need. In the meantime, you can practice being present without acting. If you succeed, you'll have a completely different understanding of help. The most common error that would-be helpers make is that they do more than the others really want or can assimilate. Here's a story that may help you understand how to help them.

The Healing

In the land of Aram—where Syria is today—there once lived an old general who was known wide and far for his courage and strength in battle. One day, this old man became ill and could not have contact with any other people, not even his own wife. He had leprosy.

He heard from a slave that there was a man in her land who could heal the illness. So the old general gathered a great column of his followers, 10 talents of silver, 6,000 pieces of gold, 10 ceremonial robes, and a letter of introduction personally written by the king, and set out to find this great healer.

After a long journey and many adventures, he reached the house in which the healer lived and he called out to be let in. He stood there with all of his followers, with his treasures and with the letter of introduction written by his king, and he waited. But no one noticed him. He became impatient and somewhat nervous. A servant opened a little side door, approached him, and said, "My master instructed me to tell you to wash in the river Jordan and you will be healed."

The general thought he was being made a fool of. "What?" he exclaimed. "That's supposed to be a healer? The very least he could have done was to come himself, call on his God, do a long and complex ritual, and then touch every sore on my body with his hand. That might have helped me. But no, this quack tells me I'm supposed to bathe in the river Jordan." He turned away in rage and went home.

Now that's really the end of the story, but since it is a fairy tale, it has to have a good ending. So, ...

As the old general was making his way home, the slave came to him again and spoke soothingly to him, "Dearest Master, if the healer had required something extraordinary of you, you'd have done it. If he had required that you sail in a ship to far lands, that you worship strange gods, that you give up your wealth and go into contemplation for many years, you would certainly have done it. But he only asked of you that you do something ordinary." The general graciously allowed himself to be convinced by her.

He made his way to the river Jordan, still very cross indeed, and bathed sullenly in its waters, quite against his better judgment. Against his expectations, a miracle happened, and he was cured.

When he arrived home again, his wife was amazed to see him healthy and wanted to know all about what had happened. "Oh," he said, "I'm feeling pretty good, but other than that, nothing special happened."

WORKING WITH RESOLUTIONS INSTEAD OF PROBLEMS

Question: Quite often when I work in groups and have clients set up the problem in a constellation, nothing happens.

Hellinger: I can tell you why. You're not *seeing*. When you look at a problem as a problem, you've got a problem. Seeing only works when you search for a solution. When you say you have a client "set up a problem in a constellation," you're already caught in a definition of the problem, or in some diagnosis. Try asking yourself, "What needs to happen? Where does the client want to get to, and what does he or she need to do to get there?" Then you can start to see the light at the end of the tunnel, and you can swim with the current. You don't need a problem to find a resolution.

Of course, it's an honored tradition in psychotherapy to treat problems as if understanding them could cause their solutions. But it's very easy to get stuck with the problem and ignore the solution.

From a systemic point of view, problems are unsuccessful attempts to love, and the love that maintains the problem can be redirected to resolve it. The therapeutic task is, first of all, to find the point at which the client loves. When I've found that point, then I have therapeutic leverage. By helping the client find an appropriate and mature way to love, the problem dissolves, and the same love that maintained the problem solves it.

Question: Is it jealousy when a woman complains that her husband doesn't give himself completely in the marriage because he hasn't separated from his mother?

Hellinger *(long pause):* Would it help if she said, "I respect your love for your mother"? *(To the group)* That's a good example of a switch of focus from a problem to a resolution. The creative force doesn't work in relation to problems, but only in relation to resolutions. The movement toward a solution is love, and *seeing* only serves good intentions and love. When I confront a person with a problem or describe it to that person, I'm in a one-up position, but we search for resolution together as equals.

Another difficulty arises when, after finding a solution, someone also wants to have a theory about it. You tend to lose the solution when you theorize about it. A theory is always less than the experience it attempts to explain, and it can't convey the wholeness of the experience. When something happens and I try to explain it with a theory, I wind up with only the tip of the iceberg. That's the reason I've slowly moved to the position of trying to avoid theory. Instead of working with a theory about how things are or should be, I have a large collection of experiences with real people, and I work hard to describe accurately different kinds of actual situations and to add them to my collection. That way, I'm always open to new experiences. I don't need to worry about seeing something that contradicts my theory, and I don't need to limit my interventions according to what my theory allows, to prove to myself that they're right or wrong. I'm free to see whether or not they help. If something new and unexpected happens, then I've got another experience for my collection.

Question: I'm impressed by the way you listen very closely to what people say, but you stop them the minute you notice that they're getting caught up in a description of their problem. That's very important.

Hellinger: Yes. When people describe a problem, they want to convince you to accept their world view. Their world view justifies their problem. That's a powerful pull. That's why you have to interrupt the description of problems quickly. If you don't, you get sucked into their belief system. Once you're caught in their belief system, it's difficult to see anything outside of it, and then you can't help them to find a resolution.

A woman once asked me, "Do you work with hypnosis?" I answered, "Sometimes." She said, "I have a client here who was treated by a psychiatrist who gave her a posthypnotic suggestion that is damaging for her. She needs someone to hypnotize her again in order to find out exactly what the posthypnotic suggestion was, and to give her another posthypnotic suggestion to interrupt the first one." I said, "That's crazy. It's a delusion. I don't work that way."

Stopping is most important in situations like that. You've got to stop descriptions of problems at the point at which you feel a pressure to accept a crazy picture of the world as if it were reality. If it were a correct description, the problem would be solved. When the problem isn't resolved, the description is, by definition, wrong.

As a rule, problems are described in such a way as to avoid a solution. That's why I don't need to hear all of the descriptions of problems from people in a group; they're certainly false. If they had the correct description, they wouldn't be talking about their problems anymore. The correct description of a problem contains the resolution to the problem.

Question: I often just don't trust myself to stop someone.

Hellinger: When you're working in a group, you can usually trust the group to know whether what's being said is relevant or not. If the group gets restless, it's a sign that it's not relevant. Then I stop the person. If you're working with individuals, you might try gently telling them that you notice that you're beginning to lose interest, and ask them if they also notice a change. See if they can get interested in their process. That's a way of stopping them that is a little less harsh.

Question: I don't understand what you mean by "the correct description of a problem." I think that there are many alternative descriptions of a problem, different ways of understanding it, and that many of them might be helpful.

Hellinger: What's right isn't a matter of choice; it either works or it doesn't. The "correct description" is the first one that offers a solution. You only need one. But finding a good solution doesn't mean that the client will implement it. It's important to understand that when people go down a certain path, for example, a path of suffering, they go down this path with love, even if their love is distorted or blind. You must not intervene without their permission.

The Wise Crack

Somewhere far in the South Seas, as dawn was breaking, a little monkey climbed to the top of a palm tree and, swinging a very heavy coconut in his hand, began to shout just as loud as loud could be. A camel, hearing the noise, came a little closer, looked up into the tree, and asked, "What's the matter?"

"I'm waiting for the queen of the elephants. I'm going to crack this coconut over her head so she won't be able to see or think." The camel thought, "But what's really the matter?"

At midday, a lion came by, heard the noise the little monkey was making, looked up at him, and asked, "Is there something you need?" "Yes," yelled the little monkey, "I need the queen of the elephants. I'm going to crack her on the head with this coconut and split her skull right open." The lion thought, "But what does he really need?"

In the afternoon, a rhinoceros came by and became curious about the little monkey, and looked up and asked, "So what's your problem?"

"I'm waiting for the queen of the elephants. I'm going to crack her on the head with this coconut until she can't see or hear." The rhino thought, "He really does have a problem."

In the evening, the queen of the elephants herself came. She scratched her back on the palm. She reached up into the branches to pick a few leaves with her trunk. Above her, it was just as still as still could be. When she looked up and saw the little monkey, she asked: "Do you need anything?"

The monkey replied, "No, nothing at all. It's true, I was yelling a little bit earlier today, but surely you didn't take that seriously, did you?" And the queen of the elephants thought, "He really does need something." Then she saw her herd in the distance and stomped off.

The little monkey thought quietly. After a while, he climbed down with the coconut and cracked it on a rock until it broke open. Then he drank the coconut milk and ate the coconut meat.

UNDERSTANDING "RESISTANCE" AS MISPLACED LOVE

Question: You don't seem to interpret resistance at all. I was trained to try to identify the resistance as quickly as possible, but you don't seem to care.

Hellinger: It's gradually become clear to me that clients have a strong tendency to use their strength to hold on to their problems and to avoid solutions. That has to do with the fact that psychological problems, unhappiness, or symptoms give us an inner assurance that we'll be allowed to continue to belong to our group. Suffering is the proof our child soul needs that we're not guilty with respect to our family. It secures and protects our right to belong to our family. Every unhappiness that's caused by systemic entanglement is accompanied by the deep contentment of knowing that we belong.

Therefore, finding solutions to our problems is threatening and unpleasant. It carries the inherent fear of losing our belonging, of feelings of guilt and betrayal, of falling out of favor, of breaking faith with the group to which we belong. When we strive for a solution, we imagine that we break the family rules that we've obeyed up until now and we feel guilty. Resolution and happiness seem dangerous because we believe they'll make us lonely. Problems and unhappiness, on the other hand, give a feeling of belonging. Often this kind of belonging is more important to people than happiness.

Because of this dynamic, solutions are often accompanied by guilt, and change requires the courage to face that guilt. When therapists feel pity for that kind of suffering, they see only one side of the situation. It's very important for helpers to understand that systemically caused suffering is always accompanied by feelings of security and innocence. Asking people to change is asking them to give up innocence.

DISTINGUISHING DIFFERENT KINDS
OF FEELINGS

Question: I've always worked to get people into their feelings more, but you often stop people from expressing what they're feeling. When you do that, it usually has a very powerful effect, and the client makes some real movement. Can you say something about what's going on?

Hellinger: I make distinctions among four different kinds of feelings: primary feelings, secondary feelings, systemic feelings, and meta-feelings.

The main difference between primary and secondary feelings is that primary feelings support constructive action, while secondary feelings consume energy that could otherwise support change. Feelings that produce effective action strengthen people, while feelings that hinder effective action, or justify not acting, or substitute for effective action all weaken people. I call those feelings that support constructive action *primary feelings*, while the others are *secondary feelings*.

Primary feelings are simple and don't require elaborate descriptions. They're intense, without drama, without exaggeration. For this reason, although they're exciting and intense, they bring a sense of assurance and calm. Of course, there are really dramatic situations, and then dramatic emotions are appropriate; for example, the difference between the fear soldiers feel in a combat zone, and the fear we feel in a bad dream.

Most feelings that are dealt with in therapy are secondary feelings. Their primary function is to convince others that one can't take effective action, so they need to be dramatic and exaggerated. When you're in the grip of secondary feelings, you feel weak, and the others present feel a need to help. If the emotions are dramatic enough, the would-be helpers don't notice that there's really nothing that can be done in the situation.

When people are clinging to secondary feelings, they must avoid looking at reality. Reality interferes with the inner images necessary to maintain the secondary feelings and to avoid change. When people who are holding on to secondary feelings 'work' in therapy, they often close their eyes and withdraw into their private worlds. They answer different questions than the ones you ask, but usually don't notice that they do. It helps to remind them to open their eyes and to look at the world. I tell them, "Look here. Look at me." If they can open their eyes and really see, and still stay with the feeling they're having, then it's usually a primary feeling. But if they lose the feeling as soon as they open their eyes and look, then you know they were caught in secondary feelings.

When primary feelings do emerge in therapy or in life, everyone present naturally feels compassion, but also feels free to respond as is appropriate. A person with primary feelings remains strong and capable of acting effectively. Because primary feelings lead to a definite goal, they're not long lasting. They come, do their job, and then go again. They take no detours. They're resolved by appropriate expression and effective, appropriate action.

Secondary feelings, on the other hand, last longer and get worse, rather than better, by being expressed. That's the main reason why therapies that encourage the expression of secondary feelings take so long.

There's also another common misconception about the loss of control that I want to correct. This is something I learned from Primal Therapy. Many people have the idea that, when they give in to their need or to an urgent feeling, they lose control. But that isn't true. When you give in to a primary feeling, for example, to the primary pain of separation, justified rage, deep longing, or reaching out, and when you completely trust the feeling, then there's a natural control in the feeling and in the need itself.

Primary feelings only go as far as is good. You won't do anything shameful if you're feeling a primary feeling, because the feeling itself has a very precise shame boundary. It's extremely rare that anyone is mocked or scorned for displaying a primary feeling. On the contrary, other people usually are profoundly moved and enter into the experience.

That's only true of primary feelings. Secondary feelings don't have the same shame boundary, and it's quite possible to make a fool of yourself when expressing secondary feelings. You can't trust secondary feelings to take care of you.

Secondary feelings do have a certain fascination. They're dramatic, exciting, and give an illusion of being alive. But the price of such aliveness is that people must stay weak and helpless.

Explanations or interpretations also distract a client. Rather than effectively leading people toward their primary feelings, they tend to keep them caught in images that maintain the secondary feelings.

Grief, for example, can be primary or secondary. Primary grief is a powerful pain of separation. If we surrender to the pain, allowing it to do its work, the grief eventually finds its own completion, and we are free to begin anew. But often people don't surrender to grief, shifting it instead to secondary grief, self-pity, or attempts to get pity from others. Such secondary grief can last an entire lifetime, prohibiting a clean and loving separation and denying the fact of loss. It's a poor substitute for primary grief.

Primary guilt leads to ameliorative action. If we accept our guilt, we naturally do what's both possible and necessary to make amends, to put the situation right, and we live with whatever cannot be changed. Secondary guilt feelings transform action into worry. They don't motivate effective action for change; in fact, they prevent change. People can worry a good problem for years, like a dog worries a bone, but nothing changes. They torment themselves and others, but there's no productive change. People who need to avoid positive change for some reason must convert their primary guilt into secondary guilty feelings.

The desire for retaliation also can be primary or secondary. Primary retaliation allows reconciliation, and it's appropriate when it frees both the wounded party and the wounder. Secondary retaliation maintains the injury and systemic imbalance and prevents resolution. An example is the clan feuds that have been taken on from previous generations. The avengers feel the need to avenge wrongs they haven't suffered themselves, and their actions often are aimed at persons who have done no wrong.

Anger has primary and secondary forms. Primary anger cleanses a relationship, and passes without leaving scars. Secondary anger at someone often follows our having done something to that person, who then has reason to be angry with us. By being angry at him or her, we preempt the person's anger. Secondary anger, like secondary guilt feelings, is often an excuse for not acting. In relationships, secondary anger is sometimes used to avoid asking for what one wants, as in, "You never notice when I need something." Another example is the man who felt that he'd earned a raise, but didn't get one. Instead of going to the boss and negotiating a raise, he went home and became enraged at his wife and children.

When suffering is primary, clients endure what needs to be endured, and then they begin to pick up the pieces of their lives and begin again. When suffering is secondary, they start another round of suffering. Complaining about something is usually a secondary distortion of consenting to what is.

The distinction between what strengthens and what weakens also applies to many other areas, to knowledge and information, for example. You can ask yourself, "Does this knowledge lead to resolution, or does it prevent it? Does this information support action, or hinder it? Does what's going on strengthen people or weaken them, support effective action for good change or hinder it?" I'm less interested in helping people to "get their feelings out" than I am in constructive change. Getting feelings out sometimes helps, but it also often obstructs change.

My recommendation is for therapists to try to avoid working with secondary feelings entirely, to distract the client's attention, perhaps by telling an appropriate joke or by shifting the client's focus of attention. My intention is not to change clients' experiences, but to guide their attention toward their primary feelings, which are the prerequisites for finding their own resolutions.

Question: The distinction between feelings that weaken and feelings that strengthen is new to me, and it fascinates me. It's so simple. But I don't know how to tell whether my crying weakens me or frees me to do something else.

Hellinger: Strength is recognized in a certain emotional continence. Do you know what continence is?

Question: Holding tight.

Hellinger: Not exactly. You know what *incontinence* is, so continence is when you don't mess in your pants. It isn't exactly the same as holding; it has a quality of competence and strength. You can watch how I work with feelings that weaken. You can learn to recognize them. They have something manipulative; they're attempts to get someone to do something, as if one couldn't do it oneself. They serve as justifications for not acting and as rationalizations for holding on to the problem. That's the reason why you usually can't do any effective work with a client as long as he or she is stuck in a secondary feeling.

The third category of feelings are feelings that have been taken on from the system; that is, when what one feels as one's own feeling is actually someone else's feeling. It's strange for most people to think that what they're feeling isn't their own feeling, but somebody else's. Nevertheless, strange as it seems, it happens a lot in the constellations, and it's usually very easy to recognize. Once you've recognized it there, you begin to see it in other situations as well. Whenever you feel a feeling that belongs to someone else, then you're caught up in something that's not of your own making. That's why your attempts to change it usually fail.

Question: I'm very interested in this idea of emotions that are taken on from the system, because I've often had that experience. Sometimes I become enraged. There's something about the feeling that's exaggerated and inappropriate. Afterwards, I always feel terrible, as if it wasn't me who was angry.

Hellinger: Yes, that kind of anger and rage is often associated with an exaggerated systemic need for justice. The need for revenge is often taken on from the system; trying to achieve justice for someone in the past. Feelings like that are usually much less intense when the injustices have been directed at you. It's as if the identification with someone out of your past actually intensifies the feelings, just as dreams intensify certain feelings.

Question: Those are the most difficult feelings for me to deal with.

Hellinger: That's clear. In order to be able to deal appropriately with feelings like that, you need to go through a process of inner clarification, or purification. You need to purify yourself from the systemic contamination that doesn't appropriately belong to you.

Question: I often feel hurt by people, especially by my husband. The hurt comes really fast, and I can't seem to do anything to stop it from happening. I've been trying to get it under control for years, but I'm still very easily hurt. Could that be an assumed emotion?

Hellinger: We'd have to set up the constellation to be certain, but judging from the way in which you describe it, it could very well be. Perhaps you are identified with someone who really was injured.

There's also a fourth category of feelings I call *meta-feelings*. These feelings have an entirely different quality. They are feelings or sensations without emotions. They're pure, concentrated energy. Courage, humility (the willingness to accept the world as it is), serenity, remorse, wisdom, and deep satisfaction are examples of meta-feelings. There's also meta-love and meta-aggression.

An example of meta-aggression might be what a loving surgeon experiences while operating, or what a therapist occasionally feels. The discipline necessary for making nonabusive, strategic interventions is meta-aggression. Strategic interventions demand absolute self-discipline on the part of the therapist if they're truly to serve the needs and interests of the client, and not to degenerate into abusive manipulations, and they cost enormous energy.

Authentic remorse is a meta-feeling. When remorse is authentic, people are centered in themselves, and they know what's appropriate for them. What they then do is immediately possible, appropriate, and effective.

When people feel bad because they're about to do something inappropriate for their souls, that's a meta-feeling. We might call it a conscience of a higher order. Sometimes it's the only thing that keeps us from going along when our group is caught up in something destructive.

Feeling what's appropriate for souls also keeps us from living out a script that we've inherited from our system. The script has an effect; it influences what we do and experience, what we believe and perceive, but it doesn't lead to the fulfillment of our own individuality. On the other hand, when awareness of meta-conscience has been developed, there's a criterion for judging what's truly appropriate. Then the limitations imposed by the systemic dynamics and scripts gradually disappear.

The crown of all of the meta-feelings is wisdom. Wisdom is associated with courage, humility, and the energy of life. It's a meta-feeling that helps us to distinguish between what really counts and what doesn't. Wisdom doesn't mean that I know a lot, but rather that I'm able to determine what's appropriate to the immediate situation and what's not. It tells me what my personal integrity requires of me in every situation. Wisdom is always related to action. The actions of a wise person are not deduced from principles, but what is required by the situation is perceived directly. That's why the behavior of the truly wise is often a surprise.

When meta-feelings appear, they're experienced as gifts. You can't make them happen; they come on their own as blessings. They're the reward for life experience—like ripened fruit.

Meta-love is a fundamental property of the bounty of life that we can feel in all areas of our lives, especially in relationships. Meta-love, in addition to primary love, gives relationships strength and security, and is the source of true responsibility, trustworthiness, and faithfulness.

CHOSEN SUFFERING AND SUFFERING AT THE HANDS OF FATE

Question: I belong to Alcoholics Anonymous and I feel very deeply touched by the atmosphere of openness and trust at the meetings. All of the members have suffered a great deal. My question is: Can that kind of being touched happen in a healthy, happy, joyful sense, or does it require some kind of suffering in order to create a sense of community and belonging?

Hellinger: Your question seems to contain the answer, so I suppose you're asking me about something you already understand. It does seem to me that that kind of community is not possible without some degree of suffering and guilt. Suffering and guilt are powerful forces that bind communities together.

Question: But isn't there a temptation to stay stuck in suffering in order to keep the feeling of community?

Hellinger: Of course, but intentional suffering doesn't create community. Only suffering at the hands of fate has the effect of granting strength and wisdom to those who go through it. Self-induced or neurotic suffering brings no good. That's an important part of the AA program, the nonintentionality. No one there is trying to change anyone else.

WORKING WITH FACTS RATHER THAN OPINIONS

Question: I set up my family of origin in one of your seminars about four years ago, but this time I observed how you work with what's in the background. Something went wrong in my mother's family. She lost her parents very early and went to live with a very strict sister of her mother's.

Hellinger: I guard against every disrespectful description, against every attribution of negative qualities, such as your word "strict." Character descriptions are irrelevant. That level of information is distracting and confusing. By omitting such descriptions, the actual events in people's lives regain their importance. It's one of the negative influences of psychoanalysis in our culture that we lend more importance to the interpretation of the events than to the events themselves. That's absurd! I'll give you an example of what I mean.

Forgetting Father's Death

In a workshop for therapists, I asked the participants to relate the most important events from their childhood. One man described how his grandfather had placed his hand on his head. That had been very important for him. Then he described getting spanked, falling down, and so on, and that when he was five, his father died. I asked the group what the most important of these events was. They guessed all of them, except the death of the father. That's the distortion from psychoanalysis.

Your mother went to live with her aunt, and her aunt was prepared to look after her—period. That shortens the whole process enormously. The descriptions of people's character make no difference in the constellations. What helps us are the simple events, and the reactions of the participants in the constellation itself. So, you can lighten the load in your head, okay?

Question: I feel attracted to the husband of my mother's sister, although I rarely see him. I only know that he helped us a lot in the refugee camp. Other than that—and I probably shouldn't say this—he was completely nuts.

Hellinger: *(to the group):* Can you feel the effect of his formulation? By ending his description of what happened by saying "he was completely nuts," he reduced his chance of resolution. Resolution is always bound up with honor and respect. He said something that deserves to be honored, "He helped us a lot in the refugee camp," but he followed it with something that negated the appreciation.

Covering good things with negative things is nuts. Doing nutty things like that distorts reality. Anything else?

Question: On the contrary *(laughing)*.

INTERPRETATIONS WORK
ONLY IF THEY TOUCH THE CLIENT'S LOVE

Question: It seems to me that what you do is reinterpret or reframe in a positive way. Do you consciously use reframing?

Hellinger: An interpretation is effective only when it fits, and it also must touch the heart. That's the therapeutic principle that applies here. Interventions are only effective when they touch the client's love, activate it, and affirm it—and the client's reaction is the criterion we use to determine the fit of the interpretation.

If you're not careful, positively reframing a harmful situation can be a capricious intervention that trivializes the seriousness of the situation, and it doesn't work. The kind of interpretation and reframing that does work arises out of *seeing* what *is*. With such an interpretation, I offer what I've seen to the client's awareness. Interpretations and reframing that are effective rest on truth.

There's a lot of discussion about the word "truth." The constructivists don't like to use it, but I've found a definition I like. Truth is whatever serves and enhances life. If you pay attention, you can feel right away whether or not a statement is true in this way—your body responds with aliveness if it's true, and with a contraction, hardening, or a sense of going dead if it's not. When an interpretation is true, clients feel it immediately; they feel a sense of relief in their body, a distinct feeling of "that's right." It's difficult to define truth, but it's not difficult to feel it. I don't need definitions about what life requires of me. If I'm awake, I feel it. People usually define concepts and goals according to what they don't want and to what doesn't conform to the imperatives of life.

When therapists interpret events or persons, they try to take control of their clients' lives, and they act as if control were possible. That's an inflation. Describing what I see is not the same as interpreting it. When I see that an event has an authentic importance, I try to get behind it and follow wherever it leads me—its leading me rather than me trying to control it. That's a humble posture, and it also protects a therapist against an inflated sense of self-importance.

AVOIDING OVERINTERPRETATION AND
INFLATED SELF-IMPORTANCE

Question: About a year ago, my brother was diagnosed with epilepsy, and several years ago, my sister contracted cancer. I would like to set up my family of origin because I want to find out what's going on in my family so that I can put it back in order.

Hellinger: That train of thought is very seductive. It seems to me that your attempt to explain these events systemically goes too far, and your implicit assumption that there's something that you can do to put it "back in order" is inflated self-importance.

Whenever people ask, "What have I done wrong that caused me to get cancer?" or "What's the psychological dynamic behind my family's craziness?" so that they can "put it back in order," they're going too far. When they start with the belief that if they only could understand enough, they would be able to "put it back in order," they act as if they could control their illness or their family's destiny by correcting their behavior. They want to avoid confronting the fact that some things happen to us that we can't control. When we're dealing with things like that, we have to bend to fate and to bow down before our destiny. Trying to control destiny often has a negative effect on the soul because of its exaggerated self-importance.

A systemic therapist recently called me. She had a seriously infected toe and the infection was spreading to her knee. She wanted to go into therapy so that it would heal. I told her to see a doctor. There *is* such a thing as sickness. You simply can't connect everything to family dynamics. If you try, you make yourself crazy. You've got to look at a concrete person. Is she avoiding her fate and her illness, or is she facing up to them and trying to live with them as best she can?

A participant once asked to do a constellation in order to see what false belief system his seriously ill sister had. I told him, "Death isn't impressed by belief systems." People are very tempted to deny the reality of their mortality.

Question: My sister told me that my father had been engaged to another woman before he married my mother. He was in a Russian prison camp for many years after the war, and no one knew whether or not he was alive, or whether he would come back. His fiancée waited a few years, and then married someone else. My father died a year and a half ago of a heart attack, although he was healthy, didn't smoke or drink, and regularly participated in sports. There must be some connection between his having been rejected by his fiancée and his sudden death.

Hellinger: That's a good example of what I'm talking about. There's a common tendency to look for psychological connections between things in order to create the sense of order and control, as you're doing now. But the more connections you find, the crazier you get. When you find all the connections, you're completely crazy. The best psychotherapy limits the connections that clients find and reduces them to a minimum.

Question: I'm still wondering what that all has to do with me.

Hellinger: What you described has no connection to you at all. Your father died of a heart attack. It happens every day. Everything else is meaningless. What does it bring? His fiancée thought he was dead and found another man. That makes sense. It's easy to understand. Those were very difficult times, and life must go on. That's just the way it is. You could find the commonsense solution too. Many people try to find an excuse for their lack of action and their unhappiness, but it's also possible to just go ahead and do what you think is best.

Question: Okay, but I still have the idea that my difficulty in trusting women could have something to do with my father's being abandoned by his fiancée. I'd like to understand that.

Hellinger: The direct way is best. Deal directly with the woman. If love is there, you'll find a way to trust her. When you think about all the things that could be interfering, and about what they might have to do with your father, you're looking at your problems and you don't see the woman. That's your problem. If you don't see her, she'll have to abandon you. It would be appropriate.

Question: That's clear.

AVOIDING OVERDRAMATIZATION

Question: It bothers me that you so often interrupt people before they've finished relating what happened to them. It's as if you don't respect what happened to them.

Hellinger: Memories are changeable and, therefore, suspect. When someone remembers something, the memory doesn't necessarily say anything about reality. The question is, "Which memory has the person chosen, and to what purpose?" Memories are often selected in the service of maintaining the victim position or a problem, and psychotherapy often reinforces this tendency.

Think about everything that average parents do for their children for 20 years or so. Then compare them with the memories that clients bring into therapy. Mostly they choose the five or six really negative experiences they have had, and forget the rest. When there was a trauma, the most important thing is usually forgotten—that the individual survived. That's often not considered at all.

One client remembered that his mother wanted to jump off a balcony carrying him in her arms. He remembered her sobbing and wanting to jump, but he forgot that she turned back and didn't do it. Or someone says, "My mother wanted to abort me!" The more important fact that she decided not to do it is forgotten, but that she was tempted to do it is remembered. Memories are often a mental armor that help to maintain a certain position and to prevent change. We're more interested in disarmament here.

FALSE CURIOSITY DISTURBS *SEEING*

Question *(Immediately after a deeply moving family constellation, in a challenging and doubting tone):* Did the constellation really change anything? Did it really change anything about your pain?

Hellinger *(to questioner):* Your question intrudes. You haven't even let him have time to digest his experience. *(To the group)* The question is a critique in disguise. If the client were to pay attention to it, it would distract him from the experience he just had.

The question shows false curiosity and threatens the effectiveness of the work. Curiosity is destructive when we want to know more than is necessary for effective action. What he just experienced is more than enough for him. If he were to answer the question, he'd have to distance himself from his experience and switch into his rational mind to formulate an answer, and the effect of the work would be interrupted. You can't even inquire about the long-term results without diminishing the effect of the work. Even trying to find out about the success or failure of an intervention in psychotherapy spoils its potency, as in, "I'm curious about what happened after our work last time."

Obviously, researching the effectiveness of certain approaches scientifically is essential, but that's different from curiosity during therapy. What I'm talking about is the inner attitude of the therapist. Sometimes therapists are tempted to ask questions like that when they're actually looking for an affirmation that they did good work. That attitude leads to a distortion in the therapists' perceptions and self-importance—if there was a positive change, the therapists think they caused it, when in fact they may have played only a minor role.

If you're able to view the therapeutic situation as being part of a larger movement in which you meet someone, perhaps give the person something, and then go on with your life, then everyone is really free. The meeting is important, but not the "therapeutic outcome." That's very supportive for the work.

Question: I keep vacillating between curiosity and skepticism about your work.

Hellinger: Neither curiosity nor skepticism is helpful. There are dynamics that lead to resolution, and dynamics that don't. We work with those that do. I'll tell you a story about curiosity.

The Man Who Wanted to Know Everything

There once was a very poor man whose wife suddenly died, leaving him alone with his many children and his many worries—he had no job and didn't know how to feed them all. As he was worrying one day, his friend told him about a hermit who knew the secret of turning stones into gold. Perhaps he could help.

The man decided to visit the hermit, gathered what he needed, and set out.

When he found the hermit, he asked, "Is it true that you know the secret of turning stones into gold?"

"Yes, I know it," answered the hermit.

"Would you teach it to me?"

"Yes, I will teach you. It isn't difficult. At the next full moon, go into the next valley to the north of here, gather five stones from the river there, and exactly one hour before midnight, lay them in a ring on a bed of pine boughs. Then sprinkle these five herbs—unfortunately, I've forgotten their names—and set the pyre on fire. At exactly midnight, your stones will be gold."

The poor man was very happy. He set off on his way to do what he'd been told. As he was starting down into the valley, he thought, "That can't be all. He certainly forgot to tell me something very important." He looked at the sun in the sky, and saw that there was still time, and so he hurried back to the hermit.

"There's more to it than you told me," he said. "You left out something important."

"Yes, there is more," the hermit said, "and it is very important, but you don't want to know it."

"Oh yes, oh yes," said the man. "I want to know everything."

"Very well," said the hermit. "There is one thing more. When you do as I have told you, you must be sure that you do not think of polar bears."

GIVING UP CONTROL

Question: I am impressed with the lightness with which we work here. It has made it clear to me how much I tend to work in a heavy and tragic mood.

Hellinger: The tragic inflates us. Ease and lightness are qualities of truth, and they bring us further. When something is difficult and requires great conscious effort, it's mostly useless. It's like a donkey carrying a heavy load down a long, dusty road. He is tired and hungry and thirsty. There are green meadows with streams of fresh water to the right and to the left of the path, but he keeps on, telling himself, "I'm on my path." That's effort.

Lars: I'm searching for something in myself, but I don't know exactly what it is. Maybe for something stable and trustworthy. I have the feeling that everything in me is so fleeting.

Hellinger (*pauses a long while*): What one holds onto becomes a burden.

Lars: I've suspected as much.

Hellinger: Exactly! Therapists have to live with the tragic fact that they so often come after the healing has already happened. They often think they're saying something special, but when they say it, they discover that the client already knows it. Sometimes they even got it from the client without noticing. The Spirit moves like the wind. Anything else, Lars?

Lars *(moved):*   Yes, I'm getting in touch with a feeling of gratitude that I know from before, but I always lose it. I wish I could hold on to it longer.

Hellinger: Gratitude is fleeting, and that's appropriate. What would it be like to be running around all the time with the feeling of gratitude?

Lars: I've been thinking about my need to keep things under control, about letting go and giving in to the flow of things. I'm going back and forth.

Hellinger: I'll tell you a story about control.

Don't Wait for Me

There once was a woman who complained to me about a horrible ritual at her house. Every Sunday, her husband got up early, dressed the children, and made breakfast, while she lay in bed. When breakfast was ready, her husband and the children would call to her, "Breakfast is ready." She'd still be in bed, or perhaps in the shower, and would call back, "Don't wait for me. Go ahead and start." But they did wait, and every Sunday, breakfast was cold when she finally came, and she got angry. Every Sunday was the same. She said, "Go ahead and start without me," they waited until she came, and then she got angry.

That was many years ago, and I was still quite naive—I still thought people wanted solutions to their problems, so I offered her a simple solution. I told her to tell them, "Thanks for waiting for me. It makes me feel good." She was so angry with me that she didn't say anything to me for the next three days.

On the last day of the workshop, I asked her what a good solution would be as far as she was concerned. She said that when she said, "Don't wait for me! Go ahead and start," they should go ahead and start. I tried to feel my way into both situations. If she said, "I'm pleased that you waited for me," something changes for the better in her, in her children, and in her husband—but she gives up control. But when she says, "Go ahead and start" and they do what she wants, nothing changes—but she keeps control. But control over what? Perfect control always turns into control of nothing.

Sandra: This afternoon, I had a wonderfully tender feeling, but it's gone now.

Hellinger: Feelings can stay as long as you leave them alone. As soon as you try to hold on to a feeling or mood, it disappears. Life is like that; it always moves on, moving on to the next thing and the next. And when you move on, it moves too. As soon as you stand still, it stands still. That's an image for what you experienced. Perhaps it will be useful.

Sandra: When you asked me to experiment with imagining myself taking my parents by the hand and leading them into my heart, I felt resistance to doing it wholeheartedly. I wanted to, but I just couldn't make myself do it.

Hellinger: Many people have a deep fear of happiness, a fear of taking the decisive step to where they can experience the depth of their love. Deep love brings both joy and pain. They go together very profoundly and inseparably. We shy away from this depth of love because we fear the pain that goes with it. The happiness we feel in this kind of love isn't exuberantly joyful, but rather full, and still, and deep. Although it's profound, sometimes it crosses over into lightness, the *Lightness of Being*. Sometimes I try to help a little bit, to give people a little push to cross the threshold of happiness.

Question: Then it's merely human, after things have been intense for while, to want to lighten up, to tell a joke or something.

Hellinger: It's like in tragedy, when the king dies, the clowns appear. Kings and fools go together. It's part of the dramatic art.

THE VALIDITY OF THERAPEUTIC STATEMENTS

Question: I really appreciate how efficiently you work. You touch a profound depth, existential issues, and it has a powerful effect. It works. In my therapy, there's so much extraneous and unnecessary talk. I thought about it, and I discovered that I avoid making statements like you do because I'm afraid of giving the impression of knowing some absolute truth.

Hellinger: I'll tell you a story about the power of therapeutic statements. There once was a young woman in a workshop who was really a beautiful person, but she had a need to help men, which I thought was damaging to her. She'd moved in with a man who had been married three or four times, had two children, and was almost

40 years old whereas she was 23 or 24. She said that she wanted to help him, but I was concerned about her need to help, and so I told her that she should leave him.

I received a letter from her a couple of months ago. She wrote that I'd been correct, that he wasn't the right one for her! The relationship had turned sour, and so she'd left him, as I suggested. Then she realized that she really loved him and moved back. Now they're happily married. So much for the absolute truth of therapeutic statements. They may sound final, but what people do with them is another thing.

Sometimes people say, "How do you dare to say something like that?" For instance, when I told Edie that she'd ruined her chances to have a good relationship because she had had so many abortions, that statement was completely outrageous. I can say things like that because I have no intention of controlling or changing anyone.

If I'd said something polite, she'd have gone about her business as usual. She wouldn't have found her own orientation. This way, she must think about where she stands, about what's right for her. I don't want to know anything more about what she does, because it's none of my business. It's not even important. I paid her great respect by being an "other" for her. The willingness to be fully "other" for someone is a form of deep trust and respect.

I think what I say is right when I say it, *but I don't believe it.* That's a very important difference. It's my momentary perception, to the very best of my ability, but I certainly wouldn't risk my life for it. I say whatever I see, and because I take it seriously, it can have an effect. Calling your avoidance of saying what you see "respect for the other" is just a form of cowardice.

A good therapist is like a good leader: A good leader sees what the people want, and then gives them an order to do it. A good therapist sees where clients' energy is pointing, and then recommends they move toward where they are going anyway.

Question: When you give people sentences to say, you're very directive. It's almost as if you're telling people what to do.

Hellinger: Yes, on the surface, I'm very directive. But the actual process is more complicated. I'm constantly watching, trying to see where people want to go and where they're stuck. When there's a systemic entanglement involved, clients can't find the liberating sentences by themselves—that requires a knowledge of the dynamics of systems that they don't usually have. If I find a sentence that might be helpful, I send it up like a test balloon and watch carefully to see what happens. I can quickly see if I've offered a sentence that helps, or if my offer was off target. If it's off target, then I let the client lead me to another. It's trial and error. It's very clear to everyone when we find the sentences that help. The client is directing me, and I do my best to follow faithfully.

Question: Did you know that some people think you're trying to be a guru?

Hellinger: Yes, I've been told that before, but I don't worry about it since I finally have found out what a guru is. During a workshop, the group climbed a mountain to celebrate at a restaurant there. When they got ready to walk home, it was pitch black outside, and they couldn't find the path down. One of them, who couldn't see either, took another's hand, they made a chain, and when they got down safely, they thought he was a guru.

ACCEPTING RESPONSIBILITY
VERSUS ASSUMING RESPONSIBILITY

Question: I've been thinking a lot about the process of surrendering to fate, about letting go and going along with whatever happens. It's especially important to me in connection with my feeling of responsibility to clients who come to me for help. I feel a great emptiness when I think about really letting go and entrusting them to their own process. I practically panic. I'm afraid that there'll be nothing there at all to support me.

Hellinger: When you accept the responsibility that comes from the client's system, you're supported by the systemic dynamic. But responsibilities that you take on yourself because of exaggerated self-importance have a negative effect for both you and the client.

Question: But isn't the responsibility already given by the fact that I belong to a helping profession? Don't I have a responsibility to help those in need? I don't grasp the distinction you're making.

Hellinger: Just surrender to the feeling sensation that differentiates between assuming a responsibility out of your need to be important and accepting one that's given to you by the client's system.

Whenever I reject a responsibility that is given to me, I feel something close up in my soul. I'm a part of a larger systemic whole, and I can't act as if I'm not. The only real freedom I have is to say, "Yes." If I consent to the responsibility, I feel my soul open up even more.

On the other hand, if I'm inflated with self-importance and seek out a responsibility that hasn't come to me, I'm cut off from the forces regulating the system.

Question: I've been thinking a lot about humility and arrogance.

Hellinger: I want to tell you a secret: You can be humbly arrogant. That's the epitome of humility. One mustn't forget the courage in humility. Every great decision must be made in *fear and trembling* and in humility. Nevertheless, every great decision appears to be arrogant, but to avoid such a decision would be cowardice. True humility also requires the courage to risk greatness.

USING LANGUAGE THAT FITS

Question: You often interrupt people when they use a word that isn't right. Sometimes you seem almost rigid about it.

Hellinger: The relationship of a definition to the thing is like the relationship of the tangent to the circle—it touches it, but it can't contain it. Still, a word like "earth" has weight. With words like "parentification" and "identification," on the other hand, it's very important to keep the clinical phenomena in mind. If we get stuck with the tangent, we don't grasp the circle. The circle is a movement. When you surrender yourself to what's happening, you don't need to rely on the definitions, and you understand better what's going on.

Language fits when you hear a word and then test it against reality: Does it fit exactly? By doing this, you continually expose yourself to reality until the word comes that does fit. You have to be willing to forget your previous words, your previous explanations and intentions, and become a mirror of reality. Then you reflect a light that leads you to the word that does fit.

Transcript

BONDING IN THE FAMILY OF ORIGIN II

The following is a transcript from a workshop in Heidelberg, Germany, in 1994. Bert Hellinger worked with an inner circle of patients with serious illnesses, together with their physicians or psychotherapists, while a larger group of mental health professionals observed. He is working here with both parents of a child with a serious kidney disease.

Hellinger *(to parents):* I invite you to come over here, sit next to me, and tell me what it is that brings you here.

Father: We're here because we found out, about nine months ago, that our eight-year-old son has kidney disease. The doctors have told us there's nothing that they can do, but they said there's a chance for a spontaneous remission. We both hope that setting up a family constellation might help us—at least a little.

Hellinger *(to mother):* Do you agree with that?

Mother: I agree with what my husband said, and I hope we can find something that will help our son.

Hellinger: We'll work with your present family. How many children do you have?

Father: Our eldest, the child who has kidney disease, is eight. Our second is a girl, almost five, and the youngest is a boy, not quite three.

Hellinger: Have either of you been married before or in a significant long-term relationship?

Mother: Neither of us has been married before and neither of us has been in a long-term relationship with someone else, but I just now remembered that we had a stillbirth about 15 years ago.

Hellinger: A stillbirth? What was the child's rank in the family?

Mother: He was our first. He died on the day he was due, while he was still inside, and then he was born dead.

Hellinger: That's very important. We'll include that child in the constellation. Okay, let's set up your present family. We'll let the father set up the first constellation, and then the wife can correct it.

Choose people from this inner circle to represent the people in your family—that is, you and your wife and your three living children. Later we'll add the stillborn child. *(To group):* When I work with couples, I let both the husband and the wife set up the constellation, so we can compare the two.

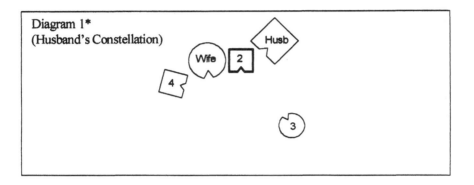

Hellinger *(to representatives):*   Now, when I ask, tell me how you felt in the first constellation, and then how you felt in the second.

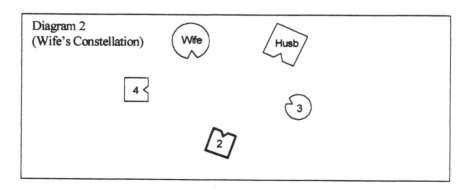

(To father's representative): How was it for you?

---

*Legend: Husb—husband's representative; Wife—wife's representative; 2—second child, an eight-year-old boy with kidney disease; 3—third child, a five-year-old girl; 4—fourth child, a three-year-old boy.

Father: Right at the beginning, I felt a pressure in my chest. It felt really tight. It was even worse for me when the eldest child was added. I had the feeling that I needed to hide, or get away. I couldn't breathe. Now, in the second constellation, I've still got a tightness in my chest, but I feel better.

Hellinger: How was it for the sick child?

Ill Child's Representative: I felt very weird in the first constellation. I really wanted to disappear. I felt the closeness to my father very strongly, but it was too close and I got a headache.

Hellinger: How was it for the daughter?

Third Child: I was very lonely in the first constellation, and I felt a strong urge to take my oldest brother and go away. The others were relatively distant. Now, in the second constellation, I feel drawn to my mother.

Hellinger: And how was it for the youngest son?

Fourth Child: I was completely confused at first, complete chaos. Now I feel wonderful.

Hellinger *(to mother):*   Now add the deceased child to the constellation.

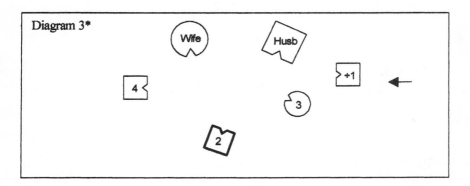

Hellinger: What does that change for the ill child?

---

*Legend addition: +1—first child, a boy who died in utero.

Ill Child's Representative: I immediately felt a pulling in my neck that drew me backwards, and there was a pressure in my head.

Hellinger: What's changed for the others?

Father: There's something eerie for me, something threatening.

Hellinger: For you, Mother?

Mother: I feel tears coming, and there's a burning in my chest.

Hellinger: What about you, Daughter?

Third Child: Something's pushing me away toward the right. I'd like to move toward my ill brother.

Hellinger: How about for the youngest?

Fourth Child: I'm curious about what's coming.

Hellinger: How is it for the stillborn child?

Stillborn Child: There's a pressure forward, but also down.

Hellinger: I'll put you next to your mother.

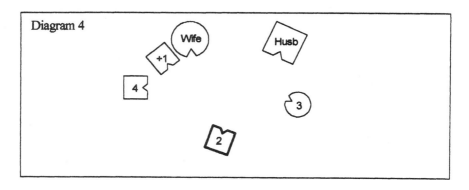

Hellinger *(to representative of stillborn):* How's that?

Stillborn Child: Better. I want to turn toward her.

Mother: It's better for me too. I feel very sad, but better.

Father: That's lovely to see.

Hellinger: Okay, I'm going to make a couple of changes now.

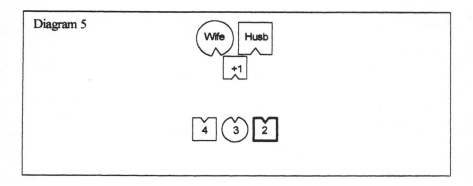

Diagram 5

(Hellinger places the father next to the mother and asks the stillborn child to sit at their feet, leaning back against them. The remaining children are positioned opposite their parents. The representative of the father spontaneously places his hand on the head of the stillborn child.)

Hellinger *(to father's representative):*   Ah! So how's this fellow feeling now? *(Father's representative laughs and looks lovingly at his wife.)*

Mother: Yes, better. Good!

Stillborn Child: Tears are welling up in my eyes. I feel like crying.

Hellinger *(to ill child):*   How are you now?

Ill Child's Representative: I'm very happy and I'm all choked up with tears too. I don't need to have any anxiety anymore. It's like a tightness is gone.

Third Child: I'm protected and well cared for.

Fourth Child: Everything's in order.

Hellinger: It's amazing what changes when an excluded child who has been forgotten is brought back into play. What a force! *(To the parents):* Now you can take your places in the constellation and feel for yourselves how it is. *(The parents exchange places with their representatives. They place their hands tenderly on the head of the stillborn child and look at each other.)*

Hellinger *(to the parents):* Did either of you blame the other for the death of the child?

Father: No.

Mother: No.

Hellinger: How did you deal with it, the death of the child?

Father: I felt sorrow and I was worried about my wife, but to tell the truth, I was also a bit relieved; I had the feeling that it was too soon for us to have a child. We didn't even make a grave for the child—we avoided *(abruptly breaks into sobs)* . . . giving . . . our son . . . a place . . . at least until now.

Mother: For me, I grieved a lot at first after the birth. Then I decided to treat the pregnancy as a beautiful, simple, and happy time, only that it ended without a child. After that, I took a lot of time for myself, had a lot of new experiences, tried out a lot of new things. I hadn't really thought at all about that child until our other son became ill and I read your book.

Hellinger: It's difficult for both parents when a child dies like that. But if you can accept your child's death as being part of your fate together, then his death has meaning and can give you strength.

Look at each other now with the feeling of willingness to carry this burden together—and give the child a place in your hearts. Your firstborn bonds you together, and he may continue to do so in the future as well. And with your first son present in your hearts, look at your ill son—with the same feeling. He can know about his older brother, and you need to do something for the deceased child so that he has a good place in your family. Does that feel right?

Father: Yes.

Mother: Yes.

Hellinger: So how do the other children feel now?

Ill Child's Representative: I'm still really fighting back the tears, but they're gradually easing off.

Third Child: I'm sad.

Fourth Child: Content.

Hellinger *(to representatives):* Okay, that's all for now. You can sit down. Thank you.

Questions

Question: I'd like to ask what actually makes this therapy work? What causes the change in the systemic dynamics and in the individuals? I can see it happen, but why does it work?

Hellinger: When we "dis-cover" an order, the correct order—I'll say it in that provocative way—then the order brings about something healing or resolving in the system.

Order is something hidden. For example, a tree grows according to an order and can't deviate from it. If it did, it wouldn't be a tree anymore. Humans and human relationship systems develop according to certain orders. The true orders of human life and human relationships are hidden and embedded in the phenomena of living. We can't always find them immediately, but it's much worse if we try to invent them to suit our wishes.

I experience the process of finding an order as turning inward while, at the same time, keeping everything in view—without intention, without fear of consequences. When I'm completely gathered in myself in this way, I'm in contact with something I call the Greater Soul. It's something secret, but there's a force that pours out of it. When I'm in contact with that force, I can recognize the structures that help people and that hinder them.

You can learn about these orders at a superficial level and then apply them in your work, or you can learn about them at a deeper level. If someone discovers an order and tells you about it, then you can work with it intellectually. You don't work from an immediate, personal recognition of the orders, but you can apply your hearsay knowledge mechanically.

If I want to achieve something at a greater depth, I must gather myself together around a midpoint of emptiness. When I'm centered in that emptiness, I'm in contact with something healing that I can't explain, but you can see its effect on people. I immediately see in the person's reaction whether or not I really was in contact—if what I say opens a movement in him or her, or if it only stimulates curiosity, objections, or questions. That's how you tell if you were in contact with an order.

Question: You've said that when we lose love, our system comes into disorder, and when we find love again, the system can return to order. Have I understood that correctly?

Hellinger: We hold valuable and meaningful whatever serves the unity and continuing growth of the systems in which we live. For that reason, order always precedes culturally relative values and has priority over them. I can't change the natural orders with personal preferences, saying, "I believe that this is the highest value of all, so the natural orders of the world must now change to conform." No, it's the other way around—personal values must conform to the natural orders. And love, too, follows the natural orders and serves them. The expression of love happens when I acknowledge that the other has just as much right to belong to the greater whole as I have, and when I treat him or her in the knowledge that I have as much right to belong as he or she does. A deep feeling of community develops out of this reciprocal affirmation. That's the love that reconciles.

There are also other forms of love. For example, there is the love that comes from bonding, as when a child who doesn't yet understand the greater connections of the world clings to the mother or father at all costs—even when the parent is dead. That's the source of the dynamic, "I will follow you into death," or "I want to be with you, even in death." That is, however, a dynamic that's damaging for a family system. It makes others want to follow someone who has died instead of staying with the living.

But, when a child recognizes that the parent he or she wanted to follow into death is still present and lives on and has a place in the child's soul, the parent is affirmed in his or her right of belonging even when dead. Then the child, too, can claim the right to full membership with love. The child can say to the parent, "Be friendly with me when I stay a while."

That's the difference between the smaller love and the greater love.

CHAPTER SEVEN

Some Helpful
Interventions

Family constellations are developed in three phases and create two different images of the family system: an image of the destructive dynamics and an image of resolution. The first phase of the constellation presents the client's memories and internal images, and is a highly subjective and personal picture of the hidden dynamics operating in the family. It furnishes a visual representation of the ways in which the family system continues to influence what the client feels and does.

This first phase generates a working *hypothesis* about the systemic dynamics operating within the family. The representatives' reactions provide information that's supplementary to what the client says. The combination of their reactions with the visual images of the constellations and the client's information is a better basis for the search for resolutions than are the client's memories and internal images alone.

After the hidden dynamic has become clear, it's possible to look for a resolution. In the second phase of the constellation, we begin a step-by-step, trial-and-error search for an image of systemic balance and resolution with love. This new constellation allows the client to see and feel a possible healing option.

The final phase of the work is a constellation that's an image of what can be, Love's Hidden Symmetry in which every member of

251

the extended family has an appropriate place and function. It's healing when clients succeed in allowing this new image to work in them, gradually modifying their old personal reality. Sometimes, the resolution constellations even affect other members of the family and the other group participants. Observers are often impressed by how quickly groups, even large groups, develop an atmosphere of alert respect, lightness, and laughter. And conversely, the group atmosphere contributes to the representatives' ability to immerse themselves in other people's fortunes and misfortunes so that each constellation of resolution is unique. The resolving constellations are frequently so powerful that they continue working change for several years.

SETTING UP A CONSTELLATION

The first step in setting up a constellation is to get an overview of the family. The task is to identify all of the persons who belong to the system, that is, all persons who systemically affect the client. The therapist begins by asking about unusual events in the extended family, such as deaths, suicides, separations, divorces, accidents, handicaps, serious illnesses, and absences. Descriptions of character and evaluations of people are interrupted because that information influences the representatives and interferes with their spontaneous reactions to the constellation.

The Conditions for Setting Up a Constellation

When clients set up a constellation, their intention must be serious and their purpose legitimate. Frivolous interest and idle curiosity don't produce the sensitivity and alertness necessary to distinguish between personal projections and systemic effect.

The effect of a constellation can go very deep. For this reason, a group atmosphere of attentive cooperation is essential. Participants shouldn't say anything while being set up, nor should the person who is setting up the constellation.

Hellinger *(to representatives doing their first constellation):*   Center yourselves, collect yourselves. Forget your own problems, your intentions, your goals. Just notice the feelings and sensations that arise as you're moved to your places, and notice whatever changes in you when others are brought into the constellation.

It's important not to try to figure out how you think you should feel in this or that place based on what you see or believe. Trust your body reactions. When you feel different than expected, report that neutrally, without judgment. You may experience feelings that are taboo and that cause anxiety or embarrassment. For example, you might feel relieved when someone dies, or you might feel drawn toward an illicit or incestuous relationship. If you don't say it, then important information doesn't come into the open. It works best when you say what you experience without censoring it, without leaving anything out or elaborating on it in any way. Whatever you experience when you're representing someone has to do with that person, and not with your personal life.

When you set up your constellation, do it by feel. Actually touch the representatives, take them by a shoulder and move them to their places so that you can feel what's right. You can forget what you thought before, because that's usually not helpful. Don't worry about gestures and sentences, and in which direction people are looking. Just find the place for each to stand that feels right.

Choosing Representatives

Question: Is it necessary that the representatives be of the same gender as the persons they represent?

Hellinger: Yes, as a general rule, but sometimes that isn't possible. It usually works out okay when someone represents a person of the opposite sex in a minor role. It is, however, a disturbance. Still, when there are too few people, you've got to make do. Sometimes, I even stand in for someone in a peripheral role.

Question: I have the impression that representatives are chosen who fit their roles, and that they're similar to the actual persons.

Hellinger: When people are choosing, they don't turn off their unconscious. Obviously, there are similarities. However, if you allow yourself to feel the effect of the position, anyone can represent anyone. It isn't too important. It sometimes happens that the same person is repeatedly chosen to represent certain persons, for example, persons who have committed suicide. The therapist should then work with the hypothesis that there's something in the person's system that could place that person at risk and protect him or her from being chosen for such roles too often.

Ignoring Interpretations and Representatives' Personal Material

Question: When you're feeling something during a constellation, doesn't your personal history come into play?

Hellinger: That's a very important question. You can't do a family constellation if you have the idea that what you feel is personal. That's too confusing. If you try to figure out whether it's your feeling or part of the system, you're already distracted from noticing how the position is affecting you. It's simpler to assume that what you feel is a function of the system and not your personal history.

You enter into a foreign system when you're a representative, and you have foreign feelings and sensations. Obviously, your personal memories and experiences can be touched, but it has a destructive effect if you allow yourself to think about them as long as you're in the role. Then you're mixing personal and external things.

For this reason, it's very important that you remain clear—although you let yourself get into the role fully, the feelings that come aren't your feelings and they don't apply to you. After you get out of the role, you can deal with your feelings if you want to. It's a little like being an actor who is playing an intense role. The feelings of Othello may touch the actor's personal feelings, but he's going to go crazy if he tries to deal with his personal issues *while* he's identified with Othello. It's better to work on your issues in the context of your system.

When you've observed a number of constellations, you see how the same participant has different feelings in each different system, and you see how the feelings constantly change within one constellation. As an outsider, you can't always tell how someone will react in a position.

Family Sculptures and Family Constellations

Hellinger: There's another distinction that I make: What we do are family constellations, not family sculptures. By family sculptures, I mean setting up the family with gestures and postures, turning people's heads to look in a certain direction, and so on. When representatives are sculpted like that, their experiences are completely determined by their positions, and they aren't free to notice the changes that occur in the course of the work. If the representatives are simply put in their places, they can follow the changes in their inner sensations as the constellation develops. If I turn their heads for them or tell them whom to look at, they can't allow the position to affect them because I've defined their experience.

Gestures and poses also make it difficult to feel the effect of the family dynamic. The very simple, almost plain constellations, on the other hand, allow us to get a much better picture of the dynamic of the family system, of how the system influences its members. If we just lead the representatives to a certain position in relation to the others and allow that to affect them, they start to get symptoms, perhaps weak knees, anger, silly ideas, or something like that. When that happens, we're getting information from a different level, not just from the protagonist's conscious concepts.

Question: While I was in the constellation, my hands felt terribly cold. I thought it was just my anxiety at being in the role, but maybe it was a part of the system.

Hellinger: Yes, that would be important information. You need to act as if the moment you step into the system, you're no longer yourself, but another whose feelings you feel. You mustn't apply to yourself what you feel in the role. Don't even think, "That might be an indication that there's something similar in me." You need a certain discipline.

Paul (*referring to a specific constellation*): When I see the parents and children in such a confrontation with one another. . . .

Hellinger (*interrupting*): That's an interpretation. You're making the interpretation that there's a confrontation because they were standing across from one another in the constellation. That's a serious mistake.

Paul: But that's how I sense it.

Hellinger: No, that's not actually how you sense it. It's how you interpret it. In this work, absolute accuracy is essential. You only could sense it if you were actually standing in the constellation. The representatives didn't have a sense of confrontation. That's a very basic principle of working with the constellations. You have to resist the temptation to come to conclusions about the system as a whole on the basis of what you think you would feel.

Paul: Does that mean that I have to place myself in the client's position in order to understand the client?

Hellinger: No, it doesn't mean that. You can't actually make an empathic connection with your clients if you identify with them completely. You need alertness and a certain distance to be truly empathic. If you contact another person with that kind of alertness, you can usually sense what he or she is experiencing. Especially, you can sense what's required for a solution. Looking for a solution requires a completely different alertness than asking the question, "What's the problem?" You can't empathize when you're looking for problems.

Working with the Minimum

Question: When people start to tell you about their families, I notice that you often interrupt them before they finish. Why do you do that?

Hellinger: People setting up their systems are often tempted to give much more information than is necessary. When they do that, they interfere with the representatives' ability to experience directly how the system affects them. Too much information confuses more than it helps. Experienced representatives will say what's important. When information comes from them out of their experience in the role, it has a different weight and effect.

It's also tempting to set up more members of the family than are necessary for resolution. Every unnecessary person in the resolution constellation diminishes the power of the image, so the therapist must make sure that only those persons are included in the constellation who are necessary for a resolution. People sometimes say, "My grandmother was living with us," or "My nanny was very important for me as a child." Mere physical proximity isn't in itself an indication of membership in the system or of importance for a resolution.

The fundamental principle is: *Always work with the minimum necessary for resolution.* People can be added to the system later as needed, but representatives who have no effect on the others must be removed from the constellation. It's confusing when too many people are set up, and it's disturbing to the representatives if you're constantly putting people in and then having to take them out again.

Family Therapy and Family Constellations

Question: Can you set up a family constellation with the members of the family itself?

Hellinger: You don't need your family to set up a family system. The constellations have a clearer effect when representatives from the group are used instead of family members. If family members set up the other members, they can't avoid setting up their conscious relationships, what they think or feel about the others. That's a very different level of information than what we need to find a resolution. Working like that can lead to good relationship clarification, but not work with the dynamics of the family system.

I'm cautious about doing therapy with the entire family. When the entire family goes to a therapist, the children tend to lose some of their respect for their parents. That's a very high price to pay, especially for younger children, so I prefer to work with the parents. I do family therapy with the parents, and the parents work with their children. The children don't even need to know what we discussed.

Sometimes it works very well to have the family watching while one member sets up the constellation with representatives from a group, but I use this option sparingly, primarily when a child has a physical illness that may have a systemic component. Then one of the parents can set up the family while the child watches.

When you set up a constellation of your family in a group, you carry away images of what happened in the constellation, and those images can affect the whole system. That's an elegant solution because no one needs to know that a therapist was involved at all. The dignity and privacy of family members are not violated, the responsibility remains in the family, and the therapist remains unobtrusive, hidden in the background.

Once the problem dynamic in the family is clear, then you can do family therapy in whatever way is appropriate to the family's situation. The family constellations are useful when the symptoms are known, but the underlying systemic dynamic isn't yet visible.

The Meaning of the Constellations

Hellinger: I want to say one thing more about the constellations, just to avoid possible misunderstandings. The constellations are images, like snapshots of what was and could be. And, like snapshots, they don't show the whole truth of the situation, just certain aspects of it. They are like scenic viewing points along a highway. When people try to make life decisions on the basis of such constellations, they easily get it wrong. The best thing to do following a constellation is not to do anything at all, but just to allow the new image to take effect on its own. Let yourself be surprised by what happens.

The representatives' feelings reveal a partial truth, but they don't necessarily tell us what actually happened in the past. They help to identify forces operating in the system that are unconscious. And they help to find a resolution. That's all that the constellations do.

A man once set up a constellation. He wasn't getting along with his wife. In the resolution constellation, he was separated from his wife, and the children were with him. He then went home and said to his wife, "Bert Hellinger said we must get divorced, and that I should have custody of the children." That's abuse, pure and simple. That's a terrible misuse of the exercise. It was very unfair to his wife, and it was unfair to the exercise.

When the sun comes up, you can use the light. You allow the light to work, helping you to see clearly. After a while, you see what you've got to do, or you see things differently, or you see a new possibility. Then you do what needs to be done, but you don't need to talk much about the sun.

The Standard Resolution Constellation

Hellinger: When you're ready to look for a resolution constellation, what you're looking for is a constellation in which everyone, especially the client, feels good. You've seen the representatives' reactions, when they could suddenly feel, "That's right!" You have to find it by trial and error, but there's a standard order you should know. There are always exceptions, but the basic internal ordering principle of a family relationship system is this:

1. Whoever was there first has priority.

2. The direction of priority in a constellation is clockwise.

3. Between a man and a woman who entered the system at the same time, the man generally comes first, and then the woman. (See Chapter Two.)

4. In the resolution constellations, the children usually come next, the oldest closest to the mother's left. Quite often, the constellation is more relaxed when the children are standing opposite their parents. (I've also had feedback from families that mealtime is more relaxed when the family sits at the table in this order.)

5. Stillborn children usually stand with their siblings in their order of birth. Aborted children, if they're important to the system at all, usually feel good sitting in front of their parents, leaning against them. When they're in that position, the other members of the constellation usually can relax, too. Aborted children aren't counted with the others—they affect their parents, but not their siblings.

Question: You said that the natural order of the family moves clockwise. What about when there's been more than one marriage?

Hellinger: The order is still clockwise: the first family, then the second family, and then the third family. For example, if the client is a man who was married three times, it starts with his first wife, with the children they had together to her left; then the second wife and children; then he; and, finally, his third wife with the children they had together on her left. Sometimes the order is different. Don't get the idea that it always has to be the same, but the resolution constellation very often will turn out to be a variant of this basic form. Actually, you can't set up some constellations in their full complexity, but you can usually get close enough to find a good resolution.

Question: Doesn't a complex family start with the client?

Hellinger: No, but the client's the midpoint.

Question: So it isn't set where the circle actually starts?

Hellinger: No. As a rule, the children from a divorce stand between their parents. The natural order within a family is that the older members entered the system first and come first, but between two systems, the new system must have precedence over the previous ones; otherwise, there's confusion and disarray. The present family has precedence over the earlier families. That's why partners have to leave their old families in order to enter into another. There are exceptions to this as well, for instance a widow and her only child. Very often, such a child has to integrate his or her mother into the new family if he or she marries. When a person has more than one family, then all of the families form one very complex relationship system.

Divorced persons are only separated from their partners as partners, but as parents they're still connected. Therefore, resolutions are possible only if that's acknowledged and the whole system is brought into balance.

Question: I'm still confused about when the man comes first and when the woman has the lead position.

Hellinger: The representatives' reactions are the only criterion. Try it out both ways if you're not sure. They usually agree as to which way is better. I'll repeat my observations since it's a point that's confusing to many people.

Since the father and mother enter a family system at the same time, their ranking is determined by their function and by their psychological weight. The person responsible for the family's external security usually has the first position, and that's usually the man. There are situations in which the woman has priority even when she isn't responsible for the family security, for example, when her family of origin has unusual weight because of its history. Then that family's fortune or misfortune outweighs the man's protective function. Feel free to experiment with the constellation to see which order is better for the participants.

When the man's place is to the left of the woman without there being a legitimate reason for it, he has a fool's freedom and he tends to wander away from his family and avoid responsibility, and the woman often feels very alone and unsupported. As soon as he's standing on the other side, he feels responsible and the woman feels protected and helped.

Question: Isn't that just the patriarchal order?

Hellinger: I don't know. The soul reacts as it does no matter what ideology you embrace. It isn't a matter of conscious choice. The constellations show clearly that whomever is responsible for the safety and living space for the family has priority, and he or she is also the one who comes first in the line of fire. It's not a question of human value, as if either men or women were more valuable.

Additional Considerations

Many couples we've worked with have discovered that it's much more difficult to change their roles and functions than they expected. Some say that's because the socialization of the roles of men and women is so entrenched, and others that there are biological or archetypal patterns that resist change.

We don't speculate about that. We observe that it generally works better when the fathers do their best to protect and serve their families, and when the mothers support them in that and follow their lead. But for many families, the traditional roles assigned to women and men are no longer appropriate. Sometimes these roles and functions may be reversed successfully, but when a man asserts his strength in a way that's contrary or oblivious to the needs and interests of his wife and children, or when wives and children claim the privileges of the lead position without truly accepting the responsibility and danger as well, the result is invariably destructive to love. When partnerships and families are having difficulties, it's often the case that the actual dynamics of the family are different from what the partners would like to believe.

Love requires that the overall power, privilege, responsibility, and freedom in the family remain balanced and well matched, and that the roles and functions of family members remain systemically appropriate. [H.B.]

The Resolution Constellation Emerges from the Process

Question: How do you go about looking for a resolution?

Hellinger: The resolution emerges during the constellation process. It's absolutely essential that you listen closely to the representatives' reports and allow them to lead you toward the resolution. There are some situations in which the therapist must trust his or her own perceptions more than the reports of the participants, especially when their nonverbal behavior isn't congruent with what they say, but, as a rule, trust what they say. Often there's missing information that makes the movement toward resolution difficult or even impossible. Then you've got to stop and wait until the information is available.

Bear in mind that you're seeking a resolution primarily for the client, and only secondarily for the other members of the system. It's my intuitive conviction that the end resolutions are pretty much the same for all members of the family. Nevertheless, the steps taken and the persons brought into the system may well differ depending on who the protagonist is, and whether childhood was experienced as a boy or as a girl.

Seeking a resolution for someone is a service that can only be done with humility. It isn't your job to create a resolution when one doesn't emerge on its own. You'll make a mess if you try. The humility I'm talking about requires that you consent to being stuck when the constellation doesn't provide a resolution, and that you trust the process to continue on its own. This kind of therapy isn't something the therapist does to the client, and your trust in the process is a model for the client.

How the Resolution Constellation Works for Change

Question: How do the end constellations actually work?

Hellinger: A resolution constellation has its greatest power for change when clients see it, take it in, and give up the attempt to do anything actively. It's as if the resolution constellation were an unconscious picture that can work if you let it. You'll do better if you just let time pass. It's like a convalescence after a serious illness—it takes time, but after a while, you're healthy again. It may take several years for the healing process set in motion by the resolution constellation to complete itself. That's nothing you can objectively measure, but you definitely can see the results.

There's another important issue. No one else in your system has to change in order for you to change. You don't need anyone to assume a different function in the system. The entire shift in the family system occurs as a result of a shift in your inner image. Occasionally, it's helpful to tell other members of the family about the constellation, but only when it's appropriate and you tell them without any interpretation. You only tell what happened and how that was for you.

When parents get their image of the family in order it affects their children. It's not necessary to tell the children anything at all about what happened. The order of the system itself has the effect, and also your honoring it in your soul. It's a characteristic of a good resolution that everyone in the system has a good place. If the resolution constellation reveals that you still owe someone something, you've got to take care of it. Some people find it useful to draw or paint their constellation, or they may look at a videotape of the constellation after a while.

Often the details of the resolution are completely forgotten, and only the effect remains. I remember a conversation I had that illustrates how the images work without actively doing anything.

I'll Pay for the Motorcycle

I was invited to lunch by a colleague. Her niece was living with her because she'd been thrown out at home. The niece, who was about 20, had been a junkie living a junkie's street life, had attempted suicide a number of times, and finally had gotten herself together at her aunt's house. She was clean, had learned a trade, and had become a more or less normal young woman. My friend told how her niece had recently made a trip to Guatemala where she borrowed a motorcycle and wrecked it. She just left it lying there, and went on her way.

I let the story work in me a while, then I said, "She'd better pay for the motorcycle, or she's in danger of slipping back into her old lifestyle." My friend had to go on a business trip right after our lunch and didn't have a chance to talk with her niece before she left. That night, her niece called her at her hotel and said, "I've been thinking. I'm going to pay for the motorcycle."

That's how the inner pictures work. I can tell you many similar anecdotes. It's the effect of "nondoing." The good image makes things happen. When insight is present, then I only need to keep my strength collected while a new pattern emerges. When the new image is clearly formed, I can do what's necessary with a minimum of effort. I can tell you of another case.

Grandmother's Serenity

A lively young couple in a group who were in their late 20s had three daughters and a fourth child on the way. The second daughter had

diabetes. When we set up the constellation, the daughter's representative was very nervous and couldn't find a place where she felt good.

Then we brought the child's maternal grandmother and great
grandmother into the constellation. They both had bad reputations
and were rejected and devalued by the client. As soon as they came
into the constellation, the little girl's representative became calm.
When we put the grandmother behind her, she radiated serenity. The
parents called home that night from the workshop and talked with
their children. They later related that the little girl had talked with
them as never before. They were completely surprised.

A couple of months later, the man's brother participated in a
group. He came up to me and told me that the little girl's blood
sugar had dropped so dramatically after the constellation that they
stopped the insulin injections for three days. Then it went back up,
and they had to start insulin again.

That seems to indicate that the good effect of the resolution constellation was interrupted, but the story still shows the kind of
change made possible by putting the inner system in order. They
hadn't told the child anything. Changes just happen when the systemic images are in order.

Here is a final example.

A Loving Telephone Call

A man in a group who was having serious trouble in his marriage
told how he had recently read in the newspaper that his illegitimate
son had been killed in an accident. He'd never seen the son and had
never concerned himself with him. He had married his present wife
shortly after the boy's birth, and the couple had three children
together.

We set up the constellation, and after a sequence of moves, the
man wound up standing next to his deceased son. Then the son sat in
front of his father, who put a hand on his head. The man broke
down, sobbing in deep grief and shame. Then it was over.

Although he was having serious problems with his wife, she tele-
phoned him at the workshop that night and talked to him lovingly.

The image had affected his wife in some way in spite of the distance. That kind of thing happens a lot, but I don't even speculate
about how it works.

Stopping as a Difficult but Necessary Intervention

Hellinger: It's not always possible to find a good resolution. After you've looked for a while without finding anything, the group starts to lose interest. When you notice that happening, it's time to quit. Usually there's information missing that you need in order to uncover a resolution. The process of watching the constellation being set up has already provided plenty of useful insight for the client, and my general principle is that it's better to quit while you're ahead. It's better to do too little than to risk doing too much.

Interrupting a Constellation

The primary issue to watch out for is how people go about setting up their constellations, whether or not they have a confusing or a clear effect on the representatives. Some constellations are very clear and have an immediate effect on the representatives. Others are diffuse, and the representatives don't get a real sense of what's going on, forget whom they're supposed to represent, and so on. After you've had a bit of experience, you can see how deeply engaged and centered someone is.

When clients are really collected in themselves, they move slowly, feeling their way into each movement. They tend to take each representative tenderly by the arm, as if physical touch helps them get the feel of what's "right." They lead the person to his or her place, make fine adjustments, and stay with the person until it's just right. Then they go on to get the next person. When clients want to make sure that they've got it right, they instinctively walk around the periphery, looking at what they've done from the outside. I don't tell participants too much about these things, because I want to be able to see how they naturally go about it.

When a client doesn't set up the constellation with this kind of genuine respect, there's a difficult and subtle test for the therapist. Everyone unconsciously watches to see if the therapist is really in charge of the situation and notices the difference. If the therapist doesn't notice, he or she might as well go home because real trust can't develop. There's something in the soul that recognizes whether the therapist truly respects life. If the therapist were to tolerate a careless or irreverent handling of issues of life and death, then people would be foolish to show their real concerns.

I'll tell you a true story that illustrates the point.

I Lost Respect for the Saw

Two years ago, a friend came to visit. While he was here, he told how his oldest son, who was learning to become a carpenter, had severely cut his leg with an electric saw and had to go to the hospital for surgery. After the operation was over and it had become clear that there wouldn't be permanent damage, he looked at his father and said, "I lost respect for the saw."

When I notice that someone is setting up the constellation according to a plan worked out ahead of time, I usually stop the constellation and tell the person that I can't work with such a constellation. Constellations like these are mental constructs, not images of what really is happening in the family. It's always more effective not to have any mental images of your constellation before you set it up. Interrupting a constellation is the most difficult intervention in systemic psychotherapy, but it's also one of the most effective.

Also, when people ask if I want them to set up the families the way they were or the way they are now, I stop. If they start out setting up their constellation by trying to do what I want, they're not respecting the truth of their own soul. Or if they try to create images according to a conscious plan, they prevent the images that could help from emerging spontaneously. It's always more effective not to have any mental images of your constellation before you set it up.

Repeating Patterns in Constellations

Hellinger: Therapists who work with constellations, or plan to do so, are often interested in knowing whether there are patterns that occur in the constellations that have special meanings, or whether there are specific solutions to specific dynamics. My experience suggests that this is, in fact, the case. However, the current state of the work is such that these are only working hypotheses. If I were to list my hunches, that might lead to misunderstandings and to the hypotheses being turned into conclusions. I want to guard against anything that interferes with people learning to *see* for themselves what's going on. I'm convinced that the best learning comes from personal experience.

As a general rule of thumb, it's better for therapists to work on the assumption that each constellation is unique and requires a unique resolution that can be discovered only in a sensitive dialogic process with the participants.

Constellations of Other Relationships

Hellinger: You sometimes can use constellations to try to understand the hidden dynamics in other relationship systems. Group participants can be set up to represent members of an institution, of the firm where one works, of one's profession, or of other important areas of one's life. In one seminar, a participant who had a constant sense of heaviness was asked what was burdening him. He set up a constellation with himself, psychoanalysis, lightness, medicine, and spirituality. Then he put them in an order so that each had an appropriate place in his life.

This technique can also be useful when a person has two professions, or when the parents come from two different countries or cultures. Setting up situations like this allows the importance of both elements to be acknowledged, and still lets you find the appropriate balance of the two. The constellations are an excellent method for seeing larger systemic wholes, for getting an overview.

Constellations with Couples

Hellinger: When a couple at a seminar wants to work on their relationship, I first have one of them, and then the other, set up their relationship using the same representatives. The representatives stay standing, and after the first constellation, the other partner moves them to new positions. Sometimes you can see that one or the other is avoiding setting up the constellation so that the issues are clearly visible. In cases like that, the representatives' comparisons of how they felt in the two constellations are especially important.

When partners join together, each brings an internalized system. For example, if a woman has internalized a distorted or dysfunctional family system, then the man's perceptions of her will be distorted, as will be her perceptions of him. When both partners set up their relationship and the important members of their families of origin, they're confronted with a more complete picture of their partner and a more objective reality. When the internalized systems are brought into order, then their mutual perceptions are also more appropriate. That has a very powerful effect on the relationship.

Summary of Things to Consider

The following is a summary of the basic points to be considered in setting up constellations and in seeking resolutions.

Guidelines for Protagonists

- Set up a constellation only when there's a burning question and a true need. Curiosity alone is not enough.

- As the representatives are chosen, it's useful to arrange them in their natural order—parents first and then the sequence of the siblings. Before the constellation itself is begun, it's useful to repeat everyone's role, to detect and avoid confusion.

- Avoid characterizations and information about how persons acted or thought. For this work, only information about actual events is helpful—illnesses, physical handicaps, separations, and deeds that had consequences for the person's life. Characterizations of the members of your family interfere with the representatives' ability to sense the effect of the family dynamics.

- Center yourself and orient yourself toward the "feel" of the family. Your ideas and plans about how to set up the family interfere with sensing the information that helps. The constellation will emerge only as you go through the process of setting it up. Allow yourself to be surprised by what emerges.

- As you look for the right place for each representative, take the person by the hand or arm and go with the person to his or her place so that you can "feel" where the person belongs. Moving him or her a few inches can make a big difference.

- Search for the proper place, but don't sculpt gestures or movements, or tell the person where to look.

- After you've set them up, go around the outside of the constellation once, make fine adjustments, and say, once again, whom everyone is representing.

Guidelines for Representatives

- Gather yourself and concentrate your attention on your reactions to being in this place. Your job is to let the position affect you and to report that as clearly and concisely as you possibly can.

- Avoid coming to conclusions about what you think you should feel based on what you see. If you feel nothing at all, then say that.

- Say whatever you notice about how this place affects you, regardless of what it might be—especially when the feeling goes against your personal values and sense of right and wrong.

- Don't worry about whether or not the sensations are your personal reaction or a response to the situation. The therapist will sort that out.

- Report what you feel, but guard against interpreting your feelings. Trust them as they come.

- Don't have any intentions other than to report accurately how the position affects you. This may include certain ideas or images that occur to you. With experience, you'll develop a clear sense of what needs to be said and what can be left out.

Guidelines for Therapists

- Your orientation is toward finding a resolution. You must seek it, but you can't create it. It's not your job to create a resolution, but to seek the one that suggests itself from what you actually see in the constellation.

- Look for those who have been excluded and forgotten, but who still have an effect on the system.

- You must stand by all those in the system who have been vilified, hated, scorned, shut out. In cases of abuse, that will often be the perpetrator. Resolution requires that the system be completely represented.

- Look for those who want to go, those who must go, and those who must be allowed to go.

- Trust the reports of the representatives.

- Trust your own perceptions, even when they are at variance with those of the representatives.

- Stop the constellation when you notice that:
  the protagonist isn't sufficiently serious;
  the protagonist isn't centered and making good contact with each representative;
  the protagonist isn't seeking the "feel" of the constellation;
  important information is missing;
  you can't see a resolution.

- Keep it simple; use the minimum number of persons necessary to find resolution.

- Pay attention to the mood of the group. It the group isn't serious and gathered, something is wrong.

Suggestions for Seeking a Resolution

- Whoever entered the system first has precedence over those who came later. Watch the order of precedence. It runs clockwise, the later persons standing to the left of the earlier one. Parents have equal ranking, but which of them stands first varies from family to family according to their function in the family.

- Between two systems, the later system has precedence over the earlier one. Thus, the present family has precedence over the family of origin, the second marriage has precedence over the first, and so on. When a person has a child with another person during a marriage, this second relationship has precedence over the first.

- When a man and a woman are set up facing each other, that's an indication that their sexual intimacy has been disrupted.

- When a mother chooses a woman to represent her son, suspect systemic pressure toward homosexuality.

- When one of the participants has an urge to leave the room or the constellation, suspect suicidal tendencies.

- When one of the parents had an earlier relationship with firm bonding, the new partner often needs to stand between him or her and the old partner; otherwise, there's no separation from the old relationship. This can get complicated when bonding has taken place with several persons since they all form one large system. There are many exceptions, especially when there are children in one or more of the relationships.

- When all of the representatives are facing in the same direction, look for a missing person standing in front of them.

Additional Considerations

Participants in our groups who have come from tribal cultures in various parts of the world have commented that our use of these constellations is like reinventing the wheel. Native healers in many cultures have utilized related methods for making visible the hidden systemic dynamics operating in relationship systems. This feedback is gratifying. Obviously, the cosmologies and world views of many native cultures are more holistic and systemic than the linear cause-and-effect thinking that has dominated Western thought for several centuries. If the therapeutic use of these constellations has the unexpected side effect of building bridges and increasing understanding among these various thought worlds, we will be very pleased indeed. [H.B.]

STORIES THAT HEAL

Question: The stories and anecdotes you tell are very beautiful. I often don't understand them, but they still have a powerful hypnotic effect on me.

Hellinger: When I tell people that they should do this or can't do that, they owe it to their autonomy and sense of honor to refuse. If I have methods for indicating where change is possible that don't require them to give up their autonomy, then they can listen to my offer and decide for themselves what's appropriate for them. That's what telling stories does. They can listen to the stories without committing themselves to change. They can then take from the story whatever they need and throw away the rest. They don't need to get into a conflict with me; in fact, they can forget me altogether. When we watch a film, we forget who's operating the projector. We just watch the film and then go home.

Stories About Bed-Wetting

A father asked me what he could do to help his daughter stop wetting the bed. I told him he could tell her how glad he was to have married her mother—no big deal, just a kind of throw away sentence in the context of another conversation. Then he should tell her a story she already knew well, but with some minor variations, for example, Little Red Riding Hood.

Little Red Riding Hood went to her grandmother's house, and as she got there, she noticed that the roof had a leak and the entrance to the house was getting wet. So Little Red Riding Hood went into the barn and got some straw to stop up the hole so that the entrance wouldn't get wet. Then she went into the house with her basket of goodies. Her grandmother was very happy to see her, and they had a wonderful party together.

Or Snow White: One of the dwarfs came to Snow White and said, "There's a leak in my room and the rain drips in." Snow White told him not to worry, that she'd take care of it. She looked at the roof and saw that there was a loose shingle, up high where the very much smaller dwarf couldn't reach it. She stretched up on her tippy toes, higher than he could reach, and put it back into place. The dwarf didn't even thank her because once everything was all right, he forgot all about it.

Or a story about a water faucet that dripped and dripped until Snow White turned it off. Or, a little girl was sitting on the toilet when a strange man opened the door and looked in. When he noticed her there, he quickly closed the door and went away, and the little girl, who had been holding her breath, let it out.

Do you understand the hypnotherapeutic background of the intervention of the last story? When she imagines the strange man coming in, the little girl automatically constricts the sphincter muscle of her bladder. That's a well-known intervention from Milton Erickson.

Six months later, the father reported in a supervision group what had happened. The intervention had been successful, but most interesting for him was his little daughter's reaction to the deviations in the stories. Normally, like many small children, she would have insisted that the stories be told exactly, but she didn't protest about these deviations.

His experience tells us something important about psychotherapeutic interventions: *Because he found a nonintrusive and respectful way to talk with her about wetting the bed by telling her the stories*, his little daughter felt his respect and didn't need to guard against his intervention. There was no capitulation or loss of face for her. Her father acted in a way compatible with his love, and in that space of nonintrusive trust, something could change without its being necessary to talk about it directly.

WORKING THROUGH IMAGES THAT BIND AND CREATING IMAGES THAT LIBERATE

Hellinger: In therapy, you often observe that people are living out certain inner images or patterns. Transactional Analysis calls those images *scripts*. The images have two different origins: Some arise out of personal experiences and trauma and some out of systemic entanglements.

When a child has a traumatic experience, it's often internalized and then organizes the child's later experiences. Many fairy tales and myths describe this kind of pattern; for example, *Hansel and Gretel, Little Red Riding Hood, The Little Match Girl, Sleeping Beauty*, and *Rumpelstiltskin.*

Sleeping Beauty for example, describes a pattern in which a girl stays "asleep" with the illusion that when she wakens after a 100 years, she'll still be 15 years old. The story actually encourages her to keep on sleeping while waiting for her prince. When it dawns on her that she's really getting older, she wakes up pretty quickly. Women who choose *Sleeping Beauty* as their favorite fairy tale are often identified with their father's former partner.

After working with fairy tales for some time, I realized something strange: Many of them contain images that limit us and the solutions they suggest are destructive illusions that serve to maintain the status quo. For many years, I've asked people to tell their favorite fairy tale, one with which they identify, and then to compare the fairy tale with their own situation. I've made some interesting observations.

When a person chooses a fairy tale about something a child can experience before the age of seven, the client's problems are most likely actual experiences. When people choose the story of *Rumpelstiltskin*, for example, their problems usually don't have to do with systemic entanglements, but with actual traumatic experiences.

The mother is missing in many fairy tales, but fairy tales are very clever and they distract us from the essential message. In *Rumpelstiltskin*, the diversion is the sentence, "Lucky for me that no one knew that Rumpelstiltskin is my name." For the people who chose it, *Rumpelstiltskin* was an image for the experience of being given away or abandoned; for example, the experience of a girl who was abandoned by her father after her mother died or left, and who, in her turn, abandoned her own son. A few had a sibling who was given away. When I suspect that might be the case, I tell a variation of the story that gives them a chance to recognize the hidden dynamic.

Rumpelstiltskin

The queen sent messengers to the far corners of her realm to discover the name of the little man. After searching day and night for many months, a messenger returned just in time and told the queen that he had discovered what she requested. She wanted to know the name immediately, but he declined, saying that he could only tell her when the little man came for her child.

At the appointed time, the little man came to get the child. He asked the queen, "Do you know my name?"

The queen asked the messenger waiting at her side, "What's his name?" He said, "Rumpelstiltskin."

"Rumpelstiltskin," said the queen. "But that's the name of my handicapped brother who was given away!"

The second kind of pattern reflected in fairy tales arises out of systemic entanglements rather than from direct personal experience. When clients identify with stories that only adults can experience, for instance, *Othello* or *The Odyssey*, my experience is that they're most likely identified with someone in their family system. There are many famous stories and myths of this type that fascinate children and adults, although they can't say why. I believe the stories have to do with another person who played an important role in the life of the family, someone who suffered tragedy or misfortune, who was shut out of the family, or who left to make place for some-one else.

Such stories are literary images of real-life events that have in-fluence on the life of the family system. Telling the story allows the missing person to be present, even if only in representational form.

In therapy, it's possible to identify the inner images that bind you and those that liberate you, regardless of whether they're related to personal experiences or to systemic dynamics. One method I devel-oped to help clients to identify the script or the image that's impor-tant for them is to tell them the following story.

All the World Is a Stage

Once upon a time, a man decided that the time had come to retire. He had worked hard and it was time to do something good for him-self. He left his home and went somewhere else, wandered around a while, and came to a house with a sign in big letters: "Theater of the World."

He thought, "This is the right place for me," and bought a ticket. It was a bit expensive, but he told himself it didn't matter. He went into the theater, sat down in a comfortable chair, leaned back, and waited. The lights went down, the curtain opened, the performance began. As he watched, he thought, "I know this piece from literature. That's absolutely nothing new at all." As he continued to watch, he noticed that it was a play in which he had played the leading role.

Ask yourself, "What's the name of the play?" It's a play that can be found in literature, a book, a play, a film, a story of someone's life. When you discover the name of the piece, it's a bit of a surprise and a little embarrassing.

HEALING RITUALS

Rituals that heal arise out of love and are performed in the service of love. Rituals that seek to change reality for any other reason don't heal. Healing rituals involve movement and they're effective in therapeutic settings only when the sincerity of all participants sup-ports the completion of the ritual movement. Therapeutic rituals of healing are offerings made to clients that, when properly performed, can change the systemic dynamics that shape their lives. That is, the rituals performed in the therapeutic situation can change the inner images that organize a client's experience of the world, and may also affect the client's situation at home. Clients frequently report that after performing a healing ritual in a therapy group, the behavior of the other members of their family changed. Completing reaching out, reliving birth, and bowing down are three highly effective healing rituals.

Completing "Reaching Out" Toward an Appropriate Goal

Question: You often speak about "bringing the reaching out to its goal." Can you explain what you mean by that?

Hellinger: There are two basic situations that lead to difficulties in relationships. One is an unconscious identification with someone else in the system. The second dynamic is an interruption of the natural movement of "reaching out toward." That movement can't develop properly when the natural reaching-out movement of the young child toward someone the child loves was interrupted— through death, illness, circumstances, or other experiences. Such interruptions are accompanied by strong feelings of hurt, rejection, despair, hate, resignation, and grief. These feelings overlay the primal love, but they're just the reverse side of love. When young children can't reach the person they love, they have a strong tendency to feel rejected, as if there were something wrong with them, and they stop practicing the movement.

Whenever such persons want to reach out to another person later in life, their memories of hurt unconsciously emerge and interrupt their movement, and they react with the same hurt as before. That's not a primary hurt that supports appropriate reaching out toward someone who could give what is needed, but secondary feelings that prevent the movement from developing and from reaching its goal.

Sometimes an interrupted reaching-out movement manifests as muscle tension, headache, or self-destructive behaviors; for example, "I'll never show weakness," or "Nothing really can help me." Instead of carrying on with the movement until it reaches its goal, such a person draws back or goes into a circular "approach/avoidance" pattern. That's the basis of neurotic behavior. When a person becomes angry at the point at which the reaching-out movement gets interrupted and the therapist encourages the expression of the anger instead of going back to the basic love and trust, the interruption of the movement is reinforced.

The expression of emotions that cover and protect the more painful earlier ones doesn't bring resolution. Resolution comes only when the movement reaches its goal and is completed. This is possible in a therapeutic setting by accompanying the person back to the point at which the interruption occurred, and then helping the person to complete it. The therapist, or another member of the group, can represent the parent and the client then actually practices and completes the movement. When he or she has made a new experience of completing the movement, then other reaching-out movements are also easier. Often the entire process lasts only 15 to 20 minutes.

Among other techniques for completing such movements are Hypnotherapy, Holding Therapy, and some forms of body or movement work. What I do is a combination of what I learned in Primal Therapy Neuro-Linguistic Programming (NLP), and Hypnotherapy. Primal Therapy involves working through the primal pain of the parents not being there in some way. The primal pain develops where the movement of reaching out is interrupted. The pain confirms that the reaching-out movement has been interrupted, but it solves nothing. Instead of concerning myself with facilitating the expression of the pain, I work to bring the reaching-out movement to completion, and then love spontaneously flows.

Question: I'm interested in your distinction between completing an unfinished situation from the past by expressing the feelings of anger that accompanied it and completing the situation by completing the interrupted movement of reaching out. Could you say more about that, please?

Hellinger: I make a distinction, as we already discussed, between feelings that originally were appropriate reactions to some situation and feelings that distract or maintain an incomplete situation. When someone is abused or injured, then saying that it hurts is an appropriate reaction and may help to finish the situation. But most of the aggression that comes up in a therapy situation actually maintains the interruption of the reaching-out movement. If you look, you can see whether or not the expression of an emotion facilitates resolution. The long-term effect of expressing secondary anger is destructive. Resolution in relationships with parents occurs only when the parents are taken as they are, and that means mastering the reaching-out movement.

Reliving Birth

Question: You occasionally allow someone to relive his or her birth. When do you do that?

Hellinger: I do that when the problem concerns a personal experience or trauma. For example, when there's a birth trauma, the reaching-out movement to the mother is already interrupted at birth. Then it's appropriate for clients to relive their birth, to reestablish a bond to the mother and father, and to recite a "Thanksgiving at the Dawn of Life."

Reaching out to our mother and the experience of being accepted by her is the most fundamental and intensive experience of relationship we can have. Even when the primary bonding to the mother didn't succeed in childhood, many people are still able to reestablish bonding through a healing ritual of reliving their birth and then being held appropriately.

Question: How do you do that, exactly?

Hellinger: I use an integration of NLP and Primal Therapy, connecting a good experience to a negative one so that they balance out. It's actually very simple, but the timing is critical. When you recognize the right moment for the client, you really don't have to do much at all. I just say, "Go back slowly in time through your life, and when you come to a place where you stop, just stay there." Then, after a minute or so, a client will start to sob or weep, and I ask, "How old are you now? What's happening?" If it's appropriate for the client, he or she will lead you to the birth experience. I help the client to relive the experience in a good way and I hold the person securely (or have another member of the group do so) so that he or she feels safe no matter what feelings come up. Sometimes, after this kind of work, I invite people to look at the representative of their mother or father, and recite the "Thanksgiving at the Dawn of Life."

Thanksgiving at the Dawn of Life

Dear Mama/Mother
I take everything that comes from you,
all of it, with its full consequences.
I take it at the full price it cost you
and that it costs me.
I will make out of it something good in memory of you—
to thank and honor you.
What you did must not have been in vain.
I hold it close and in my heart,
and if I am permitted, I will pass it on
—as you have done.

I take you as my mother,
and you may have me as your child
(son, daughter)
You are my only mother and I am your child.
You are big , and I am little.
You give, I take, dear Mama.
I'm glad that you took Daddy as your husband.
You both are the right parents for me.

Dear Daddy/Father
I take everything that comes from you,
all of it, with its full consequences.
I accept it at the full price it cost you
and that it costs me.
I will make out of it something good in memory of you—
to thank and honor you.
What you did must not have been in vain.
I hold it close and in my heart,
and if I am permitted, I will pass it on
—as you have done.
I take you as my father,
and you may have me as your child
(son, daughter)
You are my only father and I am your child.
You are big , and I am little.
You give, I take, dear Daddy.

I'm glad that you took Mama as your wife.
You both are the right parents for me.

There's no better feeling than being accepted after one's birth, so I help clients find the best possible experience, the experience of being accepted after birth, and use that as an anchor to help them to deal with whatever traumatic experiences they may have.

After we establish the experience of being accepted at birth, I let them return to the present through their memories, through all of the traumas. In this way, the negative experiences are contained and transformed by the more fundamental positive one. All of the later childhood traumas can be worked through at one time in using these anchoring compensations. I accompany them into their traumas and let them look at each experience until they're finished. Then I move on to the next situation. Sometimes a lot of analytic hours can be condensed into one session, but that's individual therapy as opposed to systemic therapy. It's the second aspect of my work that complements the systemic work.

Bowing Down and Standing Up

The ritual of bowing down before the appropriate person, paying homage, restores balance and order. In our culture, this movement has become difficult for many people; bowing down as an act of respect is easily confused with bowing down as an act of unhealthy submission. When we bow down and pay obeisance to someone who deserves to receive our honoring gesture, the soul and the body respond with release and a sense of lightness. It feels good and it has a good effect.

When we refuse to pay our obeisance to someone who has a legitimate right to receive it, the body and the soul respond with constriction, with a sense of effort and heaviness. The reasons for our refusal are irrelevant.

When families don't follow the orders of love, the children must learn to ignore their own souls and later they won't be able to recognize what's true and right for them. They may refuse to bow down before the persons for whom it's appropriate, and they frequently stubbornly insist on honoring persons it isn't appropriate for them to honor.

Like reaching out, bowing down is a movement of both soul and body. It can be completed most easily in a constellation in which the whole of the family system is represented. The completeness of the family system legitimatizes the movement.

Fall on Your Knees

A woman at a workshop told of her difficult relationship with her father. She related many horrible things he had done to her and to her mother. As she prepared to set up the constellation of her family, the therapist asked if anyone in his family had died early. She answered, "Yes. He had seven brothers and a sister who died in the war. His parents also were killed. He was the only member of the family who survived."

As representatives for the deceased were placed in a semicircle behind the representative of her father and the weight of his fate became visible for everyone, the woman spontaneously broke into deep sobbing. She covered her face with her hands and dropped her head onto her breast. After the intense sobbing had passed, the therapist directed her attention to the spontaneous movement of her head, and suggested she complete it.

She turned her attention inward, sensing the direction in which the movement wanted to go. She fell to her knees and placed her forehead on the floor between her upturned hands. She remained in that position for a long while, weeping.

In the following group four months later, she reported that, although she was in her mid-40s, she unexpectedly had become pregnant.

The movement of bowing down isn't completed until the person stands up and goes on his or her way. Appropriate bowing down frees love to flow.

ROUNDS

Question: You mostly do therapy in groups, yet your groups are different from anything I've experienced before. Can you say something about that?

Hellinger: My groups differ from the usual psychodynamic group in that members are not encouraged to interpret and confront one another. To replace this interaction between members, I do rounds. In a round, each participant has an opportunity to report what he or she is experiencing or working on, one after the other. I seldom work with an individual in a round for more than 10 minutes, but these short interactions have continuity, building on one another over the course of a seminar. The result is that some interventions with people last four or five days. I work in small doses that leave a lot of time in between for personal reflection so that no one is overflooded and no one is under pressure to do more than is possible at any moment.

In group dynamic psychotherapy, every participant can interpret everyone else. Everyone is exposed and vulnerable to everyone else. When participants do not have very strong personalities (or are not experienced in group work), they get caught up in group dynamics, which act as a collective defense, and certain important themes systematically get shut out.

Groups have a strong tendency to adopt certain principles and to make them into a group rule; for example, "Nothing can be done in this group without the consensus of all members." Consensus is important in the life of a group, but when it becomes an absolute rule, it's destructive. Then the objections of those people who don't seriously desire to explore something in themselves interrupt the process of the whole group and hinder others from doing the work they came to do. If the principle that "disturbances have priority" becomes an absolute rule, then anyone can disrupt the group, no matter how trivial the "disturbance."

The use of the group round has the advantage that interactions between members of the group are discouraged. No one can interfere with someone else's work. No one is attacked; no one can be blamed or praised. (Praise is just as damaging to group process as is blame. It directs the participants' attention away from their actual experiences and toward their effect on the other members of the group.) The round method allows everyone to feel trust in the process within the group, to be able to present their themes, and to work with those themes in a safe context.

This respect for the individual and the loving and supporting posture establish an unconscious solidarity within the group that has a more spiritual quality than that which is possible within a group-dynamic-oriented psychotherapy. There is, of course, also a certain group dynamic, but group resistance doesn't develop as strongly.

Transcript of a Round

The following is a partial transcript of a group round on the third morning of a six-day seminar. Early in the round, a constellation was made of the family of origin of one of the participants and most of the comments having to do with that constellation have been omitted. The transcript begins somewhat later in the round.

Sarah: I had an experience during a walk yesterday. I walked along a stream and suddenly I had the feeling that I had done something wrong. It was a very intense feeling. I felt guilty. I climbed up the mountain and came out of the forest, and it was suddenly very bright. I felt lighter and lighter, and the evening fog began to rise from the meadows. *(Pauses thoughtfully.)*

Hellinger: I want to say something about what you experienced. If you recognize and accept personal guilt, you no longer feel it as guilt. It gets transformed into a powerful force for action. You still know about your guilt, but it doesn't oppress you as guilty feelings. Guilty feelings develop at the point at which you refuse to act responsibly with respect to your guilt. Then you're cut off from the power to act that the guilt gives you. When you open yourself fully to your personal guilt, then you have a source of support for doing good.

Your image beautifully portrays this. You let yourself feel your guilt, you opened yourself to it, and you felt lighter. Only the support for doing good remains. You can do things now that you wouldn't have been able to do if you had blocked your guilt.

Whenever I feel guilty and try to atone for something I've done, I feel tight and limited. When I allow my guilt to empower me, the effect is totally different. For example, when I do something that reconciles victims and perpetrators, or when I do something that helps someone else, then something comes out of the victim's sacrifice.

If this were not a training group, and if you were not a therapist, Sarah, I wouldn't say anything at all, because everything important has already happened.

There's a famous story about the secrets and the wisdom of the world. It's told that they're all written in the sibylline books and are stored in a hidden cave in Italy. If anyone were to find the way to the cave and open it to learn the wisdom of the world, all the books would dissolve. Whatever is essential shies away from our curiosity, and the great secrets and mysteries of Being protect themselves.

Angela: I'm still thinking about being centered. I remember a piece I once read about prayer, the five qualities of prayer: trust, centering, gratitude, responsibility, and something else . . . faith. I really liked the article and the words, but I always have the same question: How do I recognize centering? I always have anxiety that. . . .

Hellinger *(interrupting):* I'll tell you something about centering. Some people close their eyes in an attempt to empty themselves, and they call that centering. I find that strange. Centering happens when I open my eyes and ears and take in the richness of the world all around me, and allow it to order itself in me. That's gathering and centering. Anything else, Angela?

Angela: No, that's enough.

Joseph: I am filled with thoughts and feelings, and I pass.

Ruth: I also.

Steven: I'm still thinking about what you said to Sarah. *(Looks depressed.)*

Hellinger: I don't quite trust you, Steven.

Steven: I'm really not in a good place at all. *(Shrugs his shoulders.)*

Hellinger: Right! You're leading us on a wild-goose chase. *(Steven remains withdrawn, silent, thoughtful. Long pause.)* What are your children going to do if you do commit suicide? *(Pause)* You owe the living resolution, Steven. *(Silence)* I'll tell you a story.

Love

Once upon a time, a man dreamed in the night that he heard the voice of God saying to him, "Rise up, take your son, your only and beloved son, and go with him to the top of the mountain I will show to you and make a sacrifice of him to me there."

The next morning, the man arose, and looked at his son, his only and beloved son; looked at his wife, the mother of his son; and then he looked at his God. He took his son and went with him to the top of the mountain God showed to him and he built an altar there. There he heard another voice, and instead of his son, he sacrificed a sheep.

> How does the son look at his father?
> How the father his son?
> How the wife her husband?
> How the husband his wife?
> How do they look at God?
> And how does God—if there is a God—look at them?

Another man dreamed in the night that he heard the voice of God saying to him, "Rise up, take your son, your only and beloved son, and go with him to the top of the mountain I will show to you and make a sacrifice of him to me there."

The next morning, the man arose and looked at his son, his only and beloved son; looked at his wife, the mother of his son; and then he looked at his God. He looked his God in the face and answered, "I will not do that."

> How does the son look at his father?
> How the father his son?
> How the wife her husband?
> How the husband his wife?
> How do they look at God?
> And how does God—if there is a God—look at them?

That's the end of the story, but I'll add a little more just for you, Steven.

And a third man dreamed in the night that he had heard the voice of God, and so on. He got up, looked at his son, took him to the mountain, built an altar, drew a knife, and killed him. And when he got home, he killed himself.

My comment is: It's a pity about the boy.

Suicide is a poor substitute for responsibility and guilt. That kind of atonement is just as nasty as the deed itself, and it's far easier than acting appropriately in the first place. So, Steven, I've read the riot act to you. Anything else? *(Steven shakes his head.)* Good. Irene, what's happening with you?

Irene: During the meditation before the lunch break I remembered that I was given the name of a child of my grandmother's who had died very early. I have the feeling that I'm carrying something around with me.

Hellinger: Oh! I wonder where you got that feeling from, but if it's important to you *(pause)*, there's a magic formula for situations like this. Over the years, I've discovered several magic formulas for different situations. I don't understand them, but they work nevertheless. I experience it as a great gift when one of the sentences is given to me. The formula you can use is: "Dear Aunt, you are dead. . . ."

Irene *(interrupting with amusement):* . . . and I'm alive!

Hellinger: No. You have to be sincere if you want to know, or I'll move on. *(Long pause. Irene remains sarcastically amused and silent. He speaks to the group.)* Okay, she's let the moment escape. I can't tell her now. We'll go on.

Lars: The last constellation touched me very much, and I'm still thinking about it. Other than that, I've got a headache.

Hellinger: You get what you deserve.

Lars: What do you mean?

Hellinger: Goethe said it beautifully, "Everyone is the smith who forges his own misfortune." *(Laughter)*

Eric: I notice that I have the desire to set up my family. I've always treated them as if they were unimportant, but now I see how important they really are. The exchange with Steven gave me a push.

Hellinger: Okay. We'll do it later.

Fred: I have a question about working with clients. The mother of one of my clients tried to kill her children. She didn't actually do it, but she did severely abuse them. My question is: Is there a way for this daughter to find some reconciliation with her mother? At present, she wants nothing to do with her. She feels very intensely that she's been victimized by her own mother. It would be a great relief for her if she were to find some peace with her mother, but I am very cautious when things like this have happened.

Hellinger: There is a way. It's also a magic formula. When she's ready to make peace with her mother, she can say, "Dear Mama, I agree to it." *(Silence)*

Fred *(pause):* I think I understand, but will she?

Hellinger: No, the sentence isn't exactly right yet, but it would go in that direction. Maybe it would be better to say, "Dear Mama, if that's my fate, I agree to it." Something along those lines.

Fred: Meaning that. . . .

Hellinger: No! No meaning. As soon as you comment on one of these formulas, they lose their power. What was the sentence?

Fred: "Dear Mama, if that's my fate, I agree to it."

Hellinger: A child doesn't have to forgive the parents. That's a different thing altogether. An abused child can say, "That was very bad," and the child can say, "I'm not allowed to forgive you for it," but he or she doesn't have to be damaged and bitter about what happened. The child can say, "You have to carry the burden of what you did."

Abused children usually take the guilt and the consequences of the abuse onto themselves. It's much more difficult to leave the guilt and the consequences with the parents, and also the responsibility. But children cause themselves additional damage when they feel that they have the right to get even with their parents, in the sense of, "All right, now you're going to pay for what you did to me." That has very damaging consequences. When children file a complaint or go to court against their parents, they pay dearly for it, regardless of what the parents did.

Something else, Fred?

Fred: Yes, I have another client whose father was a high-ranking officer in the SS. She never met him. Her mother went back to Austria. She suddenly developed a recurring idea to kill herself.

Hellinger: Who? The client or her mother?

Fred: The client. I've got the idea that. . . .

Hellinger: What happened to the father?

Fred: He had a very strange story. He was missing in action, and they thought he was dead, but it later came out that he was a paraplegic and was living in northern Germany. He never contacted his family before he died.

Hellinger *(thoughtfully):* A sentence that might help her is something like, "Dear Father, I leave you to rest in peace." You can help her to get to the place where she can say it truthfully. It's also important for her not to want to know more. She shouldn't dig into his past trying to find out exactly what he did in the war. She can just say, "I accept your fate and your decision, and I leave you in peace with your fate and your decision and all the consequences they had for you."

Max: Nothing at the moment.

Vera: I'm on a roller coaster of feelings. This morning there was real pain, now I'm feeling good. I'll leave it at that for now.

Fred: I'm experiencing this as completely fascinating. Brilliant. I feel more connected to people than ever before. This richness is fantastic.

Hellinger: That's a man who can be amazed. That's good to see.

Fred: Yes, really. I never thought it could be so exciting.

Hellinger: Helen, you said that something else came to you. What do you want to say?

Helen: I've got a funny feeling that my husband, Carl, paid you the seminar fee for both of us. I would have liked to have given it to you myself.

Hellinger: Do you know what that is? We call that a diversionary tactic. *(Pause)* Who was the woman? *(Laughter. Bert Hellinger is referring to an earlier intuition that her facial expressions sometimes mimicked someone else.)*

Helen *(quietly and hesitant):* My mother?

Hellinger: Guessing doesn't help.

Helen: I don't know.

Hellinger: Okay, then set up your family of origin.
(Helen sets up her family. It emerges that she identifies with her father's first wife. She was Jewish and separated from Helen's father in 1938, emigrating to the United States, where she later remarried. In a moving sequence, a resolution is found. Bert Hellinger continues after all participants are again seated.)

Being Jewish is always important in Germany. That always has an enormously powerful effect on the family system. So, Helen, how are you doing?

Helen *(laughs):* Good. I feel really good.

Hellinger: So it was an identification with your father's first wife. What now?

Helen: That makes a lot of things clear to me.

Hellinger: Yes, you must say to your father, "I have nothing to do with your first wife. I belong to my mother. Only she is right for me." Now you're nodding already. Do you know what premature nodding means?

Helen: No.

Hellinger: There's a famous saying in Goethe's *Götz von Berlichingen*: "Tell your master, 'Kiss my ass.'" That's the most subtle form of defense. Do you notice how you're still defending? Look clearly at your father and say, "This is my mother and I stand with her." That makes you less important, but that's the price of happiness. You know the saying, "Small is, beautiful." *(Helen laughs)* Here comes the other expression, do you notice it? *(Helen nods affirmation.)* Anything else? *(Helen signals "No.")*

Alexis: I've had a really peaceful, warm feeling after both of the last two constellations. It's beautiful.

Hellinger: Yes, all of a sudden everything was clear and at peace.

Fred: When we look at what emerged in Helen's constellation, does it mean that her father has lost his right to have Helen's mother?

Hellinger: No, not at all. It means that her mother can't claim him fully, not at the price the first wife had to pay. Her mother must pull back just a little and inwardly acknowledge her debt to the first wife. That's a form of respect for the first wife's sacrifice, whatever that means in actual practice. *(To Helen)* But that's none of your business, Helen. You're already back in the old expression. It takes a while before an old face like that completely dissolves. *(Bert Hellinger makes a couple of mildly off-color jokes to divert the group's attention.)* Okay, let's take a break.

Irene *(before the break):* I remembered the sentence! I don't know it exactly, but I'm not mad at you any more for confronting me.

Hellinger: Yes, that was an effective confrontation. What is the sentence?

Irene: Dear Aunt, you're dead. I'm sorry. I'll stay a little while.

Hellinger: Now I'll tell you the real sentence. "Dear Aunt, you're dead. I'll live until my time comes, then I'll die too."

That's a sentence you can use in many situations, although I'm cautious to say it, because it could be used like a vending machine token and then it would lose its effect. For example, a second wife could say to a first wife, "You lost your husband, and I have him for a while before I too will lose him." That eliminates the superiority and arrogance. It unites on a very deep human level, on a level where the passing away of everything has a right to exist. Now we'll really take a break.

Transcript

BRINGING INTERRUPTED REACHING OUT
TO ITS GOAL

Brigid is a participant in a six-day seminar. She demonstrates feelings and reactions that are typical of persons whose reaching out has been interrupted. Some minor interactions have been omitted from the transcript.

Second Day, Morning

Brigid: Yesterday, I was feeling as if I were wearing armor, but today I feel more open and there's something very fragile coming up in me.

Hellinger: I'll be very careful with your fragility, Brigid. *(She begins to cry softly.)* Breathing helps. Breathe in, breathe out. Open your mouth so that the breath moves easily, so that it flows . . . breathe . . . breathe . . . everything goes pretty quickly with you, doesn't it?

Brigid: Not always.

Hellinger: You're not used to having someone take time for you? *(Brigid begins to sob. Pause.)* Bring your chair and sit here in front of me. *(Brigid moves closer to him. Hellinger takes tissues from his pocket and gives them to her.)* I'm prepared for every emergency. Come a bit closer . . . even closer . . . just a bit more . . . *(gently removes her glasses and holds her hands)* . . . close your eyes, open your mouth, and breathe easily and deeply, in and out. *(He lightly touches the tips of the fingers of his right hand to the upper end of her breastbone.)* Go as far back as the feeling goes, far far back, until you come to the place where it belongs and to the situation where it belongs . . . mouth open, breathe . . . *(Brigid continues breathing easily for about one minute.)* Accept it as it is, whatever it is. . . . *(After about two minutes more)* What's happening? How far back are you?

Brigid: I'm about six years old.

Hellinger: What's there?

Brigid: I'm traveling with my mother in a car. I want to lie in her lap, but she won't let me. She's very cross with me.

Hellinger: Okay, look at the scene. What did you call your mother as a child?

Brigid: Mama.

Hellinger: Say, "Mama, please."

Brigid *(very softly)*:   Mama, please.

Hellinger *(after a long pause, to the group)*:   So this is a situation of interrupted reaching out. Can you notice how the scene continues to influence her?
To Brigid: Go back farther. *(After a pause.)* Looks like you've gone about as far as you can now. *(To group)*: She made a decision early in the work not to go too far, and she's keeping her word to herself. *(After a pause, he leans toward her and looks at her very gently.)* Open your eyes. What shall we do with you? *(Brigid shrugs her shoulders, looks disappointed.)* Close your eyes again. Go with your own inner movement, go wherever it wants to take you. Withdraw inwardly from your mother, farther and farther from her. *(Brigid makes a sudden movement, turning her head to the left. Hellinger waits, then very gently turns her head, as if encouraging her to look at what she was avoiding, to the right.)* Keep breathing, breathing out with power, a little faster, not violently, just strongly. *(Brigid starts to cough.)* Instead of coughing, say something to your mother, whatever needs to be said.

Brigid *(softly)*:   No more, no more.

Hellinger: Say that again, a bit louder, "No more, no more." *(Hellinger reaches behind her with his right hand and, with a light touch of his fingertips, bends her upper body forward. She lays her head on his shoulder. He holds her as she sobs.)*
"No more, no more." *(Hellinger suggests that she put her arms around him, which she does.)* Breathe deeply, keep your mouth open . . . a bit faster . . . still faster . . . breathe out deeply. It isn't necessary to hold back your crying. *(Breathing gradually slows.)* *(To*

group): Brigid has chosen the smaller happiness. *(To Brigid):* How are you doing?

Brigid: Better *(pointing to her chest),* . . . more open.

Hellinger: You got stuck halfway, but you still made it farther than before.

Brigid: Halfway back?

Hellinger: Halfway to her. Like Goethe said, "Everyone creates their own unhappiness."

Brigid: I don't think that's what he said.

Hellinger: Oh no? *(Both laugh.)* Okay, good. *(Brigid stands up and returns to her seat.)* That was a situation in which the reaching out was interrupted, and we could all see what happened when she reached that point. My observation is that a lot of neurosis starts at the point of an interrupted reaching-out movement. In fact, I see neurosis as a circular movement that always returns to the point of interruption instead on moving on. As we remember the interrupted movement, feelings and memories come up, the decision we learned as children comes up, and then instead of completing the reaching out, we turn back to the starting point and start all over again. That's merry-go-round progress.

What do I do as a therapist with this kind of pattern? *(Pause)* Brigid got stuck and couldn't complete the interrrupted movement. We must be careful not to pretend that the work brought more than it did. But even though she didn't manage to complete her reaching out, she did get a peek. Now, I turn the work over to her loving heart. Agreed, Brigid?

Brigid: Yes *(smiling).*

Hellinger: Are there any questions about this work?

Participant: I didn't understand what you meant, "Turn it over to her loving heart."

Hellinger: You can't understand it, but she did. Trusting the heart, the good heart, is always a good method. It's really astonishing how often clients find a way that no therapist could find. And secretly, without saying that out loud here, I also turn her over to her mother's loving heart.

Participant: First you suggested to her that she reach out, and then that she withdraw.

Hellinger: It doesn't matter in which direction people move, whether they reach out or pull back. The main thing is that they're in motion. When reaching out doesn't work, then try the opposite. When a person starts to move, the movement reverses itself spontaneously. You go with what's there. She withdrew, and so I followed her natural movement. When she turned her head to the left, I had the image of her pulling away from her mother. When I gently turned her head to the right, feelings came up. I was following the movement as it emerged.

Participant: That was a correction?

Hellinger: No, I don't "correct" anything. It was more nearly a support for the movement that was already happening. That's when the sentence came, "No more." Her mother was clearly present for her at that moment in the work.

Participant: Can you give those of us who have less experience with body work some suggestions on how to recognize when a person is interrupting a reaching-out movement and when he or she is not?

Hellinger: Not really. You do it with careful observation, with *seeing*. Perhaps you'll get a chance to see other examples during the seminar. When you hold on to a theory, you make it difficult for yourself to see what's there. Seeing is much more important than any specific rules. I think I've said everything important about it; more wouldn't be helpful.

Later, Same Morning

Brigid: I'm taking it all in. My mood is changing constantly. One minute I'm having a feeling of warmth and compassion—also in my eyes *(gets teary)*, and then it switches. It's always changing, and when I reach out. . . .

Hellinger: That's very good, Brigid, very good. *(To group):* Do you see how her loving heart is working? Let your good heart work on it until it finds the solution.

Afternoon, Same Day

Brigid: I'm completely present. During the lunch break, I crawled into my bed and pulled the covers up. I tried to find a connection to my mother. That was very pleasant.

Next Morning

Brigid: I was awake a lot last night. I kept thinking about my family and my mother's family.

Hellinger: What happened in your mother's family?

Brigid: My mother's sister died of typhus, and six weeks before that, her father died. My mother was 10 when that happened.

Hellinger: Was her sister younger than your mother?

Brigid: She was older, the middle child. My mother had an older brother, too. I keep thinking about the atmosphere in my family, a kind of deadly silence. There was a lot of silence and stiffness. I just thought about something else: When I visit my parents with my children, that atmosphere is gone. My parents love my children, and the children fill their whole house with life. I remember something else, too, about sitting on her lap. When my parents come to visit us, both of the girls say, "Sit on lap, Grandpa. Sit on lap, Grandma." And they're allowed to do it.

Hellinger: What did your mother's father die of?

Brigid: It was some kind of bladder infection. He went into the hospital and didn't come out again. That was in 1938. Six weeks later, my mother's older sister died.

Hellinger: That's a shock for such a family.

Brigid: Yes. There's more too. I once did a constellation with another therapist, and I set my mother up way out on one side, looking away. I can't really imagine what all she must have experienced.

Hellinger: She may be following her sister and her father, but we can set it up now and we'll see. *(Brigid sets up her family. Additional* *information emerges that Brigid's father was the youngest of four children; his brother died in childhood and he has two living sisters.)*

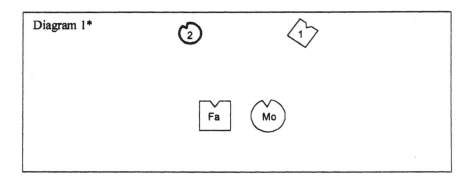

Diagram 1*

Hellinger: So, how's that for the father?

Father: I don't have any contact with my children, and my wife is just sort of there. I'm pretty much alone.

Mother: I feel very much alone. It's not good to see the children from behind. I can just barely feel my husband.

Brigid's Representative: I'm in a daze and feel like leaving. There's something behind me, but I don't know what.

Hellinger: The child who died in your father's family, was it a boy or a girl?

Brigid: I don't know.

Hellinger: What would be your guess?

Brigid: A girl.

Brother: I don't have contact with anyone. My legs are frozen completely stiff.

Hellinger *(to children):* Turn around and face your parents. What changes when you do that?

Brother: It's a bit lighter now.

---

*Legend: Fa—father; Mo—mother; 1—first child, a boy; 2—Brigid's representative.

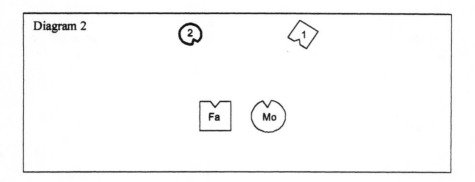

Brigid's Representative: I find it comfortable and I'm clearer in my head.

Father: Yes, I feel better toward my children, but there's still nothing going on with my wife.

Mother: The same for me.

Hellinger *(to parents):* Exchange places and see if that's different.

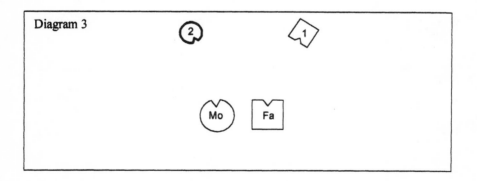

Father: Yes, my daughter is closer to me. That feels good.

Brigid's Representative: I'm feeling slightly excited about something.

Hellinger: How is it between the parents, better or worse?

Father: Worse.

Mother: I feel a little more alive.

Hellinger: We'll bring in the grandfather. *(Brigid places her pater-nal grandfather beside her father. The father and grandfather then experi-ment and find the best position behind the father.)*

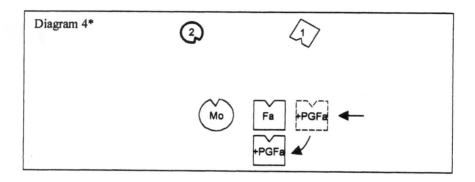

Brigid: I forgot something. My mother's father also died young, when my mother was eight years old. He had epilepsy after a war injury. He died from a seizure while he was working in the fields.

Hellinger: Put your mother's father behind her.

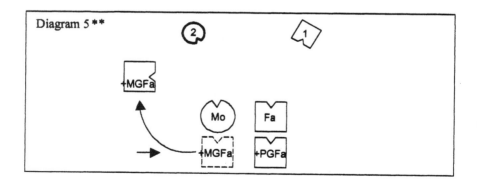

---

*Legend addition: +PGFa—paternal grandfather, died when Brigid's father was eight years old.
**Legend addition: +MGFa—maternal grandfather, died when mother was 10 years old.

Mother: As my husband's father came in, I felt a strong need to look. I was suddenly able to see my husband. Now that my father's there, the movement is more toward the left. Could he go over there, where I can see him? *(Hellinger moves representative of mother's father to left.)* That's better.

Father: That doesn't change anything in my relationship with my wife.

Brother: For me, my mother's father is very interesting. Since he's there, I find myself looking at him all the time.

Hellinger *(to Brigid):*   So that looks like your brother's identification. He's identified with your mother's father. *(Asks the parents, with their fathers, to exchange sides.)*

Brigid's Representative: That's a distinct relief. I can exhale and relax. As my mother's father was suddenly standing there, I had the feeling that I was standing across from so many men, but I didn't have any contact with my mother. There wasn't any other woman there. It's a little better now. My feeling toward my father is more relaxed. It's good when my mother's father is over there. When he was on my right, he was too close.

Hellinger: Put your mother's sister in the system, the one who died. *(Brigid places her deceased aunt behind her mother, to the right.)*
What does that change?

Mother: I'm uneasy.

Brigid's Representative: I'm looking more at her, and I can't see my father as well anymore.

Mother's Sister: I'm feeling an uneasy pull to my sister, too.

Hellinger *(placing aunt beside mother):*   What about that?

Mother: I'm getting warmer on this side *(toward husband)*. Its very nice. *(She moves closer to him, taking her sister with her.)*

Father: This place is ever so much better for me. I actually feel closer to my daughter, as well as to my wife.

Brigid's Representative: Yes, I can even see my mother, and I can see my father better. It's a complete picture, much better. Before, I was focused on my aunt.

Hellinger *(to Brigid's representative):* Stand over there next to your brother. How's that?

Brother: I'd like to exchange places with my sister. *(Brother and sister exchange places.)* That's better.

(The father wants to move away a bit. Hellinger places his deceased sister next to him. All representatives make minor adjustments, until all have a sense of balance within the system. He then asks Brigid to take her place in the constellation.)

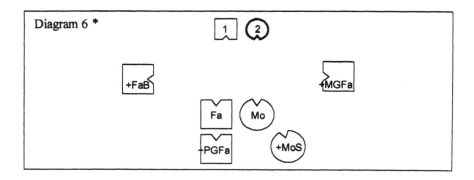

Brigid *(Looks intently at the system, especially at her mother):* Something is pulling me over there *(to the mother).*

Hellinger: It's okay to go there. *(Brigid slowly moves toward her mother and takes her in her arms.)* Brigid, if you're going to hug her at all, then hug her good and tight. *(Brigid holds her mother's representative very tightly, starts to rock back and forth.)* Calmly, calmly. Stay calm. Go slowly. Breathe deeply, mouth open. *(Hellinger brings the mother's sister to them and she holds them both in her arms. Brigid starts to cry.)* Breathe deeply with your mouth open, deeply in and . . . deeply out . . . inhaling is taking . . . no sound, Brigid . . . simply breathe in and breathe out, until you've had enough. *(Brigid starts to rush.)* No, no, Brigid. Take your time. Take all the time you need. In . . . and out . . . the silent breath has more power in it. *(Brigid does this naturally. Her body relaxes visibly. After a while, she looks around the room, and is radiant.)*

---

*Legend addition: +FaB—father's brother, died in childhood; +MoS—mother's sister, died when mother was 10 years old.

Okay, you can go back to your place. That's all, thank you. *(Everyone goes back to their seats.)*

Brigid: I'm feeling great. I feel free and my head is open and able to learn.

Hellinger: That was a beautiful movement.

Brigid *(pointing to her heart):* There's something moving here, as if it were opening.

Hellinger: Beautiful!

Brigid: Its getting freer. During the lunch break, I had such a feeling of hope that the work I did here will help me to feel more my age.

Hellinger: Surely!

Brigid: I don't want to say anything more about what happened.

Hellinger: No, that isn't necessary.

CHAPTER EIGHT

Specific Themes in
Systemic Psychotherapy

WORKING WITH DREAMS

Question: How do you work with dreams?

Hellinger: I don't work with dreams much, but when I do, I take a phenomenological, process-oriented view. I resist mythologizing dreams. Some therapists treat dreams as if they were messages from God, but I'm very sensitive to the distortion of reality that can occur in dream work and in hypnosis, especially the issue of false memory.

I remember one patient who "discovered" certain things in hypnotherapeutic dream work with a reputable hypnotherapist. As we reexamined the material, it became clear to us both that what had been "discovered" was actually invented, but it had already had a damaging effect in his life. When we reworked the material from a systemic perspective, we found something practical that he could do, and that had a very positive effect on the quality of his life. Mythological dream work and hypnosis don't get to that kind of practical action unless there's an understanding of system dynamics. If someone is avoiding doing what needs to be done, then talking about a dream isn't going to help.

Dreams are very adaptable. They adapt to the flow of energy in a person's life. If your energy is flowing into avoiding decisions and effective action, or into maintaining the status quo, then your dreams justify that posture. When you're using different techniques to put off doing what needs to be done and to justify your not acting, then your dreams do the same. You can recognize that kind of dream by the way people tell it. If people jump right into the telling of their dreams, without feeling, without respect for the dream, without an appropriate shyness and shame, then it's almost certainly one of those dreams.

I call those dreams *secondary dreams* to go with secondary feelings, and like secondary feelings, they serve to avoid whatever really is going on. Because it's "only a dream," people think that they can afford not to do anything. If you take such dreams seriously, you only reinforce the problem, and some part of the dreamer laughs at you for falling into the trap. It's similar when someone starts, "I dreamed about you last night. You were. . . ." Usually, the person just wants to take a poke at you.

I've got a great example of a secondary dream. A man dreamed that a hunting falcon saw a little bird, let it sing for a while, then held it carefully, circled high over the little bird's nest, and let it drop gently into the nest. He thought that was a wonderful dream.

His actual situation at home was that his wife had left him to live with another man. She came back three days a week to be with the children, and then returned to be with her friend for the other four days. And he accepted the situation, although he was deeply hurt. The dream described the man's situation perfectly. Instead of doing what a falcon appropriately does, his dream falcon carried the little bird tenderly back to its nest and dropped it neatly in. He had surrendered his wife to another, and she had fallen into somebody else's nest. The man thought it was a wonderful dream, a revelation. He didn't even notice that the dream only described his situation. It was a secondary dream. Secondary dreams are like bait, testing to see if you're going to bite. It's so easy to gossip about things in the images of dreams, instead of getting to work making the necessary changes in your life.

There's another kind of dream that I call a *primary dream*. Primary dreams are coded memories, and like primary feelings, they're not dramatic and loud. Dreams of water, for example, often carry the memory of birth. One woman dreamed that she was skiing with her daughter. As they started down the slope, she was holding her little daughter between her legs, and when they got to the bottom, the daughter fell into a lake. I asked her about her own birth. She said that she had arrived very suddenly while her mother was in the bathtub. So, the dream seems to be an example of a coded memory.

I also distinguish *shadow dreams*. These dreams show us the side of ourselves that we don't want to look at. We usually don't relate these dreams because we aren't ready to deal with what they tell us. They can, in fact, reveal a hidden side of us. When you want to work with such dreams, then it's necessary to take them seriously, to find a place in your heart for whatever you fear in the dream. That's the method of integration.

There are also *systemic dreams*. They don't have anything to do with the personal experience of the dreamer, but rather portray an unresolved situation in the family or in the extended family. They bring something to consciousness that's important to deal with in the family system. If the dreamer takes on the task of balancing the whole family system, then the consequences are usually disastrous.

Systemic dreams often have something brutal about them; they deal with murder, suicide, or death. The shadow of the system itself is often visible. When you try to interpret these dreams as if they were statements about the person, you abuse your client, making him or her personally responsible for something that's much larger.

Question: Would you give an example of a systemic dream? I don't get what you are driving at.

Hellinger: A man once dreamed that he found a body in his basement that was cut up into pieces. Then he called the police. He wanted to go into all of the details of the dream, about his unconscious murderous impulses and all that, but I interrupted him. I asked him who in his family had been murdered. He said that he didn't know and called his father. His father said, "I can't tell you on the telephone." What his father eventually told him was that shortly after he was born, his mother became pregnant again and complications developed. The hospital didn't have the proper facilities and the baby had to be killed and removed by dissecting it into pieces while it was still in her body. Although he didn't know about the death of his unborn sibling until he dreamed this dream, he had been unconsciously making a place for him or her in his life. He had always had two of everything—two apartments, two offices, two desks, and so on. That was the actual situation.

There's another thing that's interesting about this dream. Like most dreams, everything you need is in the first couple of sentences. The telling of a dream usually reaches its peak after about the second or third sentence. Everything that comes after that is just frosting on the cake and detracts from the power of the dream. The person relating a dream tends to become lost in the details. If you get people into the habit of telling dreams in a very concentrated way and to stop after the second or third sentence, then you have a better chance of getting a clear message with which to work.

There are dreams that do help, but they're mainly helpful to people who are already working on themselves. Such people receive additional support from their own depth. I call those dreams *meta-dreams*. The dreamer knows immediately what a meta-dream is about and it needs no further interpretation. Such dreams bring a solution into consciousness. Sometimes, when I'm working on a problem, meta-dreams provide a solution, or they show me the next step, but only if I'm prepared to demonstrate my trust in the dream by my subsequent actions.

So, if you want to work with dreams, it's very helpful to distinguish among the different types. Obviously, what I've said isn't a comprehensive theory of dream work. It's just a collection of certain observations that may help you to avoid some of the more common traps, and not set off in a nonproductive direction. It's in no way intended to replace other methods of understanding and working with dreams, but I do find it destructive when all dreams are treated as truth. There's a Chinese saying: "The wise man doesn't dream." He doesn't need dreams any longer.

Short Transcripts of Dream Work

Miriam: I keep thinking about a dream I've had three or four times. In it, I always worry about my youngest son.

Hellinger: So, tell the dream as if you were dreaming it again.

Miriam: I'm with my youngest son in a large place of business, in the building in which my sister works. I'm busy with my sister. Suddenly I hear my son calling. He's very far away and I can't find him. When I find him, he's choking. He has broken into a room into which adults can't go, and I hear his voice getting fainter and fainter.

Hellinger *(interrupting):* Your dream, strangely, makes no impression on me. How old is your son?

Miriam: He's 10 years old.

Hellinger: Did a child in your extended family system die?

Miriam: My grandparents both came from large families with a lot of children. My grandmother had 11 children herself. I don't know whether there was a stillbirth or something like that among all those kids. As far as I know, there was not *(long pause)*.

Hellinger: That's strangely distant. It just doesn't touch the heart, in spite of the dramatic images. I couldn't see you in the dream as you were telling it. There was no movement, no sense of presence. The dream leaves me cold.

Miriam: When I woke up, I immediately imagined my son in a good situation.

Hellinger: The interpretation that the people in a dream like this actually represent themselves is old-fashioned. It's a kind of *Popular Romance* interpretation.

Miriam: It actually only partially corresponds to reality. I never worry about my elder son, even when he doesn't come home at night. I'm always sure he's okay.

Hellinger: That's a distraction. What did I say?

Miriam: A *Popular Romance* interpretation.

Hellinger: Do you worry about your younger son in other situations?

Miriam: Yes, very often. *(Her mood shifts, she becomes thoughtful.)* I just remembered that my pregnancy with him was very difficult, and that I had to stay in bed a lot. Then, after he was born, he was ill. He had a very serious malfunction of his digestive system. It took a year and a half before it began to function properly.

Hellinger: Let's go ahead and consider your dream to be a memory. However, something's missing from the whole dream gestalt. That's the reason that it keeps trying to finish and doesn't leave you in peace. First, let's look at the general situation. When a trauma is worked on in psychotherapy, the most important thing is usually forgotten—that the person survived. Unless that's acknowledged, the gestalt won't close and there's no resolution. So take a minute now, get a picture of your son in your mind, and let him feel how glad you are that everything turned out all right. Okay, Miriam? *(Miriam nods affirmation, and her work develops in a new direction.)*

Thomas: I had a terrible dream last night. I woke up in a cold sweat, and my heart was pounding. I have no idea what it has to do with.

Hellinger: Tell the dream as if it were happening right now.

Thomas: I am sitting with someone in a bus. He's driving the bus. I know that he's my friend. The bus is completely full. We start to go up a steep mountain.

Hellinger: Good. Start again.

Thomas: I am sitting or standing in a bus, and a friend is driving.

Hellinger: Good! That's enough. That's the point of the dream. *(Pause)* What's the solution?

Thomas: I could drive myself.

Hellinger: Okay. Change places with the driver. Anything else, Thomas?

Thomas: Yes, something still bothers me. My dreams always have the same endings. The beginnings may be different, but they end up the same. That bothers me.

Hellinger: So, tell how they end.

Thomas: They end up with chasms and cliffs, with anxiety about falling. There's always a fear of falling and of depth.

Hellinger: Okay. When you have this dream, support yourself by imagining yourself with your back leaning against your father.

Thomas *(after a pause):*   I did it just now. It's a completely different feeling.

Hellinger: Okay. That's the resolution. When a child's in danger in a dream, the person who can help is almost always the father. It doesn't matter whether the child is a boy or a girl. Of course, there are exceptions, but especially when the danger is suicide, or a tendency to pseudosuicidal accidents or to catastrophes, the person usually will feel safe next to the father. Sometimes the grandfather is needed, as well. It doesn't matter what the father did or didn't do, or whether or not the child knew him. There's strength in the masculine.

Joseph: I had a powerful dream. My youngest son goes into the water, falls backward, and I'm afraid he'll drown. I grab for him. I feel torn because I don't have much time to save him, and, at the same time, I have to work slowly so that I don't lose sight of him. I'm afraid his clothes will rip. Then I get him back and I'm very happy. He's alive and he starts to breathe, but I worry that he might have some damage.

Hellinger: That's a secondary dream. It dramatically describes the problem without offering a solution. The solution is that *before* he falls in the water, you hold him affectionately in your arms. Agreed, Joseph?

Ralph: I fell asleep during the break, and I dreamed that I climbed a tall walnut tree. I climbed beyond the ladder into the higher branches so I could shake the branches and make the nuts fall. *(There's a quality of superficial boasting in his relating the dream.)*

Hellinger: That dream won't help you.

Ralph: And then. . . .

Hellinger: The dream won't help you. You don't respect it.

Ralph: It won't help? After the dream, I woke up with the feeling that I really wanted to crack the nuts.

Hellinger: Yes, after you woke, you wanted to crack the nuts. The image is violent, forcing things to happen. I don't work that way. I rarely work with a hammer.

Ralph: I really wanted to work.

Hellinger: There's no energy in your telling of your dream. If I stay with the dream image, you're shaking, not harvesting. The solution must come from outside. Perhaps you think I should do the work for you? That's a pretty poor basis for working together.

Ralph: No, I was certain that I wanted to crack the nuts myself. My feeling was that. . . .

Hellinger *(interrupting):* Let go of the image of cracking nuts. It doesn't help. Most dreams only affirm the problem, especially the dreams people immediately want to tell. They serve to rationalize failure.

Ralph: I was so certain that I was ready to tackle the problem.

Hellinger: That's it. Someone who is swimming around in his or her misery, always feels certain. People who have made the decision to keep their unhappiness approach the void with head held high. The truly good must be approached with fear and trembling, with profound respect. You were closer to it yesterday.

Lars: I had a dream a couple of days ago. I can only remember a fragment, but I think it could be a systemic dream.

Hellinger: Okay, tell it as if it were happening.

Lars: I am lying in my bed, about to go to sleep. The door opens and a woman comes in. Her face has a very emotional expression and she quickly moves toward me.

Hellinger: That's enough. We can work with that much. It feels like a primary dream that contains a memory.

Lars: I've got the feeling that if it's a memory, it's really bad. My whole head is getting hot.

Hellinger: Look at the eyes of the woman. Can you see them? Close your eyes and look at the woman's eyes and at her mouth.

Lars: I recognize the mouth, but not the eyes.

Hellinger: Whose mouth is it? Take your time. Observe carefully how the mouth moves—and the eyes. Those are the points at which memory is easiest.

Lars: I think it is my mother's mouth, but I'm not sure.

Hellinger: Okay. Let's leave it there for now. Perhaps the dream is a memory, but we don't want to make anything up. Let's just see if anything comes to you in the next few days.

Next Day

Lars: During the past three or four years, I've been working on my relationship with my father, on taking him, but I haven't taken my mother and I miss her, her energy. I want to take a step now.

Hellinger: I'm thinking about your dream yesterday. As you were speaking, I saw the image from the dream again. Were you in the hospital as a child?

Lars: Yes, I was often ill and I have the feeling that I just managed to escape with my life. When I was six months old, I had an abscess, and my mother had to take me to the doctor to have the abscess drained. That must have been very painful.

Hellinger: Yes, she comes into the room and you know what's going to happen.

Lars: I must have really screamed. Another time, I was in the hospital for. . . .

Hellinger: Not now, Lars. We already have something to work with. It's enough. Let's use it. We don't need more now. That's a good interpretation for your dream. Can you imagine how a mother feels when the doctor expresses the baby's abscesses and he starts to scream? A baby doesn't understand that at all.

A well-known psychotherapist who specializes in reparenting once told a story about her 16-year-old son. He took part in a group she was running in which the participants regressed and relived things from their childhood. Her son suddenly said, "Mom, you tried to starve me." She remembered the situation. The baby had severe diarrhea and the doctor had ordered a 24-hour fast.

The baby recovered, but the memory remained as an attempt to starve him. That's what sometimes happens to parents.

Another time, a therapist told how he once looked very sharply at his young daughter. She then went to her mother and said, "Papa hit me." And that was what remained in her memory.

If you're willing to feel what your mother felt when she took you, as a baby, to the doctor, you'll be able to resolve that image. It would have been much worse if she had left you in the hospital.

RESISTANCE

Bert Hellinger is a master at working with those patterns of behavior we call "resistance." In observing him at work, it quickly becomes clear how skillfully he uses the short interactions during the round to interrupt those patterns. He is extremely quick to recognize a pattern of avoidance, and he then interrupts with an explanation to the group or with a story or an anecdote. He can afford to confront rather blatantly since the groups quickly recognize how much love and respect are contained in his interventions, and how often a good resolution emerges in the end. [G.W.]

Wishful Thinking and Hypothetical Objections

Lars (*referring to a constellation in which he represented a mother's lover*): Isn't it possible for the lover and the husband to get together and be friendly? Or is that just wishful thinking?

Hellinger: It's wishful thinking.

Lars: Yes, but it's not impossible in real life. I know people who have done it.

Hellinger: The lover you represented and the husband could make peace if they wanted to have a homoerotic affair with each other by sharing the same woman. If you look carefully at the actual people involved, you'll see the price that they and their children will have to pay in the long run.

Lars: Yes, but I still wouldn't want to exclude it as a possible resolution.

Hellinger: I want to point out a basic phenomenon: You can raise a hypothetical objection to everything, even to what's right. The effect of such objections is that what was previously effective suddenly has no effect at all. Raising hypothetical objections in therapy cuts off the energy, disturbs a healing possibility, and is always a cheap shot because it's easier to come up with objections than it is to find good solutions. Whoever raises objections usually doesn't have to take responsibility for their effects.

It's very different when someone enters into the situation, and through his or her personal involvement, discovers a new variation. Then he or she can speak from personal experience and bring insight to supplement or correct what was originally said. That's a very great difference because mental effort and risk are required to bring such a contribution.

Criticizing and questioning everything with hypothetical possibilities is a game you play at the university. But when you're working with real people with real suffering, you can't do it. The consequences are too great. I can question everything, but what does it accomplish? What do you actually achieve when you bring up such objections, Lars? You can observe what happens here, what the effect of the interventions actually is. Or you can tell us about your own experience—if you and your wife's lover are good friends. When you merely raise hypothetical objections, the good effect of the work is blocked.

Lars: I have another question. . . .

Hellinger: Not now. *(To group)* Did you notice how quickly he moved on to his next thought? He didn't really even consider what we were discussing. There's something threatening about observing a process that leads to resolution—it seldom leaves much room for choice. We have a lot of room for choice with the little things, but when we're interested in a good resolution, we usually only have one way to go, especially when we are dealing with one of life's big issues. We're only too happy to escape the necessity of fitting ourselves into what life demands of us, and raising theoretical objections is a good way to escape. We have the illusion of freedom, but at what price? It's only an illusion.

Hypothetical objections have the same effect on resolutions that the scythe has on wheat before it's ripened.

Looking for Causes and Explanations Rather Than Acting

Louis: I haven't managed to make very much out of my life. I didn't finish my degree, I don't have a career. I've tried out lots of things, but I've never managed to stick with anything for very long. Do you think it could be an identification with my father? He wasn't allowed to marry his first girlfriend because he didn't have a job.

Hellinger *(after a long, thoughtful pause):*   Even if it were to turn out to be true, your method of going about it is doomed to fail. You're still looking for causes and explanations and excuses when you already know the solution.

Louis: That's all I have to do? Everything else doesn't matter?

Hellinger: What's the solution?

Louis: The solution is that I pay my father obeisance.

Hellinger: And that you tell your mother in your heart, "I belong with my father. He's right for me." Then you can forget all the other stuff.

Louis: Then everything else is unimportant, my sisters, and so on?

Hellinger: That's a case of agreement as a form of defense. *(Laughter.)*

———————————

Lydia: Right now, I'm feeling calm and strong. I had a dream last night. It woke me and I cried and cried. I had very clear images. One was of a person who had fallen into a rain barrel, and then I saw my sister, but she wasn't connected to anything at all.

Hellinger: Are those images from the dream, or what?

Lydia: They were images after the dream, and there was a lot of tears in them.

Hellinger: I don't think they're very useful.

Lydia: Good, okay! But there is a connection with a conversation I had yesterday in which I. . . .

Hellinger *(interrupting):*   Lydia, I don't think that'll help anything. I don't want to hear it just now.

Lydia: Okay, okay. But I want to tell you about it whether you want to hear it or not. Yesterday. . . .

Hellinger: No, Lydia. I want to analyze what's going on, what your process is. First, you had an experience, and afterwards you started looking for the explanation. No matter what explanation you find, you'll feel relief, but it's not likely to help you change whatever you need to change so that your life can be different in the way you want. Usually, we seek explanations for our own refusal to act, or for our unhappiness. As soon as we've found an explanation, we stop trying to understand our refusal or our unhappiness, and the process that was started by the experience is interrupted.

You can see something very similar when you study the mystics: Buddhist, Muslim, Christian, and Jewish mystics have all had experiences that are quite similar. They just explain them differently. They try to communicate what they have experienced with the tools they have available. But it's not possible to explain experience, and it requires great self-discipline to resist the temptation to do so, and to concentrate one's attention on exploring the experience itself. You have to jump into the river and swim with the current and see where it takes you. Is that clear, Lydia? Can you accept my interruption if you look at it like that?

Lydia: Thank you, but. . . .

Hellinger: I've failed again. *(To group)* If I as a therapist were to start to work with what she is going to say, or with her explanations of her tears, then I would be cooperating in interrupting the flow of the process, of the important experience itself. *(Lydia begins to cry softly.)* Now you're giving in to the experience. Take your time, Lydia. You've got lots of time, all the time you need. *(To the group, giving Lydia time)* I once contemplated pure truth and how to deal with it. The wise man deals with pure truth like a cow deals with a barbed-wire fence: As long as the cow has something to eat, she keeps away. Otherwise, she looks for a hole. *(He looks around the group.)* That's a general method for dealing with certain authorities. *(Work with Lydia resumes.)*

Stubbornness and the Joy of Contradicting

Hilda: I noticed my own pattern yesterday—I always react first with an objection. It's really difficult for me to go along with something. I'm so stubborn.

Hellinger: Those are the people who are easiest to manipulate. You can always depend on stubbornness. There are three kinds of people: The first say "yes" first, and then think; the second say "no" first, and then think; and the third think first. *(Pause, to the group)* Did Hilda understand what I said? I don't think she could, because she didn't hear it. She was too busy saying "No." *(Laughter)*

Edie: My heart's pounding. I'm still feeling hurt by your rejection this morning. *(Her eyes are closed and she's pouting.)*

Hellinger: Yes. You can hold on to it as long as it does you good, but you can only hold on to it if you close your eyes and don't look at me as I am.

Edie: I don't want to hold on to it at all, but I notice how quickly I get stubborn and . . .

Hellinger: Pay attention to your experience. It was pleasurable. You showed them.

Edie: What? What do you mean?

Hellinger: You really showed them. Of course, you lost; but you showed them anyway.
I'll tell you something about stubbornness. Stubbornness is the inability to take. The dilemma is that you have to wait for someone else to help you get over it. But as soon as someone tries to help, you have to reject the person in order to keep your stubbornness. It's a vicious circle. I've conducted research on this process for many years and I have discovered a cure for stubbornness. Do you want to know? *(Edie nods.)*
Okay, I'll tell you. You put it off for five minutes.

Do You Want Triumph or Success?

Gwen: I woke up this morning and I had the feeling that there were so many people sitting around me, telling me, "You must, you should. You must separate from your friend, you must pay him his full due before you separate, you shouldn't be angry at him."

Hellinger: You *must* tell each of them, "I will, I will, I will." That'll shut them up for a while, and then you can do what you want. *(Laughter)*

Gwen: But there are so many of them. There's one who says. . . .

Hellinger: Okay, okay. If you enjoy it so much. I didn't mean to spoil your fun. *(Laughter)* I was describing an inner strategy, and I demonstrated it. However, the strategy requires discipline—the discipline that one needs to apply all inner strategies successfully is to forego triumph. There are two mutually exclusive things: triumph and success. You can either have triumph and sacrifice success, or you can have success and sacrifice triumph. That's the discipline of success, and it requires an element of humility—lasting success, I mean. Something else, Gwen?

Gwen: I haven't made up my mind to forego triumph.

Hellinger: Exactly. You still want to have it. But a puffed-up breast is only full of hot air. You only heard the words.

Irene: My sister was widowed and she has remarried. Her new husband, also a widower, has an adult son from his previous marriage. This son is very difficult, and both my sister and her husband suffer from his behavior. Unfortunately, he lives in the same town. My sister basically understands that the young man is her husband's son, but she also sees how much her husband suffers from his relationship with him. As an outsider, she sees where her husband makes mistakes, and she tries to tell him that from time to time, but it doesn't help at all. *(Irene shows an expression of exasperation with her brother-in-law.)*

Hellinger: Obviously not. How could it? She should tell her husband, "You're the best father for your son."

Irene: That's an interesting possibility. *(Her air of superiority softens briefly, then returns.)* After you mentioned . . . .

Hellinger *(to group):* That was a very skillful avoidance. *(To Irene)* What did I say? Can you remember?

Irene: You said that she should tell her husband, "You're the best father for your son." And I wanted to . . . .

Hellinger: Okay, Irene. You heard the words, but you didn't understand the issue.

Irene: Yes I did, but I don't think you are considering . . . .

Hellinger: No, it really didn't get through yet. I want to leave it here for now.

Wanting to Know More Than Is Necessary to Act

Allen: I don't know how I feel.

Hellinger: When you don't know how you feel, you feel good. You'd know it if you weren't feeling good.

Allen: It doesn't make me feel completely good. I keep having the feeling that there's real movement in me at certain moments, but then it quickly slips away in some corner and disappears so that I can't get to it. All that's left is a diffuse fog that cuts me off from reality.

Hellinger: There are always good corners for movements to slip into to escape change. I call that the "wanting-to-know-more-than-is-necessary syndrome." That's when I always want to know more, rather than staying with the movement and acting accordingly. The minute I start trying to understand, I no longer need to act. Understanding is the escape hatch the energy of change slips into. Is there something more, Allen?

Allen: That's enough for now.

Hellinger: Did you understand?

Allen: I'm afraid I did.

Hellinger: Good. That's now the exception that proves the rule, the way in which it's good to understand. *(Laughter)*

Robert: I think too much, and I feel overwhelmed. I have the feeling that it's time to do something and to stop talking about it. I'm going to call my mother tonight after the seminar.

Hellinger: Some people like to count the drops of water while they are taking a shower. *(Pause, to the group)* He didn't get it. Did you?

I'll give another example of this process. In the United States, they have a method for teaching foreign languages. It's quite expensive, so they mostly use it to teach spies, but it's very effective and most people can learn to speak a language fluently in a short time. The method is very simple. Six or seven teachers all start talking to the student in the foreign language at the same time until he or she doesn't understand anything at all—and then the student learns, but on a different level. That's how children learn to speak; six or seven different people all say things to them that they don't understand.

Edie: I remember two dreams from my childhood and I'd like to know what kind of dreams they are.

Hellinger: No!

Edie: Why?

Hellinger: Are your chances better or worse if you ask me why?

Edie: Worse.

Hellinger: Exactly. Your question is an attempt to put me in a subordinated position, to obey your program. If you succeed in becoming superior to me, why should you trust me as your therapist? I need at least to be your equal. *(To group)* What Edie did was to put out some bait. The young and inexperienced fish will bite.

Eric: I woke up just before we started with a dream fragment. I can only remember the end.

Hellinger *(interrupting):* Eric, I want the beginning. How does the dream start? Of course, only if you want to tell me.

Eric: I don't know, I found the last scene of the dream lovely.

Hellinger *(friendly teasing):* That's very nice, but how could it have all begun?

Eric: What spontaneously comes is the start of a pilgrimage.

Hellinger: That's an interpretation of the dream. Your interpretations of your dream don't count. What did the dream itself say?

Eric: Okay. I am getting ready to leave for a strange city.

Hellinger: That's a good sentence. Let's work with that. Now you have to check out with yourself whether or not it's appropriate, whether a good energy is leading you to something better or a little devil is tempting you to leave.

Eric *(quietly):* I think it is a good energy.

Hellinger: I'm guessing it's a devil. The little devils are very tricky.

Agreeing with Contrariness

Katherine: I'm still mulling over what you said about feelings. In my relationships, I always automatically assume a contrary position. No matter how much I try to watch out, my habit is always faster. Snap, and I'm in it. When it's a conversation about justice, for example, I'm arguing the opposite position in a flash.

Hellinger: A woman once told me that her mother had told her, "You're a whore." She wanted to know how to deal with it. She always argued with her mother, "I am not." I suggested that she tell her mother, "Well, actually, there may be something to it." So the next time you're tempted to argue in opposition, tell the other person, "There may be something to it."

Katherine: That's very simple.

Hellinger: The best part is that, when you understand how it works, you can really have a lot of fun with it.

The Secret of the Path

Manuela: I hope that, sometime during this seminar, I'll get a chance to set up my family. I hope that it will work out, but I don't know if it will.

Hellinger: Judging by how you say that, it seems more likely that it will not.

Manuela: Good, if you say so. That's too bad, but maybe it's better that way. *(Begins to cry, looks at the floor.)*

Hellinger: I want to say something about the secret of the path. You make progress on the path by leaving behind everything from before, even your old insights. And there's something else about the path. You reach the goal with the last step. Everything before was only the preparation. I'll tell you a story.

The Mule

A wealthy man bought a young mule and immediately began to train it for its new life. He packed it with the heaviest loads, made it work long hours, and gave it a minimum of food and drink. And so the little mule soon became a real mule. When his master came, it bent its knee and bowed its head and allowed itself to be piled with burdens to be carried, even when it almost broke from the weight.

Passersby saw and had pity. They said, "Such a poor little mule," and wanted to help it. One wanted to give it a piece of sugar, another a piece of bread, and a third even wanted to coax it to a green meadow. But, alas, the little mule only showed them what a mule it really was: It bit the first in the hand, it kicked the second in the shin, and with the third, it was as stubborn as a mule. Then they said, "What a mule," and left it alone.

Yet it ate gladly from its master's hand, even straw, and its master praised it everywhere, "That's the best mule I've ever had." Its master gave it a special name, Mehtyoo. Later scholars were no longer sure how to pronounce the name, until one from Texas decided it should be pronounced, "Me Too."

Distinguishing Weakness from Need

Anne *(speaking in a whiney voice):* I have a lump in my throat and there are lots of things coming up for me now.

Hellinger: Resist your weakness. Look at me. Can you see my eyes?

Anne: Yes.

Hellinger: What color are they?

Anne: Dark.

Hellinger *(astonished):* Dark? *(To group)* Do you notice the difference? She has much more strength now that she's looking. When people are weakening themselves, you can help them to look clearly at something and they often get out of it. Whenever people make themselves weak, they're filtering something out of their perceptions, and they can't see, or hear, or act appropriately. Everything that weakens people interferes with their doing what they want to do. If we're interested in change, we might as well forget it. If a person really needs to feel weak, then we can tell him or her to go ahead and enjoy it from time to time, but to do it with full awareness. That's different from doing therapy.

Anne: Is there such a thing as a strong weakness?

Hellinger *(after a thoughtful pause):* Yes, when it's strategic.

Anne: I ask because, for me, weakness is an intrinsic part of life.

Hellinger: No, needs are a part of life, and that's something different. It's very important to recognize and honor our neediness, and to communicate in our relationships that we need our partners, but without misusing them. In good partnerships, both partners are needy, and that grants their relationship strength. When one or the other no longer is needy, then their relationship takes on a different quality. There are people who achieve their fullness, and then no longer are needy in the usual sense. They give by overflowing, and others can then take from them. That doesn't create a relationship in the usual sense, because they don't take. They're self-sufficient. In our ordinary intimate relationships, the other kind of give and take is necessary.

Do you know how to deal with neediness? You ask for something very concrete. Not like, "Please love me more." That isn't concrete enough. Rather, ask, "Stay with me for half an hour and talk to me." That would be concrete enough. Then the other could decide whether or not he or she wanted to do so, and when he or she did, the person would know when the request was fulfilled. With the sentence, "Please love me more," he or she could never fulfill it and would feel resentful.

GRIEF AND SEPARATION

Martha: I think constantly about a colleague who was killed last summer in a car accident. I can't get him out of my mind. I've lost 10 pounds since he died, and I've no idea what's going on. I've cried a lot, but I have the feeling that what I'm doing is somehow exaggerated and inappropriate.

Hellinger: Did you refuse to take something he wanted to give you, or did you devalue him in some way? Do you owe him something?

Martha: I had a short affair with his brother. He didn't approve.

Hellinger: Did you have a relationship with him?

Martha: No, but a friend of mine was married to him.

Hellinger: I've given you a couple of hints about where you might look. Let's leave it here for now and see if those hints have some effect. I still have the image that you owe him something, or that you need to take something from him.

My neighbor became extremely distraught when her husband suddenly died of a heart attack 10 years ago. She cried and cried, but nothing changed. I suggested to her, as a neighbor sometimes can, that she could turn to me if she wanted help. About a year later, she knocked at the door and said, "Mr. Hellinger, could you please help me?" I invited her to come in, we sat down, and I said to her, "Picture in your mind exactly how it was when you met your husband for the first time." She closed her eyes, and after a short time began to laugh. I said, "You can go home now." She got up and left. Since then, she has really blossomed and has become a very active and effective woman.

You know, good memories belong to every effective separation.

Getting Beyond the Desire to Help with Grief

Adelaide: How can you help people to get to the point at which they can live the answers to their problems?

Hellinger: Let me ask you a very basic question. Why do you want to do that?

Adelaide: Isn't that the whole purpose of doing therapy, to help people?

Hellinger: A therapist is someone who limps along behind, and with great effort just barely manages to keep up. People have a right to their own destinies, and we must be very cautious when intervening in matters of destiny.

Adelaide: I'm working with a family with a retarded son. Would you also say that to them? Is that the resolution, that the parents agree to their fate?

Hellinger: No. In a case like that, something else is needed. When people become parents, that has enormous consequences and entails risks that can last a lifetime. Procreation is the most profoundly human act. It needs to be properly respected and valued. That's the first thing.

When they fully understand and value the magnitude of parenthood, then they can accept the consequences of their action. It's a question of human dignity. They then honor and love the child, however that child is. That's the attitude that allows resolution. It's a humble attitude that expresses human dignity. When parents are able to affirm a child like that, something good and loving flows through them that can't flow otherwise.

Actually, that's how most parents of retarded children feel. It's the outsiders who are most bothered. The parents usually accept a retarded child without difficulty—unless the prejudicial attitude of some therapist gets in their way. As a therapist, you might wonder why they keep the child, or how they manage to love him, but your compassion is missing. That's why it's difficult for you, as a therapist, to truly affirm the child as he is.

That would be the first step, for the parents to affirm the child as he is. It's difficult for a therapist, and for other outsiders, to affirm such a child—truly and lovingly and without some phony "oh isn't he cute" act. It requires that you, and everyone else, keep your nose out of their business. It seems to me that that's what's appropriate in situations like that—they love their child, and you keep your nose out of their business.

I'll give you an example. Several years ago, a woman called me for some advice. She was a member of a mother–child group. One of the other mothers had a five-year-old daughter with terminal cancer. The woman on the telephone had gone to visit them to do some "death and dying counseling." After she had been there for a while, she had the feeling that something was wrong. I asked her what was going on as she arrived. She said that the child was playing happily. I said, "That's appropriate. Let the child play as long as she can, and leave her to her parents. What are you looking for there? Just stay out of it." That's what she did, and the parents did what was right for them and for the child.

Here's another example. A therapist called me after one of her clients committed suicide. She said she had the feeling that she should help the relatives with their "grief work" and wanted to know if I thought she should go to the funeral. I told her, "Don't do it. You've done your work, and now they must do theirs. You mustn't intrude into their family affairs."

No therapist has the right to feel responsible for protecting a family from life—and everything that belongs to it. The illusion that therapy can change the realities of life (or improve life) is the source of a lot of hurt, especially in relationships. Life is the way it is, with all its joys and sorrows.

Adelaide: I'll think about what you've said.

Hellinger: What does that mean?

Adelaide: I need time to think it over.

Hellinger: It sounds as though you're going to stick to your opinion, but your reaction doesn't change anything about what's actually helpful to families in grief. Still, your opinions might interfere with your perception of the effect of what you do. The question remains: Are we talking about their need for help or your need to be a helper?

When Grief Doesn't Stop

Barbara: I have a neighbor who lost her 20-year-old son in an automobile accident about 10 years ago. She's still grieving for him, as if he'd just died last week.

Hellinger: Maybe she's angry at him. When a person is angry at a deceased person, the grief doesn't stop. If she were interested in a resolution, she could say to him, "I respect and honor your life and your death." *(Pause)* I'm telling you, but you can't tell her that because it would just hurt her more.

When he was 31 years old, the poet Rainer Maria Rilke wrote a letter to a friend, "Give up looking for the answers. You wouldn't be able to live them if you found them." That's an important psycho-therapeutic axiom: Don't give anyone an answer that he or she can't yet live.

Hellinger: Our time together has come to an end. It's been a pleasure for me to be here with you, and to show you some of the things I've observed operating in families that help love to flow and to become fulfilled. I'll be pleased if what we've experienced here is of use to you in your lives and in your work; if it helps your intimate relationships to bring the satisfaction and happiness you wish for; and especially if it helps families with children to feel more at peace with one another and to be more loving.

Before we go, I'd like to tell you one more story—just for the road.

Two Measures of Happiness

In the old days, when the gods still seemed close to human beings, two singers named Orpheus lived on the same island. One of them was Orpheus the Great—the one we know from legend. He was the inventor of the kithara, a precursor of the guitar, and when he plucked its strings and sang, Nature herself was moved by the beauty of his music. Wild animals lay peacefully at his feet, and the tallest trees bent near. Befitting his greatness, he was a companion to the most powerful of kings and dared to love Eurydice, the most beautiful of women. Thus began his downfall.

The beautiful Eurydice died just as their wedding celebration began, and his overflowing cup broke before it touched his lips. But Orpheus the Great refused to accept Eurydice's death as final. Calling upon his highest art, he found the entrance to the Underworld and entered the realm of shadows. He crossed the River of Forgetting, slipped past the Hound of Hell, and still alive, reached the throne of Hades, and there he sang.

The God of Death, moved by the beauty of his music, agreed to release the beautiful Eurydice but only under one condition—that Orpheus not look back at her until they were again in the world above. Orpheus was so overjoyed that he did not notice the malice concealed within this boon.

Setting out for home, he heard behind him the footsteps of his beloved wife. They safely passed the Hound of Hell, crossed the River of Forgetting, and began the long climb up. As they saw the light of day above, Orpheus heard a cry—Eurydice had stumbled. In panic, he turned to help and saw death's shadows, released by his loving fear, closing in around her. He was alone. Overcome with grief, he sang his mourning song:

"She is dead—all happiness is gone forever."

Orpheus managed to return to the realm of light, but his sojourn among the dead had wounded him, sickening his love of life. A group of drunken women, remembering the beauty of his song, tried to seduce him into accompanying them to the Festival of the New Wine. Enraged by his refusal, they fell upon him and tore him to pieces.

So great was his suffering, so futile was his high art—but he is known to all the world.

The other Orpheus was Orpheus the Lesser. He was a singer of modest talent, singing for ordinary people, and entertaining on ordinary occasions, where he enjoyed himself. Since he could not support himself by singing, he learned an ordinary trade, married an average wife, had normal children, and committed ordinary sins from time to time. He lived happily and died at a ripe old age, having drunk his fill of life.

So modest were his gifts, so was great his satisfaction—but he is unknown in all the world, except to me.

Appendix

INFLUENCES ON THE DEVELOPMENT OF HELLINGER'S WORK

Bert Hellinger considers his parents and his childhood home to be the first major influence on his later work. Their particuliar form of faith provided the entire family with an immunity against believing the distortions of National Socialism. Because of his repeated absences from the required meetings of the Hitler Youth Organization and his participation in an illegal Catholic youth organization, he was eventually classified by the Gestapo as "Suspected of Being an Enemy of the People." His escape from the Gestapo was paradoxically made possible when he got drafted. Just 17 years old, he became a soldier and experienced the realities of combat, capture, defeat, and life in a prisoner-of-war camp in Belgium with the allies.

The second major influence was certainly his childhood wish to become a priest. At the age of 20, immediately after getting out of the prisoner-of-war camp, he entered a Catholic religious order and began the long process of the purification of body, mind, and spirit in silence, study, contemplation and meditation.

His 16 years in South Africa as a missionary to the Zulu also deeply shaped his later work. There he directed a large school, taught, and acted as parish priest simultaneously. He tells with satisfaction that 13 percent of all black Africans attending the university in South Africa at that time had been students at this one mission school. He learned the Zulu language well enough to teach and minister, but he tells amusing anecdotes about the courteous dignity of the Zulu people when he inadvertently said something rude rather than what he intended. With time, he came to feel as much at home with them as is possible for a European. The process of leaving one culture to live in another sharpened his awareness of the relativity of many cultural values.

His peculiar ability to perceive systems in relationships and his interest in the human commonalty underlying cultural diversity became apparent during those years. He saw that many Zulu rituals and customs had a structure and function similar to elements of the Catholic Mass, pointing to common human experiences, and he experimented with integrating Zulu music and rituals into the Mass. He is commited to the goodness of cultural and human variety, and to the validity of doing things in different ways. The Sacred is present everywhere.

The next major influence was his participation in an interracial, ecumenical training in group dynamics led by Anglican clergy. They had brought from the United States a form of working with groups that valued dialog, phenomenology, and individual human experience. He experienced, for the first time, a new dimension of caring for souls. He tells how one of the trainers once asked the group, "What's more important to you, your ideals or people? Which would you sacrifice for the other?" A sleepless night followed, as the implications of the question were profound. Hellinger says, "I'm very grateful to that minister for asking that. In a sense, the question changed my life. That fundamental orientation toward people has shaped all my work since. A good question is worth a lot."

His decision to leave the religious order after 25 years was amicable. He describes how he gradually became clear that being a priest no longer was an appropriate expression of his inner growth. With characteristic impeccability and consequent action, he gave up the life he had known so long. He returned to Germany, began a psychoanalytic training in Vienna, met his future wife, Herta, and they married soon after. They have no children.

Psychoanalysis was to be the next major influence. As with everything he did, he threw himself into his psychoanalytic training, eventually reading the complete works of Freud, and much of the other relevant literature as well. But with an equally typical love of inquiry, when his training analyst gave him a copy of Janov's *Primal Scream* shortly before he completed his training, (a book the training analyst had not himself read), Hellinger immediately wanted to know more. He visited Janov in the United States, eventually completing a nine-month training with him and his former chief assistant in Los Angeles and Denver.

The psychoanalytic community in Vienna was less enthusiastic than he was about this way of including body-based experience in the therapeutic process, and he again confronted the issue of what was more important—loyalty to a group or love of truth and inquiry. Love of free inquiry won out, and a separation from psychoanalysis became unavoidable. His skill in body-based psycho-therapy, however, remained an essential element in his work long after his association with Janov had ceased to be fruitful.

Several other therapeutic schools have had a major influence on his work: in addition to the phenomenological/dialogical orientation of the group dynamics from the Anglicans, the fundamental need for humans to align themselves with the forces of nature that he learned from the Zulu in South Africa, the psychoanalysis he learned in Vienna, and the body work he learned in America.

He developed an interest in Gestalt Therapy through Ruth Cohen and Hilarion Petzold and trained with them both. He met Fanita English during this period, and through her was introduced to Transactional Analysis and the work of Eric Bern. With his wife, Herta, he integrated what he had already learned of group dynam-ics and psychoanalysis with Gestalt Therapy, Primal Therapy, and Transactional Analysis. His work with the analysis of scripts led to the discovery that some scripts function across generations and in family relationship systems. The dynamics of identification also gradually became clear during this period. Ivan Boszormenyi-Nagy's book *Invisible Bonds* and his recognition of hidden loyalties and the need for a balance between giving and taking in families also were important.

He trained in family therapy with Ruth McClendon and Leslie Kadis, where he first encountered family constellations. "I was very impressed by their work, but I couldn't understand it. Nevertheless, I decided that I wanted to work systemically. Then I got to thinking about the work I'd already been doing and realized, 'It's good too. I'm not going to give that up before I really understand systemic family therapy.' So I just kept on doing what I'd been doing. After a year, I thought about it again, and I was surprised to discover that I was working systemically."

His reading of Jay Haley's article about the "perverse triangle" led to the discovery of the importance of hierarchy in families. Additional work in family therapy with Thea Schönfelder followed, as did training in Milton Erickson's Hypnotherapy and Neuro-Lin-guistic Programming (NLP). Frank Farelly's Provocative Therapy has been an important influence, as has been the Holding Therapy developed by Irena Precop. The most important element he took from NLP was its emphasis on working with resources rather than with problems. His use of stories in therapy, of course, pays tribute to Milton Erickson. The first story he told in therapy was "Two Measures of Happiness."

Those familiar with the full range of psychotherapy will recognize that Hellinger's contribution is his unique integration of diverse elements. He makes no claim that he has discovered something new, but there's no question but that he has made a new integration. He has the natural ability to throw himself into a new situation, to immerse himself in it, and when he has learned what there is to learn, to move on. Certainly, his early experiences taught him indelibly the importance and skill of listening to the authority of one's own soul—for although it isn't foolproof, it's the only real protection we have against seduction by false authorities. His insistence on *seeing* what *is* as opposed to blindly accepting what we're told, combined with the unwavering loyalty and trust in one's own soul, is the fundamental basis upon which this work has been built.

In a sense, he's the ultimate empiricist.

Through all of this, his philosophical companion has been Martin Heidegger, himself no stranger to the dangers of false authority—although Heidegger's profound quest for the true words that resonate in the soul must have commonality with those sentences clients speak in the constellations heralding change for the better, signaling the renewed flow of love.

One last influence—or perhaps better, companion—must be mentioned: Hellinger's archetypally German love of music. Yes, opera; and yes again, especially Wagner.